Wild Inside

How Nature Protects Your Child's Mental Health
and Restores Yours

Kathleen Lockyer

Otter Play Publishing

For Veda and Kira

KATHLEEN LOCKYER

CONTENTS

FOREWORD

BY HOLLY RINGLAND

Think of a place you love in nature where, when you visit, your shoulders drop. Your breath slows and a calm washes over you. You feel a growing sense that everything around you is connected. Where every leaf, wave, shell, stone, and gust of wind seems to reach out to you, inviting you to belong. This is the same feeling that Wild Inside calls us back to: a sense of belonging that is at once ancient and immediate, reminding us that we are never truly separate from the natural, living world, or from each other.

I met Kathleen Lockyer in 2018, in one such place by the North Atlantic Ocean: Connemara, on Ireland's west coast. I remember the stars overhead that night, the wind tugging at our jackets, the spray of sea salt on our cheeks as we chatted until our faces were numb from the October cold. From that very first conversation, I recognised that feeling in Kathleen's presence — the same sense of wordless connection I experience when I return to the gum trees I've known since I was a child in Australia.

In the days that followed our meeting, this feeling with Kathleen only deepened as we walked rocky shores, peat bogs and windswept cliffs, gulls cawing overhead as we talked of nature, myth, land, story, grief, joy, memory, fear, trauma, creativity, and courage. What struck me most was Kathleen's generous way of listening, her rootedness in the natural world, and her ability to weave science and story with vivid, intense lived experience.

Over the years since, I have witnessed the same truths in our conversations that Kathleen shares in Wild Inside: healing does not require us to be fully healed, but it does require our presence. This brings to mind one afternoon in Connemara in 2018 when Kathleen and I were walking along the seashore, and she paused mid-step to feel and experience the texture of giant kelp washed ashore; a small gesture of attention that revealed the care and relationality that Kathleen brings to life and writing alike.

At once tender and rigorous, Wild Inside is part memoir, part science, and part invitation. Kathleen offers us three vital threads: interoception, a sense of ourselves; ecoception, a sense of nature; alloception, a sense of each other. Which, when woven together, offer us not only resilience but restoration; a vision of how we might live more fully alive through deepening our connection with the natural world, especially with, and for, children.

This is not a traditional manual of parenting tricks or prescriptive advice. It is something far more courageous: a wise and accompanying reminder that encouraging children to connect with nature is also a powerful invitation for us to do the same, no matter what stage we're at in our lives. In every page, Kathleen reassures us: we don't need to be flawless to guide the next generation. We can heal alongside them, step by step, with the ground beneath us, the sea, forests, fields, and mountains around us, and the skies above as our steady witnesses.

One of the most striking things about Wild Inside is its refusal to pathologise struggle. For all of us who carry adversity, this book offers a vital truth: we are not broken. We are human. Part of the natural world. And, we are in relationship, with each other, our children, our history, and with the earth itself.

Through her shining writing and research – informed by her own relationship with nature, motherhood, and thirty years of practice as a licensed occupational therapist – Kathleen passionately reminds us that the natural world is not outside of us, but within us, shaping, holding, and restoring us. Whether we have children of our own, children in our lives, or are looking for ways to connect with the child that we each once were, this is a book to keep close. It guides us to remember our way back to the wild places, both around, between, and inside us.

Knowing Kathleen and her work as I do, this book carries the integrity and generosity with which she lives: honest, thoughtful, and deeply attuned to the gifts of both the exterior world and our interior one.

May you find, feel, and be transformed by the Wild Inside, letting its wisdom guide you back to what is enduring, alive, and true.

Holly Ringland

PREFACE

"The mess is the message."

Forbes Riley

I've been working on this book for over a decade. And for many of those years, it felt just out of reach. I'd draft chapters, share insights, weave in research — but something was always missing. It took me a long time to realize what it was: I was trying to write from a place of professional authority, when what this book really needed was to be more human. More honest.

Because while science is essential, it is not the whole story.

As parents, we're given stacks of information — guidelines, milestones, diagnoses, and solutions. But so often, what we need most is not more data. We need permission to connect with our child and a reminder that we're not alone. We need to know that our instincts, even in the messiest moments, are worthy of trust.

Wild Inside is about remembering what helps us feel whole — what helps us reconnect not only with our children, but with ourselves. It's about softening into the truth that parenting is so much more than a set of how to's and should's. Parenting is about, love, connection, and skill building, and for that, we need to be present for moments of *unskillfulness*. And for me, a parenting book couldn't be written without sharing my own story, and the stories of the children and families I've worked with over almost thirty years.

In the academic world, I was taught to keep the professional separate from the personal. But experience has taught me that it's our willingness to share the real stuff that opens doors to connection. When we're brave enough to be vulnerable, we give our children and each other permission to be vulnerable too. And connection, after all, is what rewires our brains.

The stories in *Wild Inside* are woven from the threads of my life — as a mother, a mentor, an occupational therapist, a child once overwhelmed by the world, and now a guide for others learning to navigate their own. You'll meet my parents and my daughters. You'll meet families I've walked beside in schools, in nature, and in living rooms filled with questions and love. And you'll meet the birds, trees, and wild places that have helped restore my nervous system again and again.

Long before I became a parent, the connection between nature and health fascinated me. In 1996, my college thesis explored the relationship between biodiversity loss and human well-being. Even then, I sensed that *the wild* we were losing outside ourselves was deeply connected to what we were losing inside. Over time, those early questions grew into the foundation of what is now the NatureLed™ Approach — a framework that honors our biological need for nature, relationship, and regulation.

We are not separate from the natural world. Our brains and bodies evolved in relationship with birdsong, sunlight, movement, and belonging. Our senses — especially those that guide emotional regulation — were shaped from crawling on forest floors, listening to shifting winds, and making sense of subtle cues from our surroundings. Children need these inputs. So do we. And when these needs go unmet, modern parenting becomes harder than it ever should have been.

This book isn't just about parenting techniques. It's about seeing your child's behavior as communication, witnessing your own story with compassion, and about understanding why you sometimes feel dysregulated, too. *Wild Inside* is about healing generational patterns through small, steady acts of reconnection.

I share science in these pages — but I also share poetic insights, personal stories, and sensory invitations. Because parenting is a wholly embodied, deeply emotional experience. Parenting is felt in our cells, our bones and our souls. And often, more effort, or more information isn't the way back to balance. The way back is through presence. Shared breath. Birds. A patch of sun lighting up a dark place.

I wrote this book for the parent I once was — tired, trying, unsure, full of love and full of questions. I wrote it for those raising sensitive, spirited, or struggling children. I wrote it for anyone who's ever looked at their child and thought — I want to help you become a confident, kind, and capable human, where do I begin?

And I wrote it with this belief at its core: *you already have what you need.* Your instincts matter. Your presence matters. And with the right support — scientific, sensory, and relational — you can create a home where your child feels seen, soothed, and supported. A home where healing happens in small moments of connection, over time — for your child, and for you.

This book is a companion. A mirror. A hand to hold. And an invitation to remember that you are part of nature, too — and that your wild, wise, wonderful child is trying to lead you back to it.

A Note on Style and Interactive Sections

Although *Wild Inside* is written as narrative nonfiction, and follows the *Chicago style of referencing* which offers clean, easy-to-read notes that support storytelling without interrupting the flow, I've chosen to include endnotes in a few key places and a detailed reference section at the end. This keeps the main text spacious and readable while still honoring the research and thinkers who inform my work. As a practitioner-researcher, transparency matters to me — I want you to be able to follow the threads, find the original studies, and explore these ideas more deeply if you wish. My hope is that this balance between story and scholarship makes *Wild Inside* both an engaging read and a trusted resource.

Interactive sections at the end of chapters

At the end of many chapters, you will find two sections designed to help you take the ideas off the page and into your life:

Try This

Offers simple, practical invitations you can experiment with right away. These aren't rigid prescriptions, but gentle ways to explore how nature, sensory awareness, and connection can support you and your child. Think of them as doorways — you choose which ones to step through, in your own way and at your own pace.

Wild Reflection

Gives you a chance to pause and turn inward. These questions are meant to spark personal insight, invite memory, and deepen your understanding of both yourself and your child. Reflection is a powerful way to notice patterns, uncover meaning, and discover what's been missing — or what's already working.

Together, the *Try This* and *Wild Reflections* are meant to support you in weaving the ideas of *Wild Inside* into your everyday family life, not as another to-do list, but as opportunities to reconnect with yourself, your child, and the living world around you.

A Note On Inclusion

I recognize that there are many issues I have not addressed in *Wild Inside*. As one very fallible human, it is not my intention to leave out or marginalize any unique person or group. I also recognize that although I have written about nature as a benevolent force, there are many who have experienced the ferocity of nature, sometimes without having experienced it as a generous and valuable part of who we are.

It is only my shortcomings as a writer that prevent me from being able to address all issues and angles in one manuscript, but it doesn't mean you, or your circumstances are not seen or valued. My hope is that this book can lay the foundation for you and your loved ones to experience the beauty and the relational inheritance that can help our species feel connected, and weather the inevitable storms of life.

I honor the uniquely beautiful you and the generous rainbow of color, orientation, expression, experiences, and creativity that life has blessed our human and nature families with. The only bias that I cling to is the hope that each individual human can one day choose to lead a life that is kind and compassionate towards all our relations.

In Connection,

Kathleen

I

FROM THE HANDS OF OUR ANCESTORS

SHAPED BY THOSE WHO'VE COME BEFORE US

Man by the use of his hands, can influence the state of his own health.

Mary Reilly, co-founder of occupational therapy

Some of us know from the start what we want to be. Others discover it along the way — in a stranger's unexpected question, a wrong turn down an unfamiliar road, or the calloused hands of those who came before us.

I discovered it at twenty-one, when a stranger's question pulled scattered memories into place and set me on a course for the rest of my life. My boyfriend and I had spent the day snowboarding with friends at a Vermont ski resort. On the ride home, I sat in the back seat of a 1988 Chevy Blazer beside a man I'd met that morning, when he turned to me and asked, "So. What do you do?"

I always dreaded that question.

It was 1991, and most of my peers were close to graduating from college, engaged in a trade job, or working towards a career. I'd been working

1

since I was eleven, when I began babysitting my two-year-old brother and a neighbor's toddler during summer break so our mothers could work. Between the ages of 11 and 21, I'd worked as a babysitter, snow shoveler, restaurant server and bus person, hotel maid, front desk clerk, preschool aide, nanny, temp agency clerk, office staff, pieceworker, house cleaner, deli sandwich maker, grocery store clerk, personal caregiver, baker, janitor, house-painter, photo store print maker, barmaid, bartender, hostess, salesperson, and gardener. I could barely remember all the different jobs I'd had.

But I still had no idea what I wanted to do with my life. I felt aimless. I looked at this stranger, who was completely oblivious to his question's effect on me. Deflecting it, I said, "Uh. Ha-ha. Well. I guess I do a lot of things. What do you do?"

"I'm an occupational therapist," he said.

"What's that?"

"Occupational therapists, we call ourselves OTs. We use meaningful occupation or activities to help rehabilitate people. I specialize in hand therapy."

"Hand therapy? Like, therapy for your. *Hands?*"

"Yeah. You know, like say someone is a carpenter and they lose a finger in an accident. I help them with hand exercises and new strategies to get back to doing carpentry."

I stared as he continued, "People usually don't realize how important and complicated hands are, both physically and psychologically — until they can't use them the way they always have!" Now, my eyes widened, and my whole body shifted in his direction. His face lit up. "Did you know that there are twenty-seven little bones in your hand and wrist?" I looked down at my right hand, palpating it with my left thumb and thinking about how much I had focused on hands as a child.

"Dude! Did you see that epic jump on that last run!" Another snowboarder shifted our conversation to the events of our fresh winter day. I went silent, my brain ticking away.

I thought, Occupational Therapy. This I totally get. Oh my. This is what I have to do.

Hands. If I could show you a picture of my father's, you would see hands that can do seemingly impossible work. His hands, and his mother's, brothers' and sisters' hands descended from ocean navigators, wild crafters, basket weavers, net makers, knitters, carvers, bread bakers, builders, gardeners, fishermen and women, stonemasons, and doers of any other work necessary to survive on one of the harshest and, some would say, most barren islands off Eastern Canada — Newfoundland.

My father is from the last generation of our family raised with the sensations, patterns, and rhythms of the North Atlantic's Labrador current — raised in close connection with weather, birds, animals, plants: all the natural world. He was the last to read those patterns and rhythms as most people today read the daily news. Standing at the front door of a little saltbox house overlooking the endless horizon of ocean and sky, he, just like his elders, could read the weather, the ocean, the birds' behavior.

My father's hands are as calloused as they are complicated. Layers of skin so thick, they once pulled a Thanksgiving turkey pan out of the oven without mitts. My brothers and I stood aghast. Dad barely noticed, mumbling in his Newfoundland brogue, "Jeez buy! That's bloody hot!" He suffered zero burns from the incident. I'd watched his hands fillet a fish as if it were soft butter. Those hands built anything we needed — shelves, kitchen tables, bed frames, fences, and eventually a pulley system to help my mother independently rise from bed in her last months of life. Those same hands could do subtle things too: pluck the strings of a guitar and carve delicate wooden birds, toy trucks, jewelry boxes, and lampshades.

If my brothers or I got unruly, those hands would clip us on the back of the head and make us believe we'd been smacked with something much harder than a hand. If Dad was upset, we might find his thick pointer finger inches from our face — causing us to freeze in place. But if one of us got a skinned knee, or had an epic bike fail, we felt those hands lift us, sensed their strength and surety, how loving and healing they could be.

His hands engulfed our small hands as we crossed the street, or when he brought one of *our* hands to his lips for a proud kiss.

I remember trying to wrap my fingers all the way around Dad's big thumb, but not quite closing the gap between my pointer finger and my thumb. We often made-up games to test the strength of Dad's hands: "I bet me and Peter are stronger than your pinky finger!" And he would amuse us by looping one end of a small rope around his pinky finger and letting us pull the other end, trying to uncurl his flexed pinky. We tried with all our might but couldn't do it. As I grew, I took pride in how capable my own hands were becoming.

When he placed a hand on our shoulder, we could feel the weight of generations holding us — generations connected with nature's power and purpose.

The day after I returned home from my Vermont snowboarding trip, I went straight to the library and researched occupational therapy. It was years before the dawn of the internet, and my more refined hands, resembling my mother's and her mother's, flipped through volumes of college reference books. My research revealed that even though women were still

4

denied the right to vote, the American Occupational Therapy Association was founded in 1917 by a board of three men and three women. With equal voting rights! My upbringing with three brothers and a dominant father made something in me quiver with possibility.

I looked up colleges with occupational therapy departments. What if I wanted to be, as my father frequently joked, "edumacated"?

I sent away for, and filled out, exactly one application. I figured I didn't have much of a chance. The cost of a college education was one obstacle. My high school transcript showing two summers of summer school to retake failed classes was another. My post–high school transcript was thin at best. I had taken random community college classes, though I'd done very well in them. Occupational therapy seemed like a long shot. I wrote a passionate and sincere letter and sent it with my application. I waited for the rejection letter.

By some grace, miracle, or accident, I was accepted into the program at Worcester State University in Massachusetts. It was there I discovered the joy of education and found that my life's purpose would come from an unexpected source: making meaning of my childhood.

Meaning rarely arrives one day at our feet or in a grand "aha" moment. We create meaning from life's moments and memories, enriching the stories we pass on to future generations if we so choose.

Making meaning of our childhoods and our parenting journey often unfolds with memories of the most ordinary moments. A conversation in a car. A parent's hands — rough, tender, capable. Our children will come to know *us* through memories in the same way. Through the things we create, build, *and do.* Through the way we hold them, feed them, fold the laundry, tuck them in, wash the dishes, bring a coffee cup to our lips.

Our children will be shaped through the stories that our hands, and theirs, will come to tell.

In the back of that Chevy, I didn't know it then, but all those years watching my father's hands were teaching me something:

His hands told a story — a story of love and hardship, safety and fear, grit and grief. A story of how trauma and tenderness can coexist in the same gesture and the same person. A story written across generations, passed down in both what one does and doesn't *do and say.*

And like so many of us, I had to learn that healing begins not necessarily with *what* we do, but with *how* we show up. With what we choose to carry forward — and what we choose to lay down from our own doing.

In occupational therapy (OT), we talk about *meaningful occupation*. Meaningful occupations are the kinds of everyday activities and rituals that shape who we are and who our children will become. OT's learn about tasks and checklists that show us everyday moments that carry emotional weight and neurological impact. These everyday moments are how the brain and the heart develop, build connection and *make meaning.*

Parenting is full of these occupations: fastening zippers, nursing and feeding, packing lunches, brushing tangled hair, guiding little hands across a street, tending a scraped knee. These are not insignificant moments. They are the moments that construct safety, build relationships, weave memory into the body and build brain structure.

Try This

Hand Mapping Connection Game

If your child is old enough, invite them to trace their hand on a piece of paper. Then trace yours.

☐ Compare sizes and lines.

☐ Ask: "What are some things your hands love to do?"

☐ Share stories of what your hands did when you were their age.

This builds intergenerational connection, body awareness, and curiosity through awareness and storytelling.

Wild Reflection

Take a moment to reflect or journal:

What memories live in your hands?

What have your hands taught you about caregiving?

What are three ways you use your hands each day to connect with your child?

2

The Cost of Survival

How childhood shapes the nervous system

Our country's 75,000,000 children represent only 20% of our population, but they are 100% of our future.

Moira Szilagyi, former head of the American Academy of Pediatrics, and professor, UCLA

Some of our stories live in the spaces between memories — in what we felt but may not have understood. They live in the reach of a hand. The flinch we had at its sudden movement. The warmth of a jolly laugh or the sting of a flash of anger.

Often, it's not until we become parents ourselves that these moments come into focus. We see them reflected in our children's eyes, in *their* gestures and reactions, and in the ways we find ourselves mirroring our own parents. These are storied opportunities for growth and healing, rising from the root system of our lives and asking not only what we'll pass on, but also what we are still working to understand — and what we are healing.

It might take a child's confused heart, a parent's exhausted mind, or the impulse to just check-out, to bring a buried story to the surface.

> *We don't need to dredge up every chal-*
> *lenging childhood memory, but by see-*
> *ing our past more clearly, we can offer*
> *something different for our children.*
> *And it's important to understand that*
> *a lack of skill on our parents' part, or*
> *ours, is not the same as a lack of love.*

As parents, we are constantly translating our past while shaping our children's future. As I learned to translate my past, many moments emerged, like the following incident. It is one of many where I cannot remember much of what I was doing prior to it, or how my body felt as it was happening. I remember as if it were a dream.

It was 1978, and I was eight years old. My family of five had recently moved from Hopewell Junction, New York, to a small coastal town in Connecticut. I sat in the backseat of our maroon-colored 1973 Dodge station wagon with my two brothers. The Dodge was the only car my mother and father ever bought brand new. Dad bought the car for two reasons. The first was that he could lay the back seat down and make a bed for us kids to sleep during our fourteen-hour drives to visit his family in Canada. The second was that he could fit eight full sheets of plywood in the back, "and still close the hatch!" Although he'd bought the car almost five years earlier, I still felt excited every time we piled in.

I was wearing my favorite dandelion-yellow polyester shorts and staring out the window. I remember trying to unstick the back of my legs from the vinyl seats, and I'd just put my hand on the shiny silver window crank when our wagon slammed to a stop. Everything happened so fast, and yet the memory arrives in slow motion. I looked up to see a man run up to the car directly in front of us. He reached through the car's open window, grabbing the male driver. I slung my arm around my little brother and yanked him in close. With needle-threading precision, the man ripped the driver through his open window and slammed him like a rag doll against the side of his steel-blue Impala. We watched the assailant's red face yelling. While gripping the driver's shirt in one hand, his other hand hovered in a pointed finger, partial fist, inches from the driver's nose. The driver was holding his hands up as if an officer had said, "Put your hands up in the air!"

My mother screamed from the front passenger seat of our car. One of her hands pressed firmly into the dash, while her other hand grabbed at her very pregnant belly. "Roch![1] Stop! Stop!" she shouted at our father. My father's crazed eyes shot away from the man in his grasp and toward our mother's scream — only then did I realize the assailant was our father. His frenzied gaze was the same that sometimes caused me and my older brother to become still as statues.

Mom's pleading command caused my father to release his grip before any real damage was done to the driver. Fast as lightning, Dad was behind our steering wheel, shouting expletives about my mother's safety and that *expletive* guy cutting us off. Our car bolted from the intersection, my head smacking the window next to me as I looked back to see the man still leaning against his car in a daze, his head in his hands.

When we pulled into our driveway, Dad bolted for the woods behind our house. I ran for the long arms of a weeping willow. I lay down under my tree, back sinking into the ground. My head rested on a pile of leaves while my ears listened to the sound of house wrens calling back and forth for each other. My head was spinny and my stomach hurt, but listening to the call and response between the birds steadied my thoughts. A dance of light through the green leaves gave my eyes a focus. Watching light create harmony with the wind, the willow, and the green earth slowed the erratic beating in my chest. Shallow, stuck breath became easier with the chatter and song of the wrens and the gentle caress of wind through my hair.

When Dad returned from communing with the woods, he was different. Calmer. Happy. Engaged. So was I.

Later that day, with the same hands that had threatened the stranger, Dad picked me up and joyfully plunked me down on his knee. While singing a ridiculously silly song, he made different cartoon-like voices. He jostled me up and down till I giggled so hard, I couldn't breathe. My concern for the man in the car, and my confusion about my father's actions, faded. I looked at Dad's jolly face, listened to his tenor voice, and reveled in his hugs. Mom smiled as she set the table for dinner.

By the time I was a freshman in high school, Dad's hands had begun to fail him. He would arrive home from his construction work with hands cracked, bleeding, and immobile. They had developed psoriatic arthritis — a painful autoimmune disorder. Now that he could not use his hands the way he always had, Dad's depression grew exponentially, seemingly overnight.

It was only then I came to understand that the 'meaningful occupations' of his youth — fishing, playing guitar, carving, wandering the wild spaces, building, creating — had kept something bigger at bay. They gave him purpose. They soothed the pain he carried.

Finding and teaching occupations will take their minds off of their misfortunes...It's not enough to give a patient something to do with their hands, you must reach for the heart as well as the hands. It's the heart that really does the healing.

Ora Ruggles, pioneer in the field of occupational therapy

I had many passionate 'aha' moments during occupational therapy school, but my truly big revelation came in a class called, *Abnormal Psychology*. It was during a heated discussion led by Dr. Mark Rosenthal, author of *Wellness and Lifestyle Renewal.*[2] The discussion centered on rehabilitating incarcerated people. He asked, "What are some ways to rehabilitate people who've been incarcerated?"

The students eagerly offered ideas.

Help them find jobs.

Help them find meaningful hobbies.

Help them find housing.

I found it challenging to take part in the discussion, distracted as I was by content from that morning's lecture. Dr. Rosenthal had covered mental health issues and the symptoms of depression, anxiety, manic behavior, bipolar disorder, and rage. He talked about how these behaviors affected a person's ability to manage daily life and how they affected the people around them, too.

Snapshots from my childhood reeled through my mind — my father's hands pulling that man out of the car window. My father's hands threading a fishing line, touching the moss on the side of a tree, slapping his knees while laughing wildly, his pointer finger an inch from my nose as he yelled at me, red faced — then immediately grabbing me (my pulse racing) and hugging me to apologize. His hands dragging one of my brothers out of

13

bed and down the stairs because he hadn't completed a chore. His hands building a campfire, baking bread, tossing us candy bars, hugging me, splicing rope for my friends and me to jump rope with. And eventually, my father's hands, idle.

Was it mania? depression? rage? that fueled his unpredictable moods? I'd never been aware that I had been navigating someone else's mental health issues my whole life. For me and my brothers — mania, depression, and rage were just, well — *normal.*

Though Dad had kept his hands busy and productive when I was young, he'd been unable to give much attention to "reaching for the heart." His heart seemed irrevocably broken. Nothing in his search, job after job, move after move, town after town, ever came close to restoring the meaning and the sense of connection that Dad experienced in his first seven years; before the collapse of the fishing culture that had lasted for generations — in a landscape so harsh, even the Vikings abandoned it. Would anything ever repair the damage caused, when abandoned by her husband, and out of desperation, his mother moved her six children away from the fishing village and the adults Dad trusted? And when his suffering of abuse by church clergy began after this move?

The class discussion about rehabilitating convicts continued, but I was remembering my father saying, "Jeezus, I can't believe I never ent up dead or in jail! Most of the guys I hung around with are either dead or in jail. Poor sons o' bitches." And I thought about his childhood and his mother, with only a second-grade education, providing for her children, often working three jobs. And my father, with a sixth-grade education, and his stories of feeling hungry, abandoned by his father, alone. I thought about the many jobs Dad quit, the houses we packed up and moved from because of an end-of-the-world riff with a landlord, boss, or neighbor, and my many schools, teachers, and friends. I thought about my mother's renewed hope — *maybe this time things would work out* — as she placed a gentle hand on his arm.

While the class discussion continued, my heart raced. I recognized that certain symptoms of mental health issues were all too like my own challenges with memory, organization, and communication skills; my vigilant mind always on the alert for danger; my all-or-nothing attitude; the constant industriousness of my brothers and me, our suck-it-up survivor-perseverance. I thought about how the happiest times in my childhood occurred when Dad was doing something that gave him meaning — like carving, building, playing guitar, or being outdoors in nature, walking through the woods, fishing, berry picking, building a fire to warm us after ice skating.

I recognized that my father's life, and by extension my mother's, was a demonstration of what happens when childhood trauma goes unseen, unheard, and unaddressed. And when there is nothing meaningful to replace what has been lost, taken, or never gained to begin with. I realized that my father's childhood, and my own, could be classified as "abnormal."

And yet, what if most of us could say the same? Not necessarily because of trauma or neglect, but because so many of the things we now know children need — consistent caregivers, time in nature, safe touch, supported regulation, freedom to explore — were missing or minimized in our own upbringings. What we called "normal" may be misaligned with what healthy development actually requires.

Suddenly impassioned, I slammed my open palm on the desk and blurted out to the class — "WAIT!"

I felt a ripple of attention. Everyone was staring at me. My face flushed, my voice cracked, but I spoke anyway. "But. But. We are having a whole discussion about rehabilitating an entire population of people who've likely never been *habilitated* in the first place."

I looked at everyone, and after an uncomfortable pause I asked, "Shouldn't we start the conversation there?"

From that day forward, I carried these questions with me:

What does habilitation really mean?
Can missing or misaligned developmental pieces be recovered?
And what does nature have to do with it all?

The profession of occupational therapy uses the term "occupation" to mean anything you do to 'occupy' your time. From simple activities like enjoying your morning cup of coffee to coding a complicated app, to driving your car to pick up your kids.

In the occupational therapy program, I found validation for what I'd intuitively known: The way a person occupies their time, and the way their thoughts occupy their mind, shapes their habits, roles, actions, and behaviors. Occupation creates brain patterns. When that occupation is deeply meaningful and aligned with purpose, it helps build healthy brain patterns. When it is meaningless or chronically stressful, it can build patterns of dysfunction.

When survival is the primary goal, the nervous system adapts. It learns vigilance, shutdown, or constant motion. It learns to normalize stress. And it wires these lessons into the body. Lessons like those become unconscious habits, like "checking-out"— which may have served us as children in situations that felt unsafe and that we had no control over. But checking out as a parent has different implications.

Looking back now, I wonder what version of *my* children's story they will remember of *me* — how my nervous system, shaped by moments like the one in the car, shaped the atmosphere *they* grew up in.

What We Normalize Becomes the Narrative

As parents, we often say: *I turned out okay... right?* But part of our healing — and our children's — is pausing long enough to ask: What did I learn to tolerate in order to survive?

From a developmental standpoint, many modern childhoods are "abnormal" — not because of any one person's failings, but because our culture is out of sync with the evolved needs of children. We've normalized disconnection from nature, fractured communities, overstimulated nervous systems, and chronically under-supported parents. By recognizing this, we can see more clearly without blame — so we can do better.

My story shows how the invisible patterns from our parents' lives become the soil we grow in. And yet, the same soil can be enriched. It can be tended differently. What we pass on doesn't have to be what *we* inherited. We can plant and water new seeds. We can create new stories.

The root of "occupation" is to *occupy*. If a child occupies their time in safety, wonder, movement, expression, they build brain patterns that support growth, regulation and thriving. If they occupy their time in fear, shutdown, or chaos, those patterns reinforce survival behaviors instead.

Understanding that so many of us were never fully habilitated isn't a reason for shame — it's a reason for compassion. And it opens the door to something else entirely: the chance to start again, with intention. To choose something *beyond* survival.

As caregivers, we can't erase our pasts. But we can change how our children occupy *their* time — and how we model meaning-making for them. And we can do this because we stand on the backs of those who've come before us.

Try This

Sacred Questions Dinner Jar

If your children are too young for this, you can do this with your husband, wife, partner, or even a good friend. Invite your family to co-create a jar of "sacred questions"— write each one on a small slip of paper and draw one at mealtime.

Try questions like:

□ What helps you feel calm when you're upset?

□ What makes your body feel strong and good?

□ What's something you do with your hands that makes you happy?

□ What do you think people need to feel safe? (Start with a specific example like: To feel safe, I need someone sitting next to me).

These questions help build emotional awareness and open the door to healing conversations—without pressure.

Wild Reflection

Take a moment to reflect or journal:

What patterns or behaviors from my childhood did I normalize that I now question as a parent? (The point here isn't to blame, but to understand. Our parents were shaped by their own stories and limitations, just as we are.)

In what ways does how I spend time with my child support their nervous system and sense of safety?

What helps me feel grounded when I feel emotionally "out of baseline"?

3

WHAT NATURE KNOWS ABOUT HABILITATION

SENSORY REAWAKENING

The behaviors and academic learning of your child are the visible expression of the invisible activity within his nervous system.

A. Jean Ayres, PhD

*H*abilitation = *To make fit, or to develop skills to function successfully in one's life and community.*

There's a moment when the weight of responsibility sinks in: How do I raise a child, and myself alongside them?

That moment might arrive as a pregnancy test, a dream that wakes us in the middle of the night, a voice in the back of our mind asking, *Can I give what I never received?* That's when we begin the long road to habilitation. Not just for our children, but for the parts of us still waiting to be seen, soothed, and shaped.

Many parents arrive at this moment, where they vow, *I will do things differently.* Maybe it happens as you prepare for childbirth. Or from the

20

surprise of feeling overwhelming love and adoration at the first sight of your newborn. It might happen after your child screams in a way that echoes your own childhood. Perhaps as you stare at a stack of parenting books, wondering why none of them hits squarely like the truth.

That moment can be like a reckoning as we come face to face with the versions of ourselves that never fully grew up, never got habilitated. The ones still learning how to be human.

Changing course starts with seeing clearly how development actually unfolds — and how nature, when allowed to lead, offers the sensory signals our neurology is waiting to respond to. It requires us to understand that habilitation is a journey shaped by the nervous system through our interactions with other people and the world.

We parent with our minds, our hearts, and we parent with our senses. Our children develop both through what we tell them, and through what they feel, hear, smell, see, and touch. Habilitation begins in the body, sensory signal by sensory signal.

Imagine a long road. At one end is a newborn baby and their senses. At the other end of the road is the result of successful habilitation — a fully developed person who has reached their full potential. To deliver us safely down the long road of development to the destination of habilitation, we need a skilled driver (caregiver). If we are lucky enough to have one, our brain feels safe and we can relax; our senses are free to engage with life, pay attention to whatever adventures we encounter, and make meaningful associations among them. If the driver seems unreliable, or even dangerous, the brain will use all its energy to find a route to safety. The senses will not pay attention to the sights and scenery and cannot make meaningful associations beyond those that will affect immediate safety. Survival is everything.

Here's another way to think about habilitation. Babies are born seriously underdeveloped. So as an analogy, if a baby were a house, at birth it would have its framing, electrical wiring, and plumbing roughed in, but the walls, flooring, paint, fixtures, insulation — many things that make a house functional and pleasant — would still need building. To speak specifically of a child, at birth the physical body is roughed in and wired with important structural parts — the bones, the organs, the circulatory and nervous systems, and the senses — but they are unfinished. Much has to happen before they become functional and skilled. Build-out must continue after birth; this is the work of habilitation.

With this wonderful design, fine-tuned by evolution over hundreds of thousands of years, we humans inherit great potential. The better we do in habilitating our young, the less *rehabilitation* they will need later, and the healthier our society becomes. The natural world has an important role to play in this.

After college graduation, I found myself so broke that I had to take the first job that came my way. A lot was happening in my life! After graduating and before taking the national exam to become a board-certified and licensed occupational therapist (OT), I'd gotten engaged. To a man I'd known for nine whole days. We moved in with my parents while I studied for the exam.

Then came another surprise, and I denied it as long as I could — until I nearly threw up on my new boss.

By the third positive pregnancy test, I couldn't deny the child growing in my womb. Recognizing that motherhood was on the horizon, I began to straighten my backbone. My under-habilitated approach to life suddenly became less than good enough. Shit got real.

I'd put myself through college to have a "better" life than my parents. They switched jobs and moved us so frequently I felt like I had whiplash! By the time I'd graduated from my third high school, I'd lived in more than twenty houses. We even spent one summer "camping" with all our belongings in storage.

I didn't want the struggle of living paycheck to paycheck, from one crisis to the next. I didn't want to keep leaving jobs and people, always looking for something better. I wanted to love my work and have long-lasting friends.

I was four months pregnant when I got married and five months pregnant when I received my license to practice occupational therapy.

In college, I came to understand that my childhood was shaped by one mental health crisis, one un-habilitated choice after another. It was a sobering realization, one that didn't erase the love I'd received, but complicated the story I'd always told myself.

When I came to recognize the negative aspects of my childhood, I felt guilty, ashamed that I felt anything less than gratitude for the good things my parents had done. After all, I had been allowed to both spend time in nature and develop a relationship with it — my most treasured and trusted ally in life. And just as importantly, I knew without a doubt that however tragically expressed, my parents loved and wanted me. But with motherhood looming, I had to face the chaos of my childhood and how it affected the habits, behaviors, and coping strategies I'd inherited.

I continued to reflect on what my parents had done well, which had helped create my capacity for putting myself through school, yet also what had been missing from my upbringing. It took time to arrive at the understanding that Dr. Gabor Mate, author of *The Myth of Normal* and addictions specialist, expresses so well: "Well, maybe your parents did the best they could? And maybe that wasn't enough? And maybe both things are true?"

During breaks from working with stroke and heart patients at my new job, I read everything I could about birth and babies. It was before the days of "gender reveal" and I listened to people's theories about why they thought I was having a boy and how to make him sleep when he was born. I couldn't wait to get home each day — first to take a nap, and then to read the newest book on my coffee table. I understood enough about myself and my childhood to know that there was a lot I didn't know about how to raise a healthy, well-habilitated child.

Book after book: *"What to expect..." and "How to..." and "Train your baby to..." and "Your guide to childbirth the (fill in the blank) way,"* all shared directives that left me confused and frustrated. Some of the advice and information made good sense, but much of it left me worried like I was going to, or already had, done everything wrong. Others had me thinking everything would be a piece of cake if I just followed a certain impossible formula. It felt like the books were delivering half-truths; none painted a whole picture. And no book addressed what an expectant parent should do if their childhood adversities had limited their own habilitation.

What's the plan when the parent still needs parenting? When the one holding the child is still sorting out their own childhood? How would I habilitate another human being if I'd not been fully habilitated myself?

When I was about seven months pregnant, my father visited without my mother. While he'd been relatively unemployed or on disability since I was in high school, my mother worked more than full-time to make ends meet.

As soon as my father walked in the door, he took one look at the stack of books and spouted, "What the hell do you need all these books for, woman? Women have been doing this for thousands of years!"

I felt tears well up.

He bellowed, "Don't be so goddamn sensitive!"

My tears erupted, and I stammered, "Well. Well. I'VE never done this before!" I grabbed a sweater, waddled out the front door, and mad-walked down the street.

I knew that some part of what he said was true. Why was I so unsure? (and why did he have to be so abrasive?) Why were so many of the women in my generation uncertain about giving birth and raising children, a process so ancient and elemental?

At a park, I sat down under a sugar maple tree.

I inhaled the smell of autumn air, ran my fingers along rough bark, closed my eyes to the cool breeze, and felt my baby kick and wiggle. I placed both hands on my swelling belly and opened my eyes. A helicopter seed twirled its way down from a branch and landed on my womb. "Hello sweet Maple Mama," I said out loud. "Thank you for your gift."

I watched as more seeds twirled from her limbs and descended, each in its own time. Some of them fell fast and straight; others danced left and right; still others seemed to linger on the wind, making time irrelevant. I whispered, "How do you know? How do you know when they are ready for release, Mama? Tell me your secrets?"

The base of her trunk cradled my back. Her body told a story. Deeply rooted, she stood. Her branches shaped by storms and sunlight. Her wisdom was responsive. Alive.

Surrounding the lake were other trees, each releasing seeds at their own pace. No artificial clocks or manuals. No sleep schedules or timelines. Just the sun and the elements. They weren't worried about doing it *right*. Why was I?

The books in my house were a yearning for a more organic parenting manual, one that speaks in something other than words, one that nudges child and parent ahead from some internal place, one that is specific to them. That's what the maple seemed to have.

The line of trees surrounding the lake moved their leaves in a cascade of rustling. Each maple tree on a slightly different timeline than the others, each helicopter seed taking its own path to the earth. *They* weren't reading books or taking classes. Why did I need to?

I hated it that my dad was right to some extent.

I closed my eyes again, breathing the autumn air and imagining my baby receiving it. My body felt calmer than it had when I left the house. My baby felt calmer, and so did my mind.

I imagined generations of stored knowledge within that one tree. Rings of wisdom held within its bark. I saw the maple tree as the mother she was — sturdy, grounded, providing roots, while allowing her seeds to release based on the alchemy of weather, water, air, sun, seasons. Storms blew her branches about, yet they held strong.

When I opened my eyes, I looked beyond this maple and noticed another maple tree a little farther from me, close to the road. Her seeds were sparse. I got up and walked to it. On its other side, I found a huge gash in the trunk. A car accident?

I placed both my hands on the gash, feeling the wound that had healed over. "Trees don't heal. They seal," I remembered a teacher saying — a reminder that a tree does not erase damage but grows living tissue over it, protecting itself while growing. Like trees, we can grow new rings around our wounds, not to hide them but to integrate and transform them, keeping pain from spilling into the next season of our lives as parents. And maybe, like the maple, we carry an inner wisdom — an ancient rhythm — that knows when to hold on and when to let go.

"Glad you are taking time to heal." I said as I kissed the palms of my hands and placed them on the tree for a moment before I turned and walked home.

When I returned, Dad seemed to have forgotten our interaction. He was heating chicken soup he'd made for us. So, I silently did what I've always done — study him — the way he moves, the intonation of his voice, his eyes, forehead, and his hands. I could see how ridiculously ecstatic he was at the idea of becoming a grandfather. "Hey Dad? Most kids were born at home in Newfoundland, weren't they?" I ask.

His whole body animates, his hands wave about; his limbs jerk and bounce from stove to cabinet, clanging dishes and dropping a spoon. He begins, "Oh well, of course. I mean, there were women. I guess they were like midwives who helped with the births. The men were never allowed, but they helped in other ways..."

As he spoke, I looked at my stack of books and our new baby backpack, its packaging portraying a happy young couple toting a toddler up a mountain, as though nothing in their lives had changed by starting a family.

Dad's stories faded into the background. My mind drifted to the ways I would do this parenting thing differently, and better. All the ways I would do it *right*.

I didn't yet understand that there would be sleepless nights, vomit, constant confusion, and many, many moments of unskillfulness — despite my books and gear, these experiences were inevitable. I wasn't yet aware that, for all of us, to do it differently for our children means we must make the journey of habilitation for ourselves. And my journey had just begun.

The Parenting Road Is Also the Healing Road

The word habilitation means building skills to fully engage with life. But what if no one helped you build those skills? What if you're doing that while parenting at the same time?

If you've ever wondered *why is this so hard for me when it seems easier for others?* — this is one reason: Many of us are raising children while still building scaffolding for our own nervous systems.

Even so, you are doing it. Every moment you choose presence, reflection, or repair — even imperfectly — is part of your own habilitation. Your children benefit from that work in ways you may not even see for years.

Nature shows us that healing doesn't look perfect. It can look like sealing wounds. Holding space. Learning to recognize inherited chaos — and choosing not to pass it on.

Try This

Grounding with a Tree

   ☐ Take 5 minutes outside with a tree — any tree.

   ☐ Place your hand on its bark.

   ☐ Breathe slowly and feel the air around you.

   ☐ Say (aloud or silently): What have you lived through? What have you learned to seal?

   ☐ Imagine that wisdom slowly becoming your own.

Try this alone or with your child. Invite them to ask the tree a question too.

Wild Reflection

Take a moment to reflect or journal:

What did you inherit that you want to heal, not repeat?

How can you know when your nervous system feels "safe enough"?

What has nature taught you about resilience, patience, or starting again?

What about your 'inheritance' can you be grateful for?

4

WHAT TO EXPECT WHEN YOU ARE NOT EXPECTING

A MILLION YEAR OLD MANUAL

Life is lived forward but only understood backward.

Holly Ringland, The Lost Flowers of Alice Hart

Not all of us planned to become parents when we did. Even those who did may still feel completely unprepared by the moment it actually happens. But one thing is true: ready or not, becoming a parent transforms you.

And transformation doesn't really care about *your* timeline.

The transformation can begin with the first intuition that you are pregnant. A phone call in the early morning hours. Or when you first hold your baby. Expected or unexpected beginnings. And while parenting may seem like uncharted territory, the sensory map for healthy development is a million-year-old technology still living inside each newborn baby.

31

My transformation began in the predawn darkness of Christmas morning, 1997, amid the first big snowstorm of the year. A heavy tugging in my body woke me. I felt an icy breeze. The slice of air through my bedroom window smelled like snow and frost. Tug. Tug. My body implored me to pay attention. I reached down and rested my palm on my belly, which was taut like stretched animal hide over a hand drum frame. I swear I could hear a rhythm beating. Fresh air caressed my cheek, and I inhaled, smiling.

I was exhausted from working 50 hours a week at the hospital. But breathing in crisp, wintry air calmed my tired body and alerted my mind. Snow and frost seen through the window reminded me of girlhood days wandering through the eastern woods.

My father would say things to me like, "You see how the moss on this side of the tree forms a shape like a pregnant woman? Let's call her the northwest mother and turn here." In this way, as we went through the woods, we created what some call a storyline based on different natural features. If we read the storyline in reverse, it could lead us back out of the woods.

I inhaled another wisp of wind and snow from the open window and thought, this snowstorm is part of my baby's storyline.

Our car crawled to the hospital, its tires leaving the first tracks in ankle-deep snow. We arrived to a skeleton crew in the pre-dawn hours of Christmas Day. My daughter was born that afternoon, making headlines in the local paper: the "Christmas Baby."

Immediately following her passage from my womb, she lay on my much softer belly. Our eyes fixed on each other. Her body trembled and flailed as if falling in a dream. I pressed my pointer finger into the palm of her quaking hand. Her tiny fingers immediately wrapped around my finger, gripping tightly. Her whole body calmed. So did mine.

In a book on my living room floor, I'd read that it often took three days for a mother's milk to "come in," and I'd worried how a baby could survive with only thin, clear, colostrum. In the moments after my daughter's birth, with our hands together, I understood that nourishment was so much more than food in a breast or a bottle.

For the first few months after my daughter was born, I felt lost, disoriented, as if I had entered a dense forest and couldn't see my way out. Despite all I'd read, my story had lost its through-line. None of the books piled on my reading table had prepared me for the vast change I was experiencing. I felt completely caught off guard. What do you expect when you are not expecting? When pregnancy wasn't the "plan?"

Those first days, weeks, and months, I was consumed by my daughter's eyes, her tiny hand on my breast, her sleep giggles. How could I possibly follow the directives about schedules, how to's and should's? My heart expanded beyond anything I could explain. My rational, intellectual brain had gone offline.

Then one morning, after the blur of a sleepless winter, numbing adoration and a newborn's vomit, my five-month-old baby and I unfolded into the first glorious spring day. It was one of those days when you open the door and know you are emerging from winter hibernation — the light was soft and inviting. Robins were singing loud and proud about the joy of making it through winter. Crocuses and hyacinths were pushing through hard ground. Everything felt fresh. That day, the book I had searched for, the organic parenting manual — landed at my feet.

I look back now and realize how easily I could have missed it.

I held my cherub in arms, stepping out onto the front step. The fresh air accentuated by a warm breeze. When I took a deep inhale to greet the world, my daughter did something unbelievably subtle, and unforgettably profound.

She turned her face into the wind — reached her hand out in front of her, with fingers splayed as if someone was there to grab them — she closed her eyes — a gust of wind enveloped us, lapping at her face — her tiny hand quivered like a tuning fork, and her little body heaved... gasped and laughed...

Then I laughed, and she looked toward me. Mesmerized, I was overtaken with joy. I gasped and laughed too. At this, she turned again to the wind, closing her eyes once more, breathing it in, laughing, opening her eyes, turning to me. I laughed again.

Over and over this went on, for perhaps ten or fifteen cycles...

A dance between my daughter and the wind, her, and me, me and her, her and the wind again. Each of us awakening to, engaging with, and integrating the pleasure of wind on skin, laughter, and our dance.

We were captivated. *We* were connected. And my stress about "doing parenting right" felt surprisingly calmed. I was finding new inspiration for my quest to learn what habilitates and can ultimately rehabilitate a human.

I have learned a lot about habilitation since that spring day twenty-seven years ago. With the wind's presence, and my permission to give her time to enjoy it, my daughter was being nourished by nature.

Nature was sending signals — invitations — to her developing nervous system. Wind awakened my daughter's touch receptors. She then turned to accept the wind's invitation, even reaching for it with her little hand. In that way, she allowed nature to guide the development of her senses.

Since the beginning of humanity, nature has called to our neurology through sensory experiences similar to this one. Our ancestors answered that call over and over.

Research reveals that at my daughter's young age, her neurology was rapidly developing. Connections between neurons were firing and wiring, or, firing and being discarded. We are born with the raw material of a nervous system, with bits and parts in place, but we must actively fire all the little bits and parts to develop them.

Our environment stimulates us through our sensory-motor system. The more we allow our bits and parts to be stimulated by the environment — especially in meaningful, relational ways — the stronger those neural pathways become.

And it's not just the stimulus that matters. It's the context of it and the importance we place on it. A caregiver's smile, coo, or gentle touch helps the baby's brain tag that sensory information as comforting, safe, important. That's when the brain and body agree: "Yes. I'll keep this information."

But if ignored or paired with tension, the brain may flag the same stimulus as unimportant or even threatening. It then gets tossed away or wired into the survival system instead of the connection system.

Although scientists have identified hundreds of senses, we have eight primary senses that guide this sensory-development conversation. The familiar five: *sight, hearing, touch, taste, and smell* — are just the beginning. Three lesser known but critically important senses include:

Proprioception: our sense of body awareness — how we experience our body through muscles and joints.

Vestibular: our sense of balance and orientation to space and gravity.

Interoception: our sense of internal states, like hunger, heartbeat, and gut sensations.

To understand how our sensory system works, imagine each of your child's senses as a beautifully crafted instrument. Each one evolved over millennia to help them interpret the world. But, like instruments, we must use and practice them repeatedly to create music. A child must practice using their instrument over and over and over for that instrument to make beautiful music.

Nature is rich with the exact sensory inputs we're wired to need: buzzing insects, rustling leaves, birdsong and chatter, twirling seeds, howls, hoots, rattles, sunbeams, snowflakes, scents of spring, gurgles, splashes, thunderous bangs, rolling hills, craggy mountains, meadow cacophonies, rhythmic waves, and so much more. These are practice opportunities.

Sensory signals from nature call to us. When we are young, we are live wires waiting to spark at those signals. I call our readiness to receive and respond to nature's invitations our *sense of ecoception*. **Ecoception** is a word I made up to describe a preconscious, evolutionary state — our nervous system's ability to notice and respond to the signals of nature. I use the word ecoception to describe a birthright that's often buried beneath the noise of modern life: the body's built-in dialogue with nature.

Ecoception:

Derived from eco- (from the Greek oikos, meaning home or environment) and -ception (to perceive or receive), ecoception refers to the body's preverbal, embodied capacity to perceive and respond to nature's signals. It is the sensory-motor system's biologically inherited ability to attune to environmental stimuli — like birdsong, wind on skin, or the changing quality of light.

Many sensory conversations discuss the senses as though they are meant to play solo concerts. But the senses are meant to work in harmony, as an ensemble, and in cooperation with each other. They are meant to play together, communicate, and adjust in real time. When they don't practice cooperating — when one sense dominates, or another falls behind — the entire system can get disorganized. Emotions become harder to regulate. Focus slips. Planning and sequencing fall apart. It's like listening to an elementary school band squeaking through one cringeworthy moment after another.

For this symphony to come together, it needs a conductor. Our original conductor is nature itself. For generations, it was nature that led the rehearsal. That guidance shaped our brains, our movement patterns, and our capacity to adapt.

When I talk about the NatureLed™ approach, I'm simply naming nature as our conductor.

Our sensory receptors — specialized cells in our bodies that detect and respond to stimuli from the environment, such as light, sound, touch, taste, smell, temperature, pressure, and gravity — wait for information. When they detect a stimulus, they send a message to the brain. The brain asks: What does this mean? Am I safe? Is this important? Will this help me survive?

Once the brain answers that question, it can decide what to do next.

The more the senses practice this loop — from reception to interpretation to action — the more fluent and melodic the body becomes.

Here are just a few examples of nature's invitations for each sense:

Visual (seeing): branching patterns of trees, animal markings, clouds shifting shapes, a hawk circling overhead

Auditory (hearing and listening): birdsong, leaves rustling, water trickling, twigs snapping, distant thunder

Olfactory (smell): the smell of damp earth or mammal fur, flowers blooming, ocean breeze, impending rain

Gustatory (taste): the taste of ripe or sour berries, salty air, bitter roots, snowflakes on the tongue

Tactile (light touch on skin): rough bark under palms, soft grass, cool mud between toes, wind on skin

Proprioceptive (how we experience our bodies through our muscles and joints): lifting stones, walking uneven ground, gripping branches

Vestibular (balance and gravity): climbing, swinging, spinning, jumping off a rock, scrambling up a hillside

Of these senses, our vestibular and proprioceptive senses are the secret powerhouses. They get little fanfare, but they organize the rhythm of the whole sensory system. They are the organizers of our brains and bodies.

Proprioception helps you figure out how hard to hug, or how much force to use when picking up a gallon of water or lifting your morning cup of coffee, cracking an egg for breakfast, or how tightly to grip a pencil and how hard to press it to paper. Consider that you don't have to think,

"Hmmm. How heavy is this cup, and how much muscle will I need to pick it up?" You don't have to look at your mouth to take a sip; you just know where your hand is, and your brain predicts the amount of force you will need to lift the cup to meet your lips without hitting your teeth. That's your body's proprioceptive sense at work.

The vestibular sense works alongside proprioception, helping you stand upright, catch yourself if you trip, navigate around the furniture in your living room, sit in a chair without falling to the floor, and move about the world without running into things. It also organizes your thoughts. Think of it like a centrifuge: it receives streams of input, swirls them together, and smooths them into one fluid, coordinated motion.

With strong senses the whole body moves in rhythm.

The nervous system says: I know where I am. I know who I am. I'm safe to learn. I'm safe to connect.

When these senses are undeveloped, our motor control is reduced, and even minor tasks can feel enormous. Emotions get big. Anxiety rises. Uncertainty builds. We lose focus. Social interactions and talking can become a struggle. We can feel quite literally like an astronaut lost in space.

The experience of astronauts helps us understand just how critical these senses are.

In space, there's no gravity, which means no push and pull on our joints and muscles. Without gravity, the feedback loop disappears. An astronaut's proprioceptive and vestibular senses disengage. It's as if the brain's centrifuge has stopped spinning — the streams of input no longer swirl into a smooth current, and scattered signals remain scattered. Astronauts lose track of where their limbs are, how much force to use, and which way is up or down. When they return to Earth, many experience what they jokingly call "the space stupids." They feel disoriented, uncoordinated, and clumsy. Their bodies must relearn themselves in relationship to Earth.[1]

In many ways, this mirrors what children experience today — under-stimulated senses make it harder to navigate the world with ease. Consider that for most of humanity, these senses worked hard for the better part of every single day. Now the inverse is true: children must work hard to be *allowed* to engage these senses at all.

We see the side effects in behaviors like toe walking, sucking and chewing on things, pulling, pushing and breaking items, bumping into objects, tripping, uncertainty, impulsivity, anxiety, depression, apathy, and big emotional outbursts.

We label it all as difficulty. But often, it's a lack of practice. Lack of sensory rehearsal. And as children rehearse less, special education departments are booming, as is demand for behavior intervention specialists.

When the senses have space to harmonize, play, and coordinate, a deeper sense awakens.

Interoception.

Interoception is known as our gut sense. It is the felt sense of what's happening inside: My belly is full. My heart is racing. This is dangerous. I am warm. I am cold. I need to rest. I feel safe.

Interoception is like the conductor's ear. It is the brain's ability to listen to the body's instruments and know what note needs to be played next. When the senses are playing in tune, the inner voice gets clearer.

We often call it intuition, but it is literally our gut instinct. And it's not magic. It's integration.

Alternatively, if the senses are not playing in tune together, you can end up feeling anxious and uncertain, something like an astronaut upon returning from space.

When nature leads the practice, and when we give our senses room to fire and wire, the entire system becomes more coherent. And sometimes that coherence shows up in unexpected moments, like saying, "That's so weird. I was just thinking about that, and then it happened."

Another element of that moment between my daughter and I, and the wind that day can be explained by research from the Harvard Center for the Developing Child (HCDC). They have named this type of interaction as, *A Serve and Return Interaction*.[2]

HCDC explains a Serve and Return interaction as the back-and-forth exchange, or "volley" between a child and caregiver. A baby smiles. The adult smiles back. A baby babbles. The caregiver responds. That volley builds neural structure. It's like a game of tennis, but instead of points, what's being built is the brain itself. Serve and Return is how we wire for connection, not just socially, but neurologically.

The more safe, responsive volleys a child receives, the stronger and more integrated their brain becomes.

We are wired for relationship. But not just between each other. We are wired to serve and return with nature too. That spring day with my daughter, the wind served. My daughter received it. She reached, laughed, turned toward it. Then turned toward me. I laughed too. And just like that, we began a multi-layered loop of serve and return:

Wind to child.
Child to caregiver.
Caregiver to child.
Child to wind.

41

She was eco-receptive — tuned to the wind's invitation. I let nature lead her, and I followed. Together, we engaged in a developmental feedback loop older than language. A loop that predates instruction manuals, algorithms, or university research. A loop encoded in our cells.

Only later did I realize I had three choices in that moment:

1. To send her the message that this moment mattered — that nature, her body, her joy was worth noticing.

2. To dismiss the moment — through distraction, indifference, or inattention.

3. To respond with negative emotion — scold, admonish, or react fearfully.

Each of the three responses would produce a different outcome.

1. Connection

2. Disconnection

3. Fear

Serve and Return

Outside—with the Senses

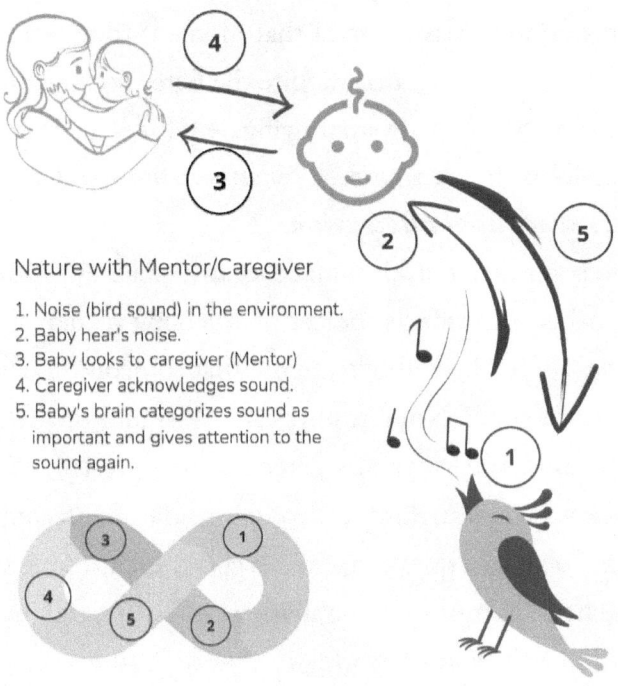

Nature with Mentor/Caregiver

1. Noise (bird sound) in the environment.
2. Baby hear's noise.
3. Baby looks to caregiver (Mentor)
4. Caregiver acknowledges sound.
5. Baby's brain categorizes sound as important and gives attention to the sound again.

©KATHLEENLOCKYER - RXOUTSIDE.COM

Serve and Return With Nature

43

How many times had I sat under a tree, or lain in the sun, closing my eyes, and allowing wind to caress *my* skin — unconsciously inhaling, receiving, and returning the gentle or rapturous serve of the wind, a reciprocal inter-action?

My parents had given me permission to receive nature's signals. To play with the wind. To laugh with the rain. To listen for meaning.

That permission was passed on at that moment to my daughter. And now, I pass it on to you. Because despite the fierce independence that so many westerners covet, we have an undying need for each other, which also means, especially as children, *we need permission to connect.*

We could say we need alloception.

Alloception is another word I've made up to explain our *need for others.* Allo means other. Ception is the act of receiving or perceiving. Thus alloception would be the embodied sense that someone else is here with you; You sense the other. Not just physically, but emotionally. Spiritually. It's the way a child knows when a parent is truly present, even without words, like the way my daughter turned toward me after feeling the wind. It's the return volley of a question asked, a glance held, a song shared. Just as ecoception helps us tune in to the aliveness of nature, and interoception helps us tune in to our inner world, *alloception is how we tune in to one another.*

Nature is so much more than an add-on, a reward, or a bonus. It is the foundation, the original source code, the sensory soil in which regulation, relationship, and learning grow. And we have shared nature with each other forever.

Nature has provided us with essential source materials — water, sticks, stones, dirt, wind, hills, and so on — to inspire and guide our learning. Nature reaches for us through stimuli, patterns, and rhythms, and we, through our ability to sense the world around us, have reached back and engaged with nature since the beginning of our species. And until the last few hundred years, humans validated and supported each other in the human-nature connection. The modern human brain and body are a testament to these relationships.

As I searched for answers about what habilitates and ultimately rehabilitates us, three things have emerged: *We need interoception — a sense of ourselves; We need ecoception — a sense of nature; And we need alloception — a sense of each other.*

Try This

Wind Dance Invitation

☐ Step outside with your child or go alone first.

☐ Stand quietly.

☐ Close your eyes and feel the air against your skin.

☐ Stretch your arms like branches. Let your body respond.

☐ Notice if your child mirrors you. If they do, let it become a shared rhythm.

☐ Say (aloud or silently): *I am listening. I am receiving. I am responding.* Let nature lead.

Try this as a daily reset. Even two minutes can shift the tone of a whole day.

Wild Reflection

Take a moment to reflect or journal:

What was one moment when your child responded to nature with delight or curiosity?

How did you respond?

When was the last time your own body felt naturally regulated, without trying?

What invitations from nature are you learning to say yes to?

What is one way you can follow the wind today?

5

COMPOSING CONNECTION

RELATIONAL RHYTHM, REGULATION, AND THE MUSIC OF BECOMING

> Many of us don't distinguish between the acts of listening
> and hearing.
>
> Bernie Krause, The Great Animal Orchestra

If our sensory system is an orchestra, then regulation is its rhythm, the living pattern that turns scattered notes into music.

And like music, rhythm doesn't arise from a single note; it is a coordinated effort.

The day my five-month-old connected with wind, I walked back inside and looked around our apartment.

Sprawled across the coffee table, kitchen counter, and even the bathroom floor were books and baby items promising to solve the "problem of parenting." Feeding schedules, baby bouncers, moon-shaped pillows, cradle, bassinet, binkies, hanging mobiles — all aimed at relieving my exhaustion, confusion, and overwhelm. But they created more.

Today, we add screens and apps to this cluttered cacophony.

This "stuff" is a symptom of something deeper: a culture that has lost its ability to listen deeply. One that teaches children, and parents, to tune into scattered, disconnected stimuli: a sound here, a flash there, a beep, a click, a glow, a pop. But the brain — like a musician learning to play — doesn't develop well in chaos. It needs to listen for patterns of sounds and silences while feeling the rhythm of how they go together.

In nature, information arrives in cohesive, patterned arrangements. A robin's call signals a squirrel nearby. A slant of light cues dusk is coming. The smell of petrichor means rain is on the way. These are notes played in sequence, not fragments flung across space. Our brains evolved to recognize this kind of music — *patterns in context*. Nature offers sensory coherence.

Modern toys and entertainment, by contrast, provide sound without a score. The beeps, blinking lights, and synthetic textures may grab attention, but they do not carry a tune the brain can organize. They create confusion through sensory dissonance, pulling the nervous system in many directions at once without offering a structure that makes sense of the signals.

Imagine a robin perched on a branch outside your window. You hear its call. You notice its movement. Over time, you learn that sound means a squirrel is nearby. One day, in an unfamiliar place, you hear the same call — and there is the squirrel. Your nervous system relaxes. Your brain recognizes the familiar motif. This is relational learning. This is sensory music. And it's happening in the natural world all the time.

The melodies of nature are not only beautiful; they are trustworthy. They repeat with variation, build a repertoire your child's brain can return to, and invite harmonies. Random notes cannot teach the brain how the world works. Without a sensory score — without a thread of relational rhythm — a child is left adrift in life's symphony.

I came to see this not only through research and observation, but in my own life. Disconnection was everywhere, and yet when my children were born, I still found myself caught in the scattered noise I now recognize as incoherent and nonsensical. Like many parents, I felt overwhelmed by modern life. But the connection with nature I'd been given permission to have became the melodic thread I wove into the larger composition of life with my children — even as I stumbled through the practice of parenting myself.

I've never met a "perfect" parent, or one who had a perfect childhood. All parents have strengths in some areas and gaps in others. Some of us grew up learning practical or academic skills, even survival skills — but not relational ones. We may not have seen what it looks like to be supported inside an affirming community, or how to repair unskillful interactions. And so, when it comes time to raise our own children, we may feel confident in some ways yet deeply unsure in others.

The inverse is also true. You may have grown up in a supportive family, but without nature as part of the picture. You may have learned to read people's moods, but not the sky. One half of the orchestra was practicing, while the other sat silent.

In the absence of role models, we turn to experts and strategies. Too often, this advice runs counter to the rhythm inside us. The more we tune out our voice, the more our inner tempo falters.

Parent confusion is not accidental. It's good for business. Entire industries thrive on selling solutions to our insecurities. The more exhausted and unsure we feel, the more likely we are to click "add to cart." But what we're really being sold is an impossible dream.

And in chasing that dream, we risk losing the very things that make parenting vibrant:

Curiosity

Connection

Relationship

If we can remember that there is already a coherence carried in our lineage — guided by the older harmony of nature — we can stop outsourcing our knowing. That knowing carried me outside one spring day, guiding my daughter's tiny hand to reach for something invisible yet undeniable. It still lives within all of us.

Even so, I struggled, caught between what I thought I should do and what my daughter truly needed. Modern life is full of contradictions.

I remember one night when my older daughter was about a year and a half old. Her father and I were hosting a small dinner party with two other couples, none of whom were parents. We were laughing, talking, and feeling like regular adults again when my daughter's bedtime arrived. I felt resentful, left out, like I was sacrificing my "fun" to meet her needs.

But I could see she was overloaded. Her body was buzzing with the dissonance of too much everything. I brought her to our room and lay down beside her. Her little body wrestled with itself — hands fidgeting, legs kicking, breath uneven. I wondered how long it would take before I could return to the party.

Lying there, frustrated and restless, I remembered something my mother-in-law, Martha — a business owner and mother of two — had told me: "Don't worry. You have your whole life to do that stuff. But she'll be gone before you know it." With that memory, I exhaled and looked at my daughter again — her trusting eyes, her reaching hand, her curious mind.

51

I let myself feel her hand clutching my arm, her leg slung over my belly, and the sanctuary my body offered her. Suddenly, it felt like everyone else was missing out. And I thought, what is more joyful and beautiful than this moment?

And as that realization settled into me, her twitchy body softened. Her breath found tempo. Her grip eased. She drifted to sleep. Our sense of alloception was fed. I stayed with her a while longer, listening to our shared breath as if it were a duet — steady, synchronized, calm.

We were connected.
We were regulated — together.

In that harmony, I could feel how we influenced each other's state of being. At first, my dissonant frustration had tangled with her overstimulation, creating a loop of mutual tension. That's the other side of alloception — it can transmit stress as easily as it offers calm.

That night reminded me: regulation isn't taught like a sheet of notes; it's offered like a tuning fork. Our internal state reflects what surrounds us — a phenomenon called entrainment. When I walk by the ocean, my heart slows to match the rhythm of the waves. My breath elongates. My body hums in tune with the sea. The same is true in human relationships. We entrain to each other.

Our nervous systems draw upon the landscape that surrounds us, the way an electric plug draws from a socket. When we are attuned, we create music worth listening to and sharing. That night with my daughter was not about "self-regulation." It was about relational regulation.

If ecoception describes how our bodies organize through connection with nature, and interoception describes our internal self-awareness, then alloception is the resonance we create in response to others — the feedback loop of attunement that tells us we are safe, held, and not alone.

It is the unspoken dialogue between parent and child:
a look,
a breath,
a hand resting lightly on a shoulder,
a soft voice saying, "I'm here."

This is the music of connection.

What many call "self-regulation" is actually the result of thousands of micro-moments in tune *with* something — or someone. Quite the opposite of a solo experience.

Lisa Feldman Barrett, known for her pioneering work on how the brain creates emotions, calls this the predictive brain.[1] Her research shows that we aren't simply reacting to the world; we are anticipating it, building patterns from what has come before. So when a child is overwhelmed, they are essentially forecasting. *Am I safe? Will someone come? Does anyone hear me?*

And our response — a slow breath, a steady eye, a calm voice — becomes part of their internal prediction repertoire. Their body begins to learn: I can trust this. I am not alone. I can relax.

That is the beginning of a nervous system in harmony.

So yes, that sticker chart, that timeout strategy, that withheld attention, may teach the child to behave — but their short term behavior might not be the long term behavior you hope for. It might teach the child that they are alone in the effort to soothe themselves. That their song must be played in silence, unaccompanied. And isolation sold as "independence" begins a road to disconnection.

What the language of "self-regulation" sells is connective disharmony.

What my daughter needed that night wasn't a strategy, boundary or technique. She needed resonance. She needed me — not to fix her or silence her, but to attune to her internal confusion and offer my own as an anchor.

And the best thing I could do as her caregiver wasn't to rush her through her emotions. It was to slow down enough to notice them. To meet her where she was. Together, we let go of societal schedules and...

We slowed down.
We listened.
And together, we composed regulation.

Moments of resonant connection are the only real antidote to overwhelm and dysregulation.

Our job is not to be perfect parents, but to become our child's steady bass-line beneath the improvisations of their becoming — to remind them of harmony when life grows dissonant. For many of us, that kind of secure relationship was not modeled. This is the sacred work of healing through parenting. It is the long road and the dynamic rhythm of habilitation, for our children and for ourselves.

Try This

Tuning the Family Ensemble

Choose one moment today to be the bass-line for your child. Resist the urge to fix their experience. Instead, offer a steady presence as they move through their own rhythm.

☐ When your child is upset or overstimulated, pause before you respond.

☐ Let your breath slow, or gently match theirs, and notice if they attune to you.

☐ Offer a simple, grounding phrase like: "I'm right here."

☐ Place a calm hand on their back, or sit quietly nearby.

You are providing rhythm, resonance, and rest (not performance).

Wild Reflection

When was the last time your child needed your nervous system more than your words?

What does "harmony" in your family feel like right now?

In what ways have you had to compose a new rhythm for your family — one that was never modeled for you?

Think back to your own childhood. Who, if anyone, offered you that steady bass-line of support? If no one did, how have you begun creating it for yourself — or your children — now?

6

RISKS AND HAZARDS

THE TRUTH OF PROTECTIVE PARENTING

"We are not given the world: We make our world through in-
cessant experience, categorization, memory, reconnection."

Dr. Oliver Sachs

My baby's receptivity to nature's invitations gave me a map home.
Every child comes into the world with that map already inside
them, a melody of belonging. But when nature's signals go unanswered,
when a caregiver's presence is muted, children lose sight of it. They experience a disorientation of self. The result is a nervous system without a
compass and when enough of us become disoriented, we begin to lose our
way as a society. We lose our sense of each other, of nature, and ultimately,
of ourselves.

Have you ever been lost? Like really lost? You might remember a time
when you were a child and lost your bearings, maybe after drifting too far
from your parents in a store or getting turned around in your neighborhood. There's a specific kind of panic that sets in with a wave of nausea and

shallow breathing; it causes you to pause, scan the immediate landscape, take inventory of your surroundings. You realize the street, tree, trail, or houses look unfamiliar. You wonder, *have I seen this before?*

Your brain scrambles to filter through what you see, hear, feel, as it tries to recall how you got there. Your body wants to move but doesn't know which way to go, so you start, and stop, and start again. You tell yourself to stay calm, but instead you get more emotional — or worse, you detach.

Now imagine a generation of children who feel that way most of the time — lost within their own bodies, untethered from their world, unsure of where to turn or where they belong.

In my nearly thirty years as an occupational therapist, I've met many children who cannot tell where the wind is coming from, where the sun rises and sets, or what an ordinary dandelion looks like. They cannot see or hear the birds outside their door.

They haven't fully experienced their senses. If they don't have a good sense of themselves, how will they sense another? Or nature?

The cost of disconnection like this is profound, especially when you consider most children can name every character in a movie franchise, and navigate the apps and settings on a smartphone. Their senses are being reduced to a single dimension, and their focus has become fantasy. Screens have colonized their senses.

When children are denied passage on nature's multi-dimensional road to habilitation, they lose access to a vitality of being. We may be living through the first era in history when, instead of actively taking part in raising our young, we have reduced nature to mere background noise and discordant notes. The road to becoming human is increasingly blocked.

Author Joseph Chilton Pearce warned as early as the 1970s that we were witnessing a quiet erosion of our sensory abilities. He referenced a study that spanned two decades, reporting that the number of color shades people could detect dropped from 350 to just 130, and the range of distinguishable sounds declined from 300,000 to fewer than 180,000. Although the original study is difficult to locate, an email exchange with one of Pearce's research partners confirmed its historical existence. His findings have since been cited by others and may have helped pave the way for more recent research in this area.

Recent developmental studies[1] show that sensory abilities don't grow without stimulation. They can narrow, dull, or become impaired depending on a child's environment and experiences. Recall that our sensory instruments must be played to make music. Idle instruments lose out. Infants naturally lose sensitivity to stimuli they rarely encounter (a process called 'perceptual narrowing').

During the early years, children's brains are wired for auditory dominance meaning they tune into sound before sight — it's part of how they learn to speak, relate, and feel safe. Around ages 6 to 10, the brain naturally shifts to rely more on vision. But when children spend large amounts of time on screens, especially before age three, this natural progression is disrupted. Studies show that their responses to sights, sounds, and touch can become scattered or delayed, making it harder for their sensory systems to grow in healthy, balanced ways.

For children with developmental delays, it's as if several instruments in the orchestra are out of tune at once, showing how easily these pathways can be disrupted.

Our sensory inheritance is eroding. [2]

Some of the most heartbreaking and well-known cases of deprivation show just how profound this impact can be. One such case is that of Genie, a girl who was discovered at age thirteen after surviving extreme early neglect. Isolated in a small room for most of her childhood, Genie had almost no sensory or relational input. Despite intensive therapy after her rescue, many of the effects of her early deprivation persisted. Her vision, for example, remained shaped by the limited depth of her early surroundings, and her emotional regulation never fully developed.

Animal research echoes these findings. In one famous study, kittens were raised in a space that contained only vertical lines. When later placed into a normal environment, they repeatedly ran into horizontal surfaces. Their brains had literally not learned to see what they'd never experienced. This kind of sensory shaping — or loss — shows how the brain prunes away what it doesn't use.

In the early years, a child's brain is like a gardener — planting new skills while also deciding which ones to keep and nurture. Just as a gardener pulls weeds to make space for what will thrive, the brain lets go of skills that aren't as useful so the most important ones can grow strong.

Studies show that deprivation goes far beyond the senses. Emotional regulation is one of the first casualties. Research from the Bucharest Early Intervention Project, which examined children raised in the stark deprivation of Romanian orphanages, offers one of the clearest pictures of how neglect affects developing brains. The orphans spent their early years in bare rooms with little touch, comfort, or caregiving. Their (very) basic needs were met, but emotional and sensory needs were entirely ignored. The study revealed that even after interventions, these children struggled to calm themselves, understand their feelings, or use relationships for comfort. Their brains showed structural differences, including enlarged, overactive fear centers, and abnormal stress hormone patterns. Some showed chronic anxiety; others had stress systems so blunted they barely responded. Even after adoption into caring homes, these children had trouble forming close relationships, especially during adolescence.

But research also revealed that when children were moved into responsive homes early — ideally before age two — their outcomes were far better. Their sensory systems and emotional capacities had a chance to catch up.

The global shifts in early experience for Western children are not the extreme examples like the ones we've just covered. They are a more insidious form of sensory deprivation.

When essential sensory experiences are absent or distorted, children lose access to internal cues that help them regulate, relate, and respond to the world. What begins as a disruption in perception soon echoes outward into emotion, behavior, and connection.

If you're like most parents today, you might be living with your own subtle form of sensory deprivation. Without realizing it, many of us spend only about seven percent of our lives outdoors. [3] That's about the time it takes to sip a latte at a café, far less than what's needed to feel the wind on your face, follow the sun across the sky, or notice the way the day breathes in and out. Our children aren't much different—most spend just 28–49 minutes outside each day. [4] As our connection to natural cues fades, so does our ease in reading the cues of our children.

I hear it often: *My kid doesn't like going outside. My kid gets bored. My kid doesn't know what to do out there. My kid would rather be on an iPad.* Every time I hear these words, I know the neural-nature gap has widened a little more.

Our wild insides don't stop needing nature just because our schedules are busy or our lives are indoor-centric. No invention, no screen, no shortcut will ever replace a million years of evolutionary fine-tuning.

Children are not rejecting nature. They are reacting to unfamiliarity. If their brains have not yet had the chance to form strong connections with the outdoors, they treat the natural world as something uncomfortable and unimportant. As we explored in chapter four, the brain works like a prediction machine. It learns from repeated experience, deciding what is worth paying attention to and what can be ignored to save energy. What may appear to be disinterest is often a nervous system doing its best to stay safe in unfamiliar territory.

One mother shared with me how her son would whine and ask to go home within minutes of arriving at the park. She would pack snacks, try different playgrounds, and offer games to keep him engaged, but the pattern was always the same.

"Shouldn't kids love nature?" she wondered. After meeting with me, she tried something different — short, low-pressure visits with no set agenda. She brought a blanket, let him collect sticks, and simply stayed present with him. Slowly, his time outside began to stretch. One afternoon, he pointed at a crow and said, "I think he's watching us," and she realized he was beginning to notice nature.

What changed was not his personality, but his nervous system. His brain began to re-categorize nature as familiar and meaningful. That shift rarely happens all at once, but it does happen, especially when a caregiver can stay present through those early moments of resistance. This is how the brain rebuilds its map.

If we mistake that early resistance for disinterest, we risk missing what is really needed. The answer is not more stimulation or structure. It is permission. Permission to be uncomfortable at first, to stay in the moment, and to reawaken the natural drive to explore.

Exploration, movement, and testing physical boundaries, what we often call risky play, are inherent needs children have in order to come alive in their bodies. Yet many children today are growing up without the freedom to follow that wiring. They are surrounded by what looks like protection, yet are often starved of agency. They may be kept physically out of harm, but emotionally they remain unanchored.

Agency is the ability to make choices and take action in your own life. It means feeling like you can influence what happens to you—not passively being controlled by others or by circumstances.

Instead of scrapes and bruises, many kids now carry invisible wounds: a chronic sense of uncertainty, low confidence, anxiety, and a disconnection from their own instincts. These are developmental injuries that show up in how a child navigates the world later on.

And that's where permission comes in.

Permission to *be nature* is how we give back to our children the things that for-profit culture has taken: the right to explore, to feel fear, to test limits, and to know their body and their world.

As we have moved away from nature-led parenting practices, we've confused safety with avoidance. This confusion didn't happen because parents don't care. In fact, it often comes from a place of deep love and fierce protection. But again, parental fear is good for business.

Many parents today are deeply afraid of injury, judgment, and of doing something "wrong." Ironically, it's this fear-driven protection that denies children the very experiences they need to grow resilient. Real safety comes from just-beyond-the-edge adventures that strengthen our prediction systems and show growing kids what they're capable of.

What we're seeing now is the long-term consequence of shielding children from nature-connected, risk-rich, movement-centered play. When children are deprived of sensory depth and relational grounding, focus fades, regulation becomes harder, communication breaks down, connection frays, the doors to awe and beauty close without notice and depression and anxiety take root.

If you are worried about your child's mental health, you are not alone. The absence of risk-rich, outdoor engagement is showing up in the mental health of an entire generation. It's alarming that across all age groups, depression and anxiety are the leading causes of disease burden world-wide. At its worst, depression leads to suicide, the second leading cause of death among 15–29-year-olds.[5] Seventeen percent of 10–24-year-olds report regular serious suicidal thoughts.[6] Suicide is the eighth leading cause of death in children ages 5–11.[7]

Sensory integration is the foundation for emotional regulation; and depression and anxiety are regulatory disorders rooted in the nervous system's inability to efficiently process and respond to internal and external signals. Lisa Feldman Barrett describes how the brain mismanages the body's energy budget when its predictive systems fail, leading to chronic emotional dysregulation.[8] Elizabeth Stanley shows that trauma narrows the nervous system's window of tolerance, trapping individuals in survival states that manifest as anxiety or depression.[9]

Studies by Grahn and by Touloumakos & Barrable demonstrate that nature-based experiences enhance regulation and resilience, especially in those with histories of adversity.[10]

Interoceptive research by Ceunen and colleagues further supports the view that affective disorders arise when the body's internal cues are mis-read or ignored[11]—reinforcing the need for sensory-based, embodied approaches to healing.

That's why risky, adventurous play matters so deeply. It's not a luxury; it's a lifeline.

Kids need all the opportunities they can get to develop their sensory symphony. Children who regularly engage in unstructured outdoor play—especially the kind that includes manageable risk—experience fewer symptoms of anxiety and depression, and greater emotional resilience.[12] These effects are even more pronounced in children facing adversity, suggesting that risky play can serve as a potent form of mental health support across all backgrounds.[13]

By giving children space to climb, balance, leap, chase, and take social and physical risks, we're not only meeting their sensory and developmental needs—we're offering them a form of protection.

Risky play doesn't need to be forced or scheduled; children want to do it. They play longer, move more, laugh more, and build emotional strength along the way. With this kind of play it becomes hard to pull them back inside — because their survival intelligence recognizes the nourishment from this kind of experience.

Permission to play in meaningful ways fuels the development of agency. When a child is allowed to explore and test boundaries in safe, supported ways, they begin to internalize a sense of personal agency.

One summer day, my older daughter reminded me how important even a little permission can be in the development of agency. She was about four, and it was a humid summer day on the east coast. She shed her clothes and was playing in the relief of cool water from our garden hose. I don't know where she came up with the idea, but she carried a bucket of water to the top of our play structure. Pouring water onto the yellow fiberglass slide, she sat down at the top of the slide, and before I could stop her, she flew down the slide, skidding her bare back across the grass. She got a bit scratched up, but I bit my lip at her wide-eyed surprise. Beaming, she stood up. Then she became a scientist. She brought more water and poured it down the slide, testing objects — different sizes, weights, textures — observing how each slipped and slid down the slide and across the yard. She busied herself for more than an hour, exploring flow, friction, and force. At only four, she was already conducting sensory-based field research!

For generations, children have chased the thrill of fear and laughter woven together — that sweet spot where excitement and caution meet. Research shows that when adults don't interfere, children's meaningful play is rarely tidy or tame.

Risk researchers, Sandseter and Brussoni, highlight the value of what's called "risky free play"—climbing trees, building forts, running fast, or hiding out with friends.[14] This style of play invites kids into a space where they experience both exhilaration and a little fear — right at the edge of their comfort zone. That is where they learn to stretch.

When I interviewed Dr. Brussoni for a podcast, she shared that "risk involves uncertainty." She explained how this form of play isn't about "courting danger, but about granting children the autonomy to assess and navigate risks on their own terms" — like my daughter learning how to measure risk with the water and the slide. Minor risks in childhood prevent bigger risk-taking behavior in the teen years and early adulthood when the stakes are so much higher.

Sandseter's research named several kinds of play that children are most likely to engage in when given the chance. [15]

Play at great heights.
Play at high speed.
Rough-and-tumble play.
Play with dangerous tools.
Play near dangerous elements.
Play where children can "disappear" or get lost.

Scary-funny play — the kind that ends in laughter after a shriek.

If we strip all risk from a child's experience, we also strip away meaning. We send the message that their curiosity is dangerous and convey that the world is to be feared, not explored.

Another point of confusion for parents and caregivers is what risk actually is.

There is a key difference between a healthy risk and a dangerous hazard. Brussoni, Sandseter and others distinguish between "risk" and "hazard" within the context of children's play. They explain that risk involves a challenge that a child can see and chooses to tackle, such as deciding to climb a higher tree or jump from a tall step. This type of engagement is crucial for empowering children to assess their capabilities and limitations, fostering essential skills like problem-solving, confidence, and resilience.

A hazard represents an unseen danger that children cannot anticipate and therefore cannot safely navigate, such as a broken piece of playground equipment, fast-moving water, obscured sharp objects or toxic waste. Adults should consciously manage or eliminate hazards to ensure safety while allowing for the benefits of free play. Our job as adults is not to eliminate risk but to remove hazards and stay present enough to let children explore.

With my daughter and the slide that day, she clearly understood that water would make her go faster, giving her the excitement of a thrilling risk, but she had not anticipated the hazard of the slide's material when wet. After her skid across the grass, she taught herself how to turn that hazard into a mitigated risk.

If I had revoked my permission for her to play with water because she'd underestimated the swiftness of her body on the slippery slide, what would she have learned? Perhaps that exploration isn't safe? Maybe the world is too risky? Or worse, she may not have built foundational skills to assess risk later in life. Thankfully, I won't know because I breathed through my discomfort (while standing a bit closer!) so that she could play and learn how to measure her risk-taking. That's resilience building.

Risky play helps children process emotions — like when my daughter stood up, a bit shaken, but realized she was okay and kept playing. It refines the sensory systems, as she learned to calibrate weight, speed, and timing. It builds problem-solving skills, like when she figured out what could safely go down a wet slide (maybe not her). Risk connects kids to meaning because it engages their whole being — body, mind, and spirit — in the task of becoming themselves.

Healthy risk-taking in the early years can even reduce future unhealthy risks. Like how maybe, because of that unforgettable moment with the slide, my daughter's future teenage self recognized when a risk was too great — like a slick rock face — and walked away, critical injury avoided despite a dare.

When you understand the difference between a real danger and a healthy challenge — and recognize your child's natural drive to explore — you can create a playful environment that helps them grow strong, confident, and capable.

If we want children to go outside and play, we need to make sure we are letting them do that.

A further complication for parents today is the widespread belief that academic learning is superior to playful learning. From baby genius apps to early literacy programs promising Ivy League futures, the pressure to prioritize achievement over play is constant. And once again, the science tells a different story.

In a 2024 report by the National Institute for Play, researchers point to a strong inverse correlation: as play has decreased over the decades, rates of anxiety, depression, and behavior challenges in children have gone up.[16] Meanwhile, children today are often described as louder, pushier, or less respectful — so society turns its finger toward parents, blaming them for being too permissive, too restrictive, or not teaching enough manners.

Even if there are fragments of truth in those stories, they are far from the complete picture.

Parents are just plain overwhelmed by constant judgment, and by deeply ingrained messages they've carried since childhood. Many were taught that play is frivolous, dangerous, and that real success comes from worksheets, enrichment programs, and structured achievement. Most parents of the last two generations didn't learn that play is the original curriculum.

Yet, that's exactly what research and experience confirm: engaging in play — especially outside, together — is possibly the most effective way to build the skills that will raise skillfull, successful kids. Confidence, coordination, communication, creative problem-solving, resilience, and emotional regulation are all born through real-time interaction with the world — not through passive consumption or rigid academic drills.

And now, more than ever, that kind of real-world, whole-child development is essential. As our world rapidly changes with the rise of artificial intelligence and automation, the old academic paradigm is crumbling right in front of us. We simply don't know what the future will require — but we *do know* that creativity, problem-solving, flexibility, and strong social-emotional skills will matter more than ever.

Play has been so essential to our survival that evolution built a core impulse for it right into our children. Their natural affinity for fun and exhilarating play is like an internal insurance policy for growth. When children climb, leap, balance, chase, or pretend to escape danger, they are practicing the very survival-based behaviors that helped our ancestors thrive.

Dr. John Medina, author of Brain Rules, puts it simply: our ability to do calculus or write computer code is a lucky byproduct. Our most meaningful occupation, first and foremost, is survival. Play is the meaningful way children learn survival skills.

The thrill of mastery is what transforms a child's mindset from *"I don't like playing outside"* to *"Can I please go play outside?"*

Play prepares us for life, building and shaping our skills, and it shaped my skills too. People often ask how I overcame what I did to raise such grounded, capable children. I point to the many moments in my own childhood when healthy risk and imaginative play became a kind of training. Playing with my brothers and cousins, I learned adaptability through action. I remember so many moments that blended challenge and hilarity — the kind of wild, full-bodied laughter that follows a fright. Like when someone jumps out from behind a door, everyone screams, and then collapses in a heap of laughter. Those experiences were more than amusement. They were practice in fear and recovery, risk and regulation, separation and reunion — all braided into the music of connection.

One such time happened when I was about eleven. I spent a few weeks in the summer with my older brother and two cousins in northern Ontario, Canada, at our grandmother and grandfather's home. Their home is on the edge of Algonquin Provincial Park. The town is relatively remote and at the time had a population of less than one hundred residents. We frequently saw bears, tracks of wolves, played in meadows where the grass was taller than we were, and once accidentally surprised a big bull moose.

One day, my brother and cousin took their fishing poles, a can of worms, a sack lunch and walked down a dirt road to a local creek. Another cousin and I sneakily trailed behind them. We waited until the boys had cast their fishing lines and quietly snuck close, making sure to stay camouflaged. As they chatted with each other, we grabbed a birch sapling, shook it vigorously and made deep growling sounds. The boys dropped their fishing poles and ran out of the woods faster than we'd ever seen them move!

Later that day at dinner as they shared the story of the "bear" in the woods. My cousin and I couldn't keep our secret and burst out laughing. I'll never forget my grandmother's face as she said slyly, "Oh. You two girls! You've got the dickens in you!" Me, my brother and our two cousins are still laughing about that "scary-funny" moment over forty years later.

Scary funny play can help build awareness. After that day, all four of us became more aware of our surroundings and of bear signs in the woods. A key point to understand about scary-funny play is that the person isn't alone in the aftermath; it's a shared experience. For my cousins and I, we had each other.

What makes play like this meaningful isn't just the adrenaline. Sandseter's research found that children use these experiences to build emotional flexibility. They are literally inoculating themselves against fear — learning, one heart-racing game at a time, how to navigate life's uncertainties. Adults who allow play that is exciting to unfold are not being irresponsible. They're offering a developmentally essential experience.

Those summer days were exhilarating for us. We felt truly alive and vital, and it motivated us to play more.

Recent studies by Sandseter, Kleppe, and others, show that children who engage in risky play learn to regulate emotions, assess danger, and rebound from stress.[17] Another study linked this kind of play to long-term mental and physical health.[18] In nature school programs, researchers found kids became more confident, more connected, and more joyful.[19] They weren't just getting stronger bodies. They were getting what we all want for our children: a meaningful childhood.

On the other side of exhilarating play like that of my childhood is the unfortunate reckoning many parents face today: The moment when your instinct to say "yes" is overridden by fear of judgment.

Maybe you have felt the inclination to allow your child to do more but have stopped them for fear of being judged? I've seen this as a primary cause of parents revoking permission to connect with nature or play in meaningful ways. The glaring eyes of family, friends or strangers, the sidelong glances, the unsolicited advice, the unspoken pressure to conform to an image of "good parenting" that prioritizes cleanliness, convenience, and control over curiosity, resilience, and risk.

Admonishing feedback is the echo of misguided legacies — those with tangled origins and no foundation in developmental science, only in outdated beliefs. Back in 2003, when my children were young, and I had co-founded the non-profit organization to get families outside, I experienced a moment that has stayed with me, reminding me of what parents are often up against.

During one rainy program day, I, the other mentors, and the children in our programs spent the day on a grand adventure walking up a cold creek. The kids had seen fish, frogs, newts, and ruby-crowned kinglets. They had spent the day building a living willow tree bridge. After its construction, they took turns traversing the bridge without falling.

Even though the kids were wet, they were lit up with joy. We had a small fire to keep warm, and because it was coastal California, it really wasn't too cold, especially for this East Coast girl! Later after the program day ended, the two mentors and I sat outside at a coffee shop with our three children. Our kids wanted to sit outside even though it was still drizzling on and off. The kids sat at a table next to us, sipping hot chocolate and laughing. As we debriefed the day, discussing successes and challenges, a man in an expensive suit, shiny leather shoes and carrying an umbrella approached. He slammed a $10 bill on the table, and shouted, "Buy those kids some damn shoes!" We were speechless. He had judged the bare feet and wet clothes as signs of neglect.

Walking barefoot might seem risky, but not long ago, it was common. Walking barefoot offers profound benefits, helping children learn about hazards while encouraging them to slow down, move softly, stay aware, and support tactile and proprioceptive development.

Have you ever walked barefoot across small pebbles? Think about how your body changes — you slow down, lower your center of gravity, bend your knees, widen your stance, and let your hips absorb the impact. You place your feet carefully, unconsciously testing for sharp stones before committing your weight. This exercise helps children develop their tactile and proprioceptive systems — which both support joint health, back health, muscle strength, and which are as we've discussed earlier, essential for emotional and physical regulation. Plus, going barefoot is free and accessible to everyone.

The biggest challenge I've faced in encouraging outdoor (and barefoot) experiences or allowing kids to get wet and dirty, or engage with nature, isn't sharp objects or stinging things, but the biased opinions of other adults.

I've thought about that man for years, wondering who took his connection to nature from him. Who taught him that children joyfully engaging with nature was neglect? Maybe a preoccupied caregiver missed his laughter of delight as the wind touched his infant skin. Perhaps no one shared his stories or let him play. Perhaps they didn't give him the permission I received.

I've wanted him to know it's not his fault, and he could reconnect with nature anytime.

The children in our group that day were with caregivers who cared deeply for their well-being, who were attentive and playful. If all children had that reality, maybe instead of anger, that man would have felt joy and remembered his own need for nature.

So when people say, "My kid doesn't know what to do outside," I don't hear laziness or disinterest. I hear a need for permission. A need for context that restores meaning. A need for adult allies who will stand in the rain with them — metaphorically and literally and say: *Yes. This matters.*

You might need to be the first among your parent group to give this kind of permission.

It might need to be you.

You can say yes now. Yes, to muddy feet and scratched-up knees, to joyful laughter in the woods. To play on purpose — because play is how children build the selves they will live inside for the rest of their lives.

So, if you've been looking for someone to give you that permission — here it is:

Let them play. Let them feel. Let them discover who they are by moving through the world in their own skin.

Consider this your permission slip — not just for your child, but for yourself.

Six Categories of Risky Play (Sandseter, 2010)[20]

1. **Great Heights** — Activities that involve climbing or being at elevated places (trees, playground structures, rocks) where falling is a possibility.
2. **High Speed** — Play that includes rapid movement—running, biking downhill, swinging fast, sliding, or sledding.
3. **Dangerous Tools** — Use of objects like knives, hammers, ropes, or saws that require skill and attentiveness.
4. **Dangerous Elements** — Playing near potentially hazardous natural elements such as water, fire, or cliffs—with supervision and safety awareness.
5. **Rough-and-Tumble Play** — Friendly physical play like wrestling, play fighting, and chasing, where children test boundaries of strength and social rules.
6. **Disappearing/Getting Lost** — Play where children wander out of sight or play hide-and-seek, giving a sense of independence and self-reliance.

*Go to kathleenlockyer.com to download safe practices for risky free play

7

THREADS TO ROPES

AFFORDANCES AND THE NERVOUS SYSTEM'S CALL TO EXPLORE

The tongue has no bones, but is strong enough to break a heart. So be careful with your words.

Unknown

L et's return to the day my daughter laughed into the wind. What began as play became a defining moment in our shared journey of attention. That morning, the natural world became a partner in *relationship*. Each gust, glance, and reach were part of a living conversation. A pattern was forming, one sensory exchange at a time, laying down the early threads of a lifelong bond.

When the wind died down, my baby's laugh calmed, and her eyes widened. I waited to see what she delighted on next. Her neck craned and her arm extended towards the shaking needles of a pine tree. I walked to the tree where she reached out her hand to touch the needles, quickly pulling back when they gave her a poke. I laughed. She looked at me, turned to the tree and reached out again. The pine poked her again. She laughed and pulled her hand back, looked to me, I laughed. When she reached her hand towards the tree again, I reached mine out next to hers, moving my fingers past the tip of the needles and stroking them from middle to end. She made the same attempt. We both laughed. Her eyes looked deeply into mine before she jerked her head towards the call of a nearby robin. Her hand moved toward its chula-leep, chula-loo sound, and she said, "OOO ooo ooo!" I followed her hand as though it was the magnetic needle of a compass, pulling us toward our shared North Star of connection.

The morning unfolded with this dance of discovery — more trees, birds, stones, and grass until her eyelids became heavy and my breasts filled with milk.

I observed all the ways nature called to my baby and all the ways she responded, first to a stimulating invitation from nature, then to me. It particularly enthralled me how she attended to bird sounds and behaviors. Each time she responded to a birdcall or the sway of a branch, I saw the intricate weaving of her sensory system and the living world around her.

Once again, I considered my father's, my mother's, my grandparents hands, and the ways they had invited me to connect with a blade of grass, the tickle of a ladybug crawling on the back of my hand, or the awe of catching lightning bugs at dusk. Their permission to love nature had always been there. Remembering their gifts filled me with joy, calmed me.

The memories of those early nature-led moments with my daughter became profound reminders of what it means to be in relationship with the world. Each gesture, each reach, each shared laugh beneath the trees planted a seed of connection, between her and me, and between her nervous system and the earth. As I deepened my awareness of our shared sensory interactions, I wondered where I might find others who saw what I was seeing.

My curiosity eventually led me to a group that would help water my seeds of connection and sharpen the lens I looked through.

Almost seven years after that windy spring day, my husband, our two daughters, and I had moved from Connecticut to California. The first year we lived in California, I met a man named Jon Young, international wildlife tracker, bird-language expert, cultural observer, and author. Jon had bright eyes and a quick wit. His body animated when he told stories, and his eyes closed as he listened to the words of others.

I also met Paul Raphael, a wisdom keeper from the Odawa people of upper Michigan. Paul had a quiet strength — a backbone held straight by experience, eyes that missed nothing, ears practiced in listening. Paul has a big heart. Despite being stolen from his family at five years old and forced into state-mandated Catholic boarding schools, where he and his peers suffered horrendous abuses [1]— he moves with grace, and his words ripple with forgiveness.

Paul and Jon were co-presenting at a weeklong workshop about nature connection and mentoring. Jon had already been teaching people to build relationships with nature for over two decades by the time I met him in 2003. Paul works as a peacemaker among his people.

At the workshop, facilitators created an immersive experience of a mentoring culture. Jon advocated for children to have the freedom to roam and explore outside. Paul instilled how important it is to have unconditional love for children and to honor our elders.

During the workshop, they taught about five "voices" of birds: song, alarm, companion calling, youth begging, and territorial aggression (later detailed in Jon's book, *What the Robin Knows*). I'd had a love affair with nature my whole life but had never actively listened to these distinct sounds. What had once been background sound became new invitations. By actively listening to and discerning nuances of sensory information like "bird language," one can step into the ongoing conversation unfolding right outside their door.

That week, I discovered I wasn't the only one carrying the fierce desire to protect our children's wild insides.

Over time, Jon became more than a teacher. Through ongoing programs, shared adventures, and long kitchen table conversations, he became a colleague, and we grew into family woven together by this work. Paul's influence and support in my life remain immeasurable.

Years later, at a workshop I was now co-teaching with Jon, I met another colleague of his: herbalist, researcher, and TV personality from the History Channel's Alone show, Dr. Nicole Apelian.[2] Drawing from their shared time with the Naro-San people of the Kalahari desert, Nicole and Jon introduced me to the concept of "threads to ropes."[3] According to their interpretation, each time a person gives something active attention, or acknowledges what they have noticed, such as a particular bird, tree, or breeze, they begin a thread of *relationship*. Each time we notice and acknowledge it again, with a nod, a hello, a whistle, or a conscious inhale, another thread grows, deepening the relationship. Eventually, threads weave together, creating a thick, unbreakable rope (connection) to that being and *its* place in the world. Many ropes like this create an entire map of relationship with a place, shaping not only our minds but our sensory systems'. It reminded me of what I had witnessed in my daughter that spring morning — how a single gust of wind, or the call of a bird, could become a compass.

More specifically, we first notice the bird by seeing it — one thread. The second time we see it, we notice the bird is busy and scratching the ground — two threads. The third time we see it, the bird is making a noise that sounds melodic and gives us a pleasant sensation in our belly

— three threads. The fourth time I see the bird, it is sitting at the top of a bush making a harsh sound and seems upset — fourth thread. By the time I have noticed the bird twenty times, that bird becomes more than "a bird." It becomes *this bird.* It doesn't fly away when I walk out my door; it sings at sunrise; it comes close to me when a cooper's hawk is hunting; and it alarms in a specific way when a snake is near. A rope of connection stretches between us.

Serve and Return, Call and Response, and Threads to Ropes are different names for the same understanding: one act of attention at a time builds relationship, and connection.

We build connections with people and nature in similar ways. It all starts with simple gestures, like saying hello, or noticing the direction of the wind, or turning to look where a bird called out nearby. We often dismiss these moments as distractions during conversation, but in reality, they are connections. When we focus our attention on these small sensory interactions, we lay the groundwork for purposeful and respectful foundations for shared experience, and emotional and physical regulation.

This process, once woven into thick rope, isn't easily interrupted. It takes force — a sharpened and systematic effort to fray thick rope. Yet this is exactly what has happened. Colonialism didn't just seize land. It severed story, outlawed language and criminalized relationship with our more-than-human world. [4]Colonialism disrupted ropes woven over generations, fraying not only cultural practices but also the embodied inheritance that tethers us to belonging.

When the stories and songs are outlawed, the children forget. And when the children forget, the silence deepens.

PAUSE: Think about the way you talk about nature. Does it frame nature as positive or negative?

Every dismissive word is like a thread snipped before it has a chance to weave.

One day, prior to the pandemic, while consulting for a public school, I made a list of how children had learned to talk about nature. On the next page is a list of what children said.

I invite you to pause, take a deep breath between each statement.

It's just a weed.
What's a robin?
I can't touch that, it's dirty.
Eew, it's slimy.
Flowers make me sneeze.
Step on it!
Birds are annoying.
I'm allergic to grass.
It will bite you, smoosh it!
Gross.
I'm not allowed to walk on the grass.
You're gonna get in trouble if you touch it.
Bugs are dirty and they'll give me germs.
I don't really play outside. There's nothing to do.
Birds don't matter.
We're not allowed to dig.
I hate rain.
We can't climb on that tree; we'll get in trouble.
Stop playing in the water. We can't waste water.
Nature is boring.

On the next page, you will find another list I kept from that same day. A list of all the things that the adults said.

I hate weeds.

Birds are such a nuisance.

Don't touch that. It's dirty.

Eew, go wash your hands.

You should kill it!

I'm allergic to nature.

It will bite you. Smoosh it!

Gross.

Don't walk on the grass.

No running!

Bugs are dirty and they give you germs.

Stop looking at the birds and pay attention.

Don't dig holes.

I hate rain.

No climbing on that tree. You can get hurt.

Stop playing in the water. We can't waste water.

And also heard exasperated statements like:

Remember when we were kids? We played outside all the time!
Why don't kids play outside anymore?

When our language turns nature into a nuisance, we revoke permission. We declare the wild world unworthy of attention. We shrink our circle of care.

Language is love. Language is hate. Language is power. Language is a weapon.

Language connects, and *language severs.*

If our focus becomes too human-centric, we stop threading our connection and put down ropes that our ancestors painstakingly wove and handed to us. Negative nature talk implies that nature is inconsequential. While direct engagement with nature induces people to care about its welfare, to realize the stakes involved if we ignore threats to it. And those threats are growing.

In 1996, during my last semester of college, I wrote a research report titled, *The Loss of Biodiversity and Its Impact on Human Health.* This endeavor marked the beginning of my career, which has spanned twenty-nine years thus far. A quote from the report shows that the burning questions of that time remain with me and my work today: "People must begin to treat the natural world and its diversity as a great historian — one that can, and given the chance, will teach us life-sustaining laws of nature." Another of my critical concerns appears in the report: "The biggest problem with human action is that by finding temporary solutions for real and extreme problems, we are only creating long-term disasters." I was young and only just waking up to what indigenous populations around the world had known and carried for generations.

While researching that report, I learned about Rachel Carson and her book Silent Spring, published in 1962. Carson was a marine biologist, and her book was an alarm call that meticulously investigated the detrimental impact of widespread pesticide use, particularly DDT, on ecosystems and wildlife. Carson vividly portrays the interconnectedness of nature and reveals the devastating effects pesticides have on birds, wildlife, and human health. She was a catalyst for change who implored the public and the politicians to pass laws that would help conserve the environment, and ultimately save the health of our children.

Carson's alarm echoes today, and yet the numbers have only grown more dire. When I wrote the report for my senior project, I included predictions about the harm to the environment caused by human activity or neglect, and those predictions were sadly conservative compared to what actually transpired in the almost three decades since.

There has been a concerning 69% decline in wildlife populations over the past 50 years.[5] with tens of thousands of species transitioning from threatened to endangered annually.

Cornell University reports, the North American bird population has plummeted by 2.9 billion breeding adults.

Forests alone have seen a loss of 1 billion birds, while grassland bird populations collectively have declined by 53%, equivalent to 720 million birds.[6]

Twenty-six years after I first argued to my professor that biodiversity and occupational therapy were inseparable, U.N. Secretary-General António Guterres called on delegates at the COP15 biodiversity summit to "seize the opportunity to halt this orgy of destruction" and forge a peace pact with nature[7].

We are in a developmental crisis.
We are in a relational crisis.
We are in an ecological crisis.

And it's no wonder. When we condition children to see nature as something "other," we sever not only their sense of wonder, but the very roots of regulation, resilience, and belonging. If we don't pay attention and course-correct, we may tragically discover what it's like to live through a true silent spring.

But nature — our nature — keeps reaching out its hand.

The wind still touches our babies' cheeks and waits for them to notice.

The birds still sing at sunrise, hoping someone will listen.

And the ropes, though frayed, are still there, waiting for us.

We can reach back. We can pick up the thread. We can remember.

Even now, even here in this time that seems so difficult.

8

FLY THE BABY

FOLLOWING NATURE'S LEAD

The world begins with yes.

Terry Tempest Williams

The way we speak to and about nature shapes how our children relate to it. Our words teach them what to fear, what to love, and what to ignore.

During the same week I recorded all the negative nature statements from the public school I was consulting for, something else happened — and it gave me hope.

At another school I supported that same week — Weaving Earth, an outdoor program where mentors had completed the NatureLed™ Mentorship — I documented the language spoken throughout the day. What I heard was striking: a stream of nature-positive language.

Following are some of the statements those mentors offered their students.

A weed is a plant whose virtue is yet to be discovered.

Wow, feel how rough that is.

How does it feel in your hands?

Thank you, bees, for collecting the pollen.

Oh no! I think we just stepped into that ant's house!

I love how grass smells!

Hmm, does it even have teeth to bite?

Aren't snails amazing?

Let's walk softly through the grass.

How fast can you run!

Did you know that bugs help us?

Quick, point to the nearest bird.

Who might live under there?

Thank you, rain! Let's go puddle jumping.

Remember to use 3 points of contact when you are climbing.

Did you see any hawks on the way home?

How many petals did that flower have?

Next, read how children echoed this language of connection. On the next page are the *children's* statements from the same day.

Can I eat it?

Is it poisonous?

I think I saw a Robin?

I heard a Crow!

What does it feel like?

It feels soft.

I love flowers!

Don't step on it, it lives here!

Can I take my shoes off?

Will it bite?

What does it smell like?

Can we roll down the hill?

Can we play eagle eye?

Did you hear that [bird] alarm?

Birds are so cool.

Let's see what's under there.

It's going to rain again, let's build a shelter!

Trees are my friends.

Nature loves me.

The voices from mentors and children were a reminder of how much the threads of connection are still possible. Their language reflected what I had been cultivating for decades since meeting Jon, Paul, and others in the nature connection community — the practice of conscious attention — building ropes of relationship with place and guiding others to do the same.

In my journey, birds have been among my most consistent teachers. They are clear and reliable narrators of the living story unfolding just outside our doors. Their voices and behavior guide my work, my parenting, and my healing.

Listening to "bird language" is a practice that has transformed my understanding of sensory processing, focus, and relationship-building more than any other. To understand how, consider that bird vocalizations offer insight into both our worlds — human and non-human.

Though every bird voice carries meaning, I like to begin with two that offer a gentle entry point: companion calls and song.

Companion calls are the voice of connection.

Companion calls function as daily check-ins, offering a steady rhythm of connection, much like casual chit-chat.

"Hey. Are you there?"

"Yeah. I'm here!"

Song is a sign of safety and vitality. Song signals no threat is present. Birds sing at sunrise, sing to attract mates, and to express contentment.

Both companion calling and song vocalizations are indicators of baseline safety.

Children aren't so different. They too vocalize their baseline state. When their needs are met, we see their true baseline. Companion calling shows up in the serve-and-return rhythms we explored in earlier chapters. Song appears in the delights of play, with laughter, storytelling, and spontaneous creativity. When a child is safe, they don't just survive. They sing. They create. They learn. They connect.

At the 2003 workshop with Jon and Paul, a number of parents and older participants expressed grief. Grief for unknowingly blocking their children's connection to nature. Grief for the parts of themselves that had been blocked in childhood.

Before the workshop ended, Paul stood before this mostly white, relatively affluent group and said,

"It's OK. You didn't know any better. But now that you know better, you have to do better."

His words landed in my body like an invitation.

One week later, I stood on the threshold of my front door, my three-year-old on my hip and my six-year-old at my side. As my first foot crossed the doorway, I heard myself say aloud, *"I wish someone would just create a learning place that makes sense."*

And then it hit me. Now that I knew better, I had to do better. Not just for my children, but for our community and for the ones still to come. That day, I sent out a companion call to four acquaintances. They answered: "Yeah! Let's do this."

That was the beginning of *The Central Coast Village Center* — also known as *Outside Now!*, our local nonprofit. My husband and I invested our entire savings, started filling out paperwork, purchased a van, and rented a space. Nature became the core curriculum — not just for the children, but for us, the adults, too.

In those early years, the internet wasn't part of daily life, so we hosted several public gatherings. At each gathering I shared the story of my daughter and the wind. The response was always the same. Mothers, fathers, and grandparents' eyes would light up. Audible exhales. Whole-body nods of recognition.

They remembered. They remembered the weave that had once connected them.

One day, I received an excited call from a preschool parent. It was Lindsay, a mother who had recently left Silicon Valley's tech boom. She and her family had moved to the country to live a more connected and sustainable life. They went from the hustle and bustle of city life to a home among almond orchards, rolling hills, and frequent wildlife visitors.

When a pregnant Lindsay first brought her preschool-age son to our Coyote Pups program, she often lingered. She sat with us in morning circle, offered to help with snacks, filled water bottles, then applied sunscreen. Eventually she became a weave in the fabric of our days — lending a lap, a hand, or an ear to our young ones. She even organized lunches for us mentors!

What unfolded next was one of those moments that reminds us just how much nature is trying to connect, if we're paying attention.

After taking a break to give birth to her second child, Lindsay returned with her preschooler and brand-new baby, snuggled in a carrier on her chest. Mentors and children welcomed the new nestling with her beautiful wide eyes. She became our new village baby.

About six months after her daughter was born, Lindsay called me, breathless with joy. "Oh my gosh, I get it! I just did Fly The Baby, and it was amazing!"

I laughed and asked, "What *is* Fly the Baby?"

Lindsay had remembered my story of the wind and taken her daughter outside. She discovered that her daughter's tiny hand would move in a certain direction, and when she walked that way, her daughter's little body would fill with energy, wiggling and smiling. They arrived at almond blossoms, barnyard animals, and finally they followed birds flitting from tree to tree in their orchard. After following her daughter's tiny hand again and again, Lindsay realized it wasn't random: her baby was leading her to nature's wonders.

> *"I never would have noticed before, but now it's so clear! She's connecting with nature, and all I have to do is share it with her. All I have to do is Fly The Baby!"*

It was the perfect term to describe how nature leads developmental processes and the youngest among us arrive highly eco-receptive. It's what my daughter taught me on that windy spring day. It's what Lindsay re-discovered in the orchard. And it's what every one of us still has the opportunity to do.

In that simple act of following her baby's lead, Lindsay had tapped into something ancient. She was touching a biological inheritance:

Our neural-nature network. Our design for connection.

This design is not merely poetic. It's measurable. Researchers like Matthew Lieberman have explored this in the brain. Leiberman writes:

> Our sociality is woven into a series of bets that evolution has laid down again and again throughout mammalian history...
> To the extent that we can characterize evolution as designing our modern brains, this is what our brains were wired for: reaching out to and interacting with others. These are design features...[1]

We could say that Lieberman is describing our alloception *and* ecoception — our need to attune to others and to the environment. To interact is to make connections. And Lieberman and others have proven, connection is what we are built for.

When we don't use our "design features," we lose essential parts of ourselves. We may find ourselves constantly searching for meaning, for place, and for wholeness without knowing what's missing. We become strangers in our own bodies, disconnected in our homes, and alienated from the natural world.

This is far more than an individual problem. It's a public health crisis.

In a May 3, 2023 report, the U.S. Surgeon General, Dr. Vivek Murthy, declared a crisis of loneliness, isolation, and disconnection in the general population. At the same time he declared children's mental health a national crisis.[2] The U.S. Department of Health and Human Services states:

> ...young people are facing "devastating" mental health effects as a result of the challenges experienced by their generation... The physical health consequences of poor or insufficient connection include a 29% increased risk of heart disease, a 32% increased risk of stroke, and a 50% increased risk of developing dementia for older adults. Additionally, lacking social connection increases the risk of premature death by more than 60%.

Loneliness causes more than emotional pain — *it shortens lives.*

And it often begins early.

Adults who report feeling lonely have double the risk of developing depression compared to people who rarely or never feel lonely. Loneliness and social isolation in childhood increase the risk of depression and anxiety both immediately and well into the future.

It's no surprise, then, that researchers and authors across disciplines — from neuroscience to happiness studies — echo this same truth:

We need each other. And we need nature.

Gretchen Rubin, in The Happiness Project, underscores this when she writes, those nurturing strong relationships with family and friends is a consistently reliable pathway to joy and fulfillment.[3]

The Harvard Study of Adult Development, one of the longest-running studies on human well-being, confirms it:

People with satisfying relationships are happier, healthier, and live longer.[4]

And as Dr. Murthy reminds us, the solution is not complicated: [Social] connection is a medicine hiding in plain sight.

Clearly more than isolated insights, these studies form a chorus that validates what many of us have long felt in our bodies.

The conclusions shared by Rubin, Lieberman, and the Harvard study show that meaningful relationships nourish our health—emotionally, physically, and even neurologically.

Just as our connections with people matter, so do our connections with place.

To have a genuine connection with place, our biology expects natural rhythms, and none are more essential than light itself. For example, when we sync with the slow light of dawn, or the exhale of sunset, it activates our nervous system's responses — stress pulses soften, sensory harmony returns, sleep improves and joy wakes.

Light, like other aspects of nature, is not simply about illumination. It is information for our cells. It calibrates our biology to the day, the season, and to life itself. Our brains depend on morning light to regulate mood and sleep-wake cycles,[5] and our emotional well-being is directly shaped by how consistently we experience those natural cues.

Continuing with the example of light, many have long sensed that our mental health depends on daily exposure to natural light. A 2023 study of more than 85,000 people found that greater exposure to daylight — especially in the morning — significantly reduced the risk of depression, anxiety, PTSD, and self-harm. Those who were most attuned to nature's light cycle showed the greatest protection from psychiatric distress, while those exposed to light at the wrong time of day (like bright artificial light at night) faced up to a 30% higher risk of mood disorders.[6]

Sunlight is one of Earth's original relational-regulators. It helps us orient, metabolize, and remember that we belong to a constantly waking world. When we step outside into that light — whether walking to school, drinking tea on a porch, or looking up to the star-filled sky before bed — we are realigning ourselves with a wisdom far older than any clock. Nature has endless supports for our neurology similar to light.

Combining connection to others with connection to nature, such as witnessing a sunset together, creates a synergistic effect. The benefits of each relationship enhance and expand the other. A walk through the forest with a trusted companion does more than calm the body or lift the mood. It regulates the nervous system, strengthens emotional bonds, and creates conditions for learning and repair. For a child, playing outside with an attuned adult creates an enriched environment where the brain and body can organize, grow, and feel more fully alive.

What we get is a kind of neurological superfood made of the potent synergy that supports regulation and vitality.

Pediatric and family care professionals are putting this kind of synergy into practice.

Dr. Nooshin Razani, a pediatrician and public health advocate, has been a leading voice in bridging medicine and nature. In 2009, she began writing "nature prescriptions" for her patients at UCSF Benioff Children's Hospital Oakland—encouraging families, many of whom faced poverty, racism, and health disparities, to spend time in nearby parks as part of their care plans.[7] At the time, this was a radical shift from conventional treatment. But Dr. Razani understood that her patients needed more than pills or pamphlets. They needed connection.

Her approach was evidence-based and grounded in love. As the founder of the Center for Nature and Health, she helped lead research demonstrating how time in nature supports mental, emotional, and physical health in children. She didn't stop at prescribing the outdoors—she joined families in the experience. She walked beside them in green spaces, listened to their stories, and helped them feel at home in nature.

By 2013, the initiative had evolved into a formalized program. In partnership with East Bay Regional Parks, Dr. Razani launched SHINE (Stay Healthy In Nature Everyday), one of the first structured park prescription models in the United States. Her work inspired a national movement. Today, thousands of clinicians use platforms like ParkRx America to prescribe time outdoors, knowing that nature supports sleep, mood, immune function, physical activity, and family connection.

These are measurable outcomes observed again and again — in park programs, occupational therapy sessions, outdoor classrooms, and in family life. We've seen it in research and in practice: when children experience nature-connection with a safe and responsive adult, their nervous systems reorganize. They become more regulated, more resilient, and more capable of responding flexibly to life's challenges.

I've seen this in my clients, in my children, and in myself. When I feel lonely or lost, I return to three things:

A walk in nature.

A conversation with someone I love.

A few minutes of listening to birdsong.

Each one helps. But when I combine the eco and the social, when I inhale the fresh scent of pine needles while I walk and talk with a friend, or when I pause on a trail to listen to the birdsong with a client, the shift is profound. It is physical, emotional and neurological.

When ecoception and relational safety come together, healing begins to happen in ways we cannot always measure but we can feel.

That feeling is what brings people back to the wild. It's why parents are forming outdoor schools; why therapists are moving their sessions outside; why educators are rethinking what counts as curriculum. Because somewhere inside we know: nature remembers how to help us grow, and heal.

'Eco-Social' connection can happen on a large scale. And in fact, something miraculous is happening all over the world. Even without massive funding or national mandates, the movement to reconnect families with nature is gaining traction and infiltrating the consumer economy. Parents, educators, and health professionals are paying attention. They are stepping outside, looking around, and asking: What kind of learning really nourishes a child? What kind of environment really supports healing?

In 1997, Richard Louv helped spark a global conversation with his book, *Last Child in the Woods: Saving Our Children From Nature-Deficit Disorder.* His work called out what many were already feeling but hadn't been able to articulate. Children were spending less time outdoors. They were missing critical sensory and developmental experiences. And something vital was being lost in the process.

Louv's book was a signal flare, like Rachel Carson before him, who warned of the harm caused by environmental toxins. Louv's work awakened a collective knowing.

In response, families around the world began forming small schools, programs, and communities dedicated to restoring the link between nature, education, and well-being.

Many of these organizations started with little more than a tarp and a trail map. Some began around kitchen tables or campfires.

What they have in common is a shared belief that nature connection and human development belong together.

Today, those efforts have grown into a global web of action.

Outside Now in San Luis Obispo, California (which I co-founded in 2003)

8 Shields/Connection First in Santa Cruz, CA

Wilderness Youth Project, Santa Barbara, CA

BEin Nature, San Francisco Bay Area, CA

Wild Harmony, Madison, Wisconsin

Wild Roots Preschool, Santa Barbara, CA (1996)

Backyard Basecamp, Washington, D.C.

Sassafras Earth Education, Martha's Vineyard, Massachusetts

The Guelph Outdoor School, Ontario, Canada

Wisdom of the Earth, British Columbia, Canada

Vermont Wilderness School, VT

Wilderness Awareness School, Duvall, Washington

And there are many more — across the globe including the United States, Canada, Australia, Ireland, the UK, Germany, Austria, South Africa, and Singapore. Some follow forest school models. Others draw from Indigenous cultural frameworks. They serve both urban and rural communities. Each is helping to restore an ancient and future-altering truth: when we root children in nature, they thrive.

The perceived value of these schools has grown significantly in recent years. When *Outside Now!* began in 2003, many people needed convincing of its relevance. But in March 2020, as the world faced the uncertainty of pandemic lockdowns, families began turning to nature for stability and renewal. When restrictions eased, these small but mighty nature schools saw a surge in interest. Waitlists formed, and daily requests for new programming rolled in.

This rising interest has also opened doors for integrating nature connection into more traditional systems. Recently, I partnered with occupational therapy doctoral student Clare Weible from the University of Wisconsin to pilot a Tier Two intervention at a low-income public school.[8] Over six weeks, Clare led a small group of elementary students with documented behavioral challenges through a nature-connection program. At the end of the six weeks, every participant showed positive outcomes.

Even more encouraging is that this kind of work is beginning to move beyond small programs and into public systems. In Canada, for example, formal training pathways now prepare public school educators to include nature connection as a core part of the curriculum. These initiatives are framing nature as necessary.

In many Indigenous communities, the land has long been understood as teacher, healer, and relation.[9] Indigenous traditions hold wisdom that Western systems are barely beginning to remember. The forest is a classroom. The bird is a messenger. The wind carries information. The child is not separate from the world, but part of its living song.

I dream of a world where nature-positive mindsets are embedded in every school, clinic, and community. Where educators, parents, and therapists recognize that connective experiences are foundational human needs.

Let's imagine a world where no child is told to quiet their instincts, to sit still when their body needs to move or to fear the rain, snow or wildness inside them.

I hope you will join me in my dream to see a nature-positive mindset at the core of all educational institutions — reversing the mindset that attempted to train the "wild" out of our children. Whether we're flying the baby or answering a bird's call, it starts the same way: by paying attention. By saying yes to wonder. By letting nature lead.

If you are reading this and you didn't have an adult who "flew you" or you didn't receive that kind of permission as a child, if your children are older now and it feels like the moment has passed — please know that it's never too late.

Nature is *relentless* in its offer, in its invitations. Your sense of eco-ception is *designed* to respond.

9

JUMPING MONKEYS

MISBEHAVIOR AS A MESSAGE

Ten little monkeys jumping on the bed! One fell off and bumped his head. Mama called the doctor, and the doctor said, no more monkeys jumping on the bed!

You have a one in three trillion chance of life. It's difficult to conceive how rare that is. Picture a trillion as a stack of one-dollar bills reaching from the Earth to the Moon and back, not once, not twice, but about 200,000 times. You and your child are living proof that life has called to you — and it longs for your response.

We are designed for yes.

Even amid the noise of disconnection, children keep reaching out to life. If we're willing to watch closely, we'll see it: small hands climbing, feet jumping, bodies exploring.

One day in my kitchen, I nearly shut down my three-year-old's response to life. It was another moment where she reminded me how easy it is to overlook a child's natural drive to grow.

I heard it first from the other room: SLAM.

The sturdy wooden bench my father had built for her, shoved up against the kitchen sink. Then the water running. Then quiet. Next came the faint sound of her climbing down. I peeked in, turned off the faucet, and gently reminded her: "Honey, Mommy's okay with you playing in the water, but you need to turn it off before you climb down." She nodded silently, watching me as I left.

Moments later: SLAM. I hear water running and her climbing down. I returned, turned off the tap again. "Honey, we don't waste water. Do you understand?" She nodded again.

Once in the other room, again I heard: SLAM. Water. Climbing down. This time, I moved the bench to another room. "The bench is having a time-out," I sighed. "No more using the bench until Mommy says so."

Her steady gaze followed me as I walked away.

But once more, from down the hall I heard: SLAM.

She'd dragged the bench back. I raced to the kitchen in time to see her climbing down for the fourth time. But this time, she raised her hand like a tiny traffic cop.

"MAMA. WAIT!" she commanded.

I froze.

Slowly and deliberately, with her hand still in the air, she held my gaze, lowered herself to the floor, and placed her ear flush with it. I held my breath. Fifteen seconds felt like an hour; then she popped her head off the floor and with a triumphant squeal shouted:

"MAMA! WATER!"

Her face beamed. Her voice rang with delight.

And I understood. She hadn't been defying me. She'd been following the logic of her body, her senses, her brain. In order to hear the water traveling through the pipes beneath the floor, she left it running. Her nervous system needed to connect the sound in the floor with the water at the sink. What I'd mistaken for disobedience was actually a natural, embodied act of learning.

Over the years, many parents have asked me, "Why does my child keep jumping on the couch, no matter how many times I tell them to stop?"

Jumping and climbing are two of the brain's strategies to get those senses down the road to habilitation. Children have such an intense need to engage their muscles, joints, and balance that at some point, they override their desire to please us. Telling a child to stop jumping and climbing confuses their brain, which is shouting: "Jump! Run! Climb! Move to develop this body!"

It's a better use of energy to build a crash pad[1] beside the couch — or to let go of societal expectations and remember: a nice couch will go out of fashion in a few short years. A well-developed child lasts a lifetime.

What my daughter showed me in the kitchen — and what every child shows us — is what psychologist James J. Gibson called an affordance: the way the world offers itself for interaction.[2] A hill invites rolling. A puddle invites splashing. A faucet invites pouring. A floor invites listening.

Children don't just see objects. They see possibilities.

Affordances speak directly to the child's senses, affirming a child's *yes*.

The week after my daughter's discovery, I watched her explore every water-related affordance she could find. She pressed her ear to walls and floors, turned faucets on and off, followed a small creek next to our house. She flushed the toilet, asking over and over, "Where that go?"

And then, a moment of integration. Standing at the sink, sipping water from a cup, she declared, "Mama. I like water." Then, with cup still full, she climbed down, carried it outside, and poured it into the birdbath.

"Birds like water too!"

I thought about how, in this same scenario, I might have been scolded — or worse — for what looked like disobedience. A week earlier, I might have stopped her from climbing down with a full glass and lectured her about spills. But this time, I paused, watched, and said, "Yes, honey. Birds get thirsty too." Then I handed her a dish towel, helped her wipe the small spills on the floor, and added, "I'm sure the birds say thank you."

That week of exploration was richer than any theme park or playground. I witnessed an original wonderland of curiosity, learning, and joy, and we never even left home.

> *Every ability in our intellectual toolkit was engineered to escape extinction... We don't survive so we can learn. We learn so we can survive."*
>
> Dr. John Medina

For most of human history, survival was the curriculum. It gave us every reason to reach, explore, and engage with the world. Our daily occupations were inherently meaningful, functional, and shared.

Sensory-motor development was a natural outcome of those daily occupations.

Survival *skills* drove development down the long road of habilitation.

Consider the act of gathering plants. To do it safely, one had to ask: What is the shape of these leaves? Is this the edible version or the poisonous lookalike? Where does this water come from, and where does it go? These questions and more required careful attention to shape, color, soil, weather, animal behavior, scent, and season. Over time, people shared what they learned. Through cooperation, they built deeper abilities: recognizing bird calls that signaled water, or animal tracks that led to prey or danger.

Understanding at this level is contextual, relational, and orchestral.

In the sensory symphony of our survival, our ancestors didn't merely gather. They read the landscape like a living story — interpreting the slant of sun, the veins of leaves, the rush of wings overhead, the scent on the wind. Sitting still and listening wasn't idle curiosity. They were practicing and honing their sensory instruments in humanity's ongoing song.

Our ancestors survived by sensing.

And though the world looks different today, that sensory need still pulses inside us. The drive to learn, to connect, to respond to the world hasn't vanished. It's waiting — beneath the surface. Ready for us, and for our children, to say yes.

Childhood is a season of extraordinary skill-building. Every day, your child's brain is expanding its capacity, its flexibility, and its resilience. A well-developed brain prepares kids to meet basic needs for food, water, safety, and social connection. When those needs are met, the brain has energy left over for things like writing sentences and solving math equations[3].

Pyramid of Human Habilitation

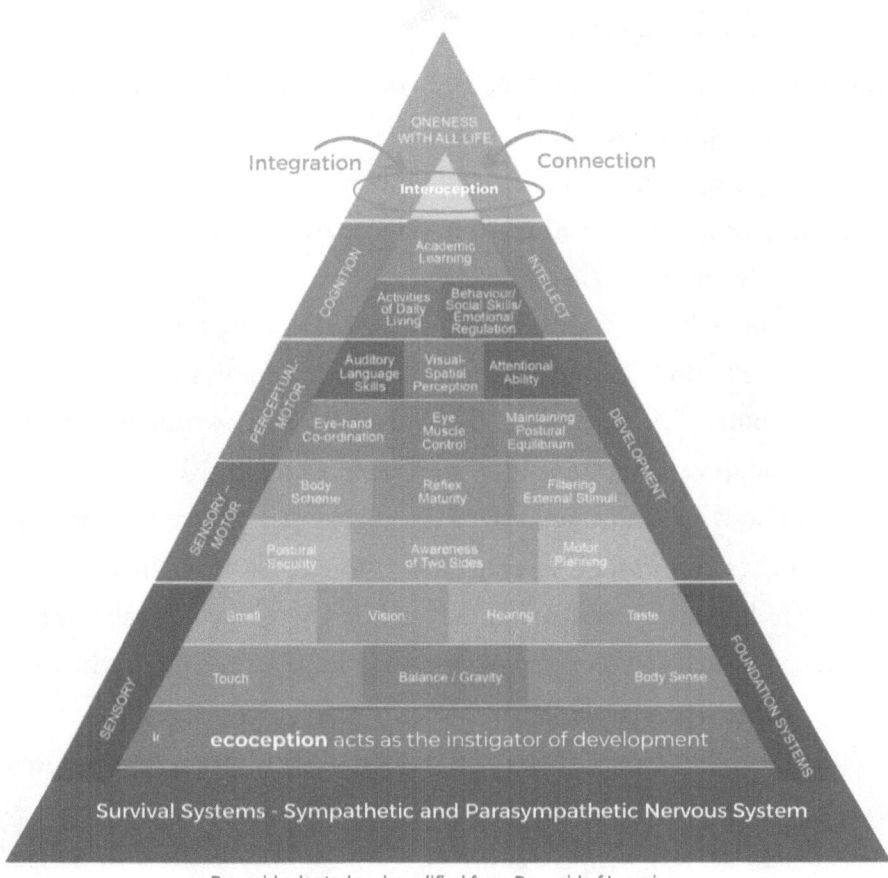

Pyramid adapted and modified from Pyramid of Learning.
Williams and Sheilenberger. (1-4)

©kathleenlockyer and rxoutside

Pyramid of Human Habilitation

Go to kathleenlockyer.com for a printable color PDF of the Pyramid of Habilitation

You may have seen diagrams like the "Pyramid of Habilitation," showing some of the many layers needed before a child can be ready for academic learning.

What you see at the top — academic learning and interoception — relies on deep foundations below: sensory processing, balance, body awareness, coordination, attention, and more. If those foundations are shaky, the learning on top wobbles.

A developing brain and body will do everything it can to get sensory nourishment and build a strong foundation. An undernourished system is frequently interpreted as "misbehavior."

That child who won't stop talking in class, shouting across the room? Maybe their brain is still working hard to process sound, to communicate clearly, to build social confidence. That child who keeps whacking the stick at everything, even after being told no? Their proprioceptive and vestibular senses — body awareness and balance — are begging for input. That child who touches everything? They are not trying to be annoying; they are literally feeling their way through the world by engaging their tactile sense (touch). These children are practicing how to make better music with their sensory instruments.

When a child's world doesn't offer enough rich, meaningful sensory experiences, their behavior isn't simply defiance. It's a message. Their nervous system is saying: *Help me build this skill. Help me find the input I need.* It's a plea from a body and brain doing exactly what it's wired to do.

Our role as parents and caregivers is to listen beneath the behavior and recognize the opportunities. What affordances are they craving? What skills do they lack? Every time we see behavior through these questions, we can help our children build skills for a stronger foundation.

Let's take a closer look at one of the most common, and often misunderstood, sensations behind behavior: sound. In many children, it's the auditory system calling out through their actions. Hearing is passive. Listening is a learned skill. And many children aren't struggling because they won't listen, but because *they can't* — yet.

Sound presents both a human dilemma and an ecological concern. As children strain to listen, the natural world is falling silent.

Researcher Bernie Krause spent decades recording the soundscapes of nature in various places.[4] Then he returned to record the same places years later. His recordings revealed what our eyes often can't see: places that looked "intact" had grown quieter. Much quieter. The creatures that once made up nature's cacophony are rapidly disappearing.

As natural sounds disappear, humans are also losing the ability to truly listen. In his TED Talk "Losing Our Listening," sound expert Julian Treasure explains that while we're surrounded by more noise than ever, the sounds themselves are less meaningful.[5] Artificial noise bombards children's senses, while the grounding, rhythmic sounds of nature quietly vanish.

Pause here. Open a door or window and close your eyes. How many natural sounds can you hear right now? How many are you surprised by?

Disappearing natural sound clues us into a loss. Children, too, are giving us clues. Behavior is a message that requires us to look closer, and listen differently, to make sense of what a child is really trying to tell us. Like with Jose, a boy I worked with years ago.

I met Jose when he was four years old, attending preschool in an early intervention program. His teacher called me in for an occupational therapy consultation. "Jose's brilliant," she told me. "But he keeps having these outbursts. One minute he's fine; the next he's screaming, throwing toys, hiding behind the bookshelf. I've tried everything. He just won't listen."

His mother looked tired. "We've tried time-outs, rewards, behavior charts, taking things away. Nothing works. People think we're too soft on him, but they have no idea how much we've tried."

I watched Jose for an hour in class. At first, he sat quietly building with Legos. Then, without warning, he threw a block, shouted "No!" and bolted behind a shelf.

"Does he do this outside too?" I asked his teacher.

"Not really. But when he's outside, he mostly stays by himself near the tree, just watching."

Later that day, I followed Jose and his aide on a trip to the bathroom. The school's hallways were outdoors, leading to a separate building. Jose stopped at every tree, every garden barrel, every butterfly along the way. He seemed calm—until he reached the bathroom. "Promise you'll stay right there!" he begged his aide over and over. I could almost see the stress-sweat on the aide's forehead as she winced in my direction from the doorway. I waited, listening to him ask her every five seconds, "You're still there?!"

And her calm reply, "Right here."

Finally, out came Jose. He ran past me, pancaking his back against the cement wall. He looked terrified, like a deer in headlights. A moment later, the toilet flushed and out came the teacher's aide. She shrugged, saying only, "Evvv-err-y time!"

I looked back at Jose, who was now in a crouching tiger position, his hands pressing hard against his ears. My attention shifted to the echo of water flushing, reverberating off the cold cement walls of the bathroom.

"It sure is loud in there," I said.

The aide nodded. "It's awful."

Jose wasn't willfully acting out. He didn't want to be feeling the way he felt. Who would?

Jose's hearing was excellent, but his brain was a jumble when it came to processing the sounds he heard. Listening is an active process. His auditory system was working overtime, constantly misinterpreting benign sounds as threatening. For Jose, everyday sounds like the school bell, a classmate's greeting, a distant airplane, the scrape of a chair — were "heard" by his brain as if each one was urgent information. Every unfiltered sound piled on until the smallest additional input, like a question from a peer or a simple instruction from a teacher, overflowed his bucket.

When Jose exploded, although it appeared sudden, it wasn't "out of nowhere." His body had been shouting for relief long before his voice.

Outside, Jose preferred the edge of the playground, where sounds were fewer and less chaotic. Sitting at the center of unpredictable noise was simply too much.

His parents had done everything they knew to do. His teachers had tried every reward system. But no one had yet understood that his "behavior" wasn't about choice. It was about sensory survival.

Negative behavior is a flag waving: Something's missing here! I don't have the skills I need! For Jose, that missing piece was auditory processing. His brain wasn't categorizing sound, wasn't creating the internal filing system that lets us tune out a humming fridge or background chatter. Every sound was new, and equally important every time. Each sound demanded his full attention. When that happens, a nervous system operates in chronic overload.

Discipline had been ineffective because Jose needed first to build his brain's *capacity* to organize sensory input.

We started small. I introduced a bird sound: the California Towhee, common near his school and home. First, we listened indoors, using a sound app and a small toy bird that played the Towhee's call. Then we mimicked it together, both in sound and movement. Then we moved outdoors, listening for it in real life. We turned it into a game — pointing, looking, listening and noticing. Over time, his brain learned to hold that one sound in a category: familiar, safe, known.

And from that one familiar sound, his system could begin making space for others.

Play was our tool. Nature was our ally. Technology bridged both. We worked from close up to far away, building his listening map by following his body's *yes*.

Sensory integration doesn't happen all at once. It builds over time through moments of familiarity and safety. Every day, your child's behavior is telling you a story. Sometimes it's a story of frustration. Sometimes it's a story of an unmet need. Sometimes it's a story of their brain sorting through incoming information for patterns and meaning. When we learn to listen beneath the behavior, we begin to hear the invitation: *Help me build this skill. Help me say yes to this world.*

And when we answer with patience and play, we help them move one more mile on the road to habilitation.

Try This

Follow the Yes

☐ Spend 20 minutes simply following your child's curiosity.

☐ Notice what draws their attention: a puddle, a bug, a clattering sound, a patch of sunlight.

☐ Resist the urge to redirect or narrate. Instead, observe quietly. If they invite you in, join without leading.

☐ As you observe them, ask yourself: What is this place, this moment, affording them? How are they using their body, senses, and attention to explore?

If you don't have a child with you, try it for yourself. Let your senses guide you: What are you drawn to touch, smell, listen to, climb, balance on? How does it feel to follow your innate yes?

Wild Reflection

Take a moment to reflect or journal:

When was the last time you followed your child's lead, without an agenda?

What "yes" did you hope for when you were a child... that someone said no to?

How did you learn to trust — or mistrust — your body's impulses and sensory curiosity?

How can you offer your child more chances to say yes to the world around them?

And: What's one small way you can clear space for wonder, movement, and sensory joy — today?

10

THE FORTY-FOOT JOURNEY

EVERYDAY ADVENTURES

It is good to have an end to journey toward; but it is the journey that matters, in the end.

Ursula K. Le Guin

How many trees are growing within 100 feet of your front door?

No two children travel the developmental journey in quite the same way. On the road to habilitation, some race ahead, some take detours, and some stop often to explore the scenery. Yet all are moving toward the same destination.

Even within one family, siblings have unique sensory personalities and genetic profiles. An individual's profile is the base from which they develop; environment shapes the rest. (For example, Jose's younger brother didn't need intervention for auditory processing.)

Here's a NatureLed™ gift to parents and caregivers: you don't need to engineer an ideal environment for growth. Nature already does the heavy lifting — without the cost of indoor sensory gear, gyms, calming sound machines, packaged curriculums, or screen-time tech. Nature has spent millions of years designing "programs", and the human nervous system arrives ready to enroll.

Even the short walk between a front door and a car can be rich with opportunity. The trouble is, that pace of learning often collides with the pressure to be efficient and on time.

If you've cared for a young child, you know the front-door-to-car journey can feel endless. Children, closer to the ground than we are, notice every stone, twig, bug, and hole along the way. These moments are not distractions; they are the body's way of becoming habilitated through environmental interaction.

And the impulse doesn't disappear when they leave nature. In the grocery store, no matter how often you say, "Don't touch," what do they do? They touch. To touch is to develop.

We often misread this drive as resistance, but it's an effort to connect with the world.

I recently witnessed this familiar scene at a park.

A mother with two young children, an infant and a toddler, took nearly twenty minutes to walk forty feet from their car to the playground. The moment the mother opened the car door, her toddler kicked at the back of the driver's seat. Her mother offered a hand, and the toddler swiped it away. Little fingers clung tightly to the seatbelt buckle, squeezing with all their might before the girl threw her whole body backwards against the seat.

Mom's hand offered support a second time, and the toddler, holding her palm in the air, wagging it back and forth shouted, "No, no, no, no, no! I do it!" Mom took a deep breath, looked up at the sky as if praying for more patience, and with a big exhale, she threw her hands up in defeat.

The child continued to make adjustments, wiggling her body for a better grip, turning the buckle, kicking her feet, and finally, voilà! The belt was unbuckled! A big smile spread across the little girl's face as she looked up to celebrate her success with her mom. Mom clapped her hands and reached for the toddler when, in a not-so-strange turn of events, the toddler buckled herself back into her seat and repeated the sequence once more. Mom clapped again, reaching a third time for her toddler, who pushed Mom's hand away. Mom stood back and breathed more deeply. The toddler finally climbed out of the SUV like a pro rock climber on a slab of stone in the Sierras.

That was only the beginning of their forty-foot journey. Instead of rushing toward the playground, the child paused again and again — first at a yellow flower, which she bent to sniff, admire, and kiss; She began walking towards the park, stopped, plopped herself down on the ground, kicked off her shoes, stood up, and continued on.

She ran towards a rock pigeon. The bird flew into a nearby tree, and the girl looked back at her mom. The girl attempted the gutteral sound of the pigeon and turned to look at her mother again. Her mother repeated the sound. The girl approached the tree, repeating the sounds again. When the pigeon flew off, the girl turned back toward the park, stopping another half a dozen times on the way — to explore a bug, a stick, a stone, to wipe dirt off her feet twice, and lastly to get a drink from the water fountain.

The fountain became its own adventure. For several minutes the toddler pushed the button for the water leaned in for a drink, but the water went off. She repeated this press-and-sip game until she got frustrated and grabbed Mom's pant-leg, pulling her to the fountain and demanding help.

To a casual observer, these detours might look like dawdling. To a developing brain, they are the real destination.

The whole scenario in their forty-foot journey made me smile and laugh. I couldn't resist approaching the mother and saying, "Hi, I'm an occupational therapist, and I just have to say how much I appreciate the space you gave your toddler to explore just now."

"Honestly? I'm not sure what you mean. It's so exhausting, just getting from the car to anywhere. I've kinda given up on any agenda I have! I just try to keep her safe!"

"I so get it!"

"I know that I'm supposed to be drawing boundaries and making her listen, but honestly, I think maybe she just needs to be herself." The baby who snuggled in the fabric carrier on Mom's chest fussed and Mom began bouncing.

"Haha!" I laughed in solidarity. "To a child, just waking up in the morning is a grand adventure!"

Mom's eyes softened a bit. "Oh. That's so true. Everything with her! I'm just so overwhelmed sometimes, but also, sometimes I just want her to do what I tell her to do when I tell her, and not take like a million years to get her shoes on!"

"Oh my gosh. I can so relate. I have two very free-spirited children! They are grown now, but they've been my greatest teachers."

"I know that everyone says this time will pass so quickly, but some days I secretly pray for it to be over."

"That's so honest of you to say that! So many of us parents think it but never say it out loud. You're in good company."

"So, can I ask? What was it about our very frustrating walk that you appreciated? Just that your kids are older, and you're done with all this?"

We both laughed.

I glanced over at the little girl, now absorbed in picking up pebbles and stacking them on the bottom of the yellow slide. I shared the following information with the girl's mother:

From the first attempt the little girl made to manipulate her seat belt, she engaged with her environment's affordances — the varied nuances of experience. The seat belt buckle was a perfect opportunity to practice using over thirty muscles and tendons in each of her growing hands. Her drive to master the latch outweighed her desire to please her caregiver — a common source of conflict between child and adult. If her developing neurological system could speak, it would say: "My fingers need this experience to develop strength, coordination, and fine-motor muscles."

Parents, often rushing to keep the day on track, want something different: for the task to be done quickly and quietly. But a child's hands, whether handling something made by nature or by humans, crave mastery. Each task completed strengthens the brain for next time, saving energy for higher-level work. These moments of practice are what build the foundation for emotional regulation, communication, and sustained attention. What looks like a slow walk is, in fact, the groundwork for human potential.

On some level, the mother at the park sensed that those forty-feet offered more than any playground slide could. Her stress wasn't from her daughter's pace, but from the unrealistic expectations our culture places on parents and young children. She may not have consciously known that these encounters — the flower, the pigeon, the seat belt — were exactly what her child's brain and body needed. Yet she allowed the pace, giving her daughter space to master the world on her own terms.

When children don't get these rich, real-world experiences, their brains search for stimulation elsewhere — but often in places that lack the same coherence or benefit. Car noise, TV shows, and busy screens may grab attention, but they don't build the harmony a child's sensory system needs. Nature, by contrast, offers patterns that organize the brain.

The eco-receptive brain seeks natural stimuli, yet modern life floods it with man-made noise. Many of us no longer recognize the patterns outside our own doors: who lives there, what grows there, when the sun rises or the moon sets. We hand children plastic toys but take away sticks, stones, and mud. We've been taught to overlook nature's invitations, replacing them with activities built for convenience, not deep development.

Nature calls to every sense. Birdsong or ocean waves train the ear. The color of a tulip or the shape of a maple leaf sharpens the eyes. Hillsides and tree limbs challenge balance and strength. Soft grass invites stillness, awe, and wonder. To a young child, every stone, leaf, and bird on a short walk can feel as thrilling as summiting a mountain.

When we miss or stop these moments of serve and return, we lose a chance to strengthen developing senses, closing the field guide nature offers. Touching, looking, listening, moving, climbing, and exploring teach children how to read the world in their own context, building the sensory and cognitive maps they'll use for life.

And context matters. A person's sensory system becomes fine-tuned by practicing — repeatedly firing its neurons — in a specific environment. The needs of a baby born in the Panama jungle differ from those of a baby born in the Arizona desert. Sensory receptors gather specialized information from that environment to develop vision, hearing, smell, taste, touch, and body awareness. As we saw earlier in the kittens-raised-on-vertical-lines study, what the brain is exposed to shapes what it can later perceive, and what it may never notice.

This process is intricate, yet it doesn't require special training or costly adventures. A week in the wilderness is wonderful, but a child's learning can begin the moment you step outside your door. Morning air, a bird's call, the feel of wind on the face — these are nature's invitations. Letting children follow them, and joining in, turns the world into both playground and classroom.

Every stone lifted, every bird call answered, every buckle mastered is part of the brain's deeper work at learning how to predict, respond, and stay steady in a changing world. What might look like dawdling, stalling, or even resistance is often the body and brain moving to an ancient rhythm that keeps us well. This rhythm has a name: allostasis.

Allostasis is the process by which the brain anticipates the body's needs and works to meet them *before* they arise. It's your brain's way of saving energy by staying a step ahead. You see it when you pack a snack before leaving the house because you know your child will be hungry mid-errand — instead of waiting for a meltdown to remind you. Or the way you put on a raincoat before getting wet. The brain is always scanning inside and out, gathering sensory information to predict what might happen next. A well-tuned sensory system makes these predictions accurate, which supports regulation.

Dr. John Medina, in *Brain Rules*, describes this as a constant loop of questions the brain tries to answer. One of the most important in a new situation is: Have I seen, heard, smelled, or felt this before? This is where a child's sensory experiences matter most — each new sound, sight, or texture adds a note to their internal library of patterns, making future predictions easier, more accurate and requiring less energy.

I saw this the day my daughter first heard water moving under our floor. Her whole body tuned in, testing the sound against her other senses, gathering data for the next time she heard something similar. Just like the toddler in the park, she was saying yes to the world — the same yes that begins every meaningful forty-foot journey. The more we as parents can take the role of co-adventurer, the more our children learn to trust themselves and their exploration.

Nature knows how to lead, if we are open to following.

Ecoception — the nervous system's readiness to receive nature's invitations — lets the natural world do the heavy lifting of development. By embracing the simplicity and richness of nature-led experiences, we can shift from contrived, equipment-laden approaches to those that value spontaneous, unhurried exploration. The subtle moments — a seatbelt mastered, a flower kissed, a bird call echoed — are monumental in the orchestra of sensory and neurological growth.

I invite you to take in this wisdom from nature: the greatest gifts we can offer our children — and ourselves — are not found in the latest gadgets or structured programs, but in the freedom to explore, the patience to observe, and the wisdom to value the natural rhythms and teachings of our original home, Earth. By fostering an eco-receptive approach, we nurture healthier, more adaptive minds and deepen our reverence for the world that sustains us. In this sensory symphony of discovery and growth, may we all find our place, grounded in the beauty and simplicity of nature, moving ever closer to the harmony that defines what it means to be truly human.

II

RELATIONAL PARENTING

FROM CONTROL TO CONNECTION

Real listening is a willingness to let the other person change you.

Alan Alda

C an you point to the direction of where the last storm came from?

Relational connection begins in small moments. Moments that seem ordinary at the time but subtly shape how we pay attention to the world. For me, it began at home, with a simple daily ritual.

I must have been about four or five. My fists rubbed at sleepy eyes as I spotted my father standing just outside the back door, looking toward the horizon. No matter where we lived — house or town — this ritual was one thing I could count on. He would stand still, scanning the distance, inhaling the air. I remember wondering intently what he saw and smelled.

"We'll get a storm tonight," he said, placing his heavy hand on my shoulder.

I sidled up to him, turning my still-clouded eyes to the sky and savoring the rare calmness in our day. The little hairs on my arms rose in the chilly, moist air as I studied the clouds with him. The cool air wrapped around us as we stood side by side. Finally, I asked, "But Dad? How do you know?"

"The land tells me."

"How?'

"Do you feel the wind?"

I closed my eyes to feel the wind.

"Do you smell the air?"

I sniffed the air.

"Do you see the sky way over there?"

I looked into the distance.

"What do you see the birds doing?"

"Uh, hmmm. I don't know?"

"What's the sky saying?"

My ears strained to hear the landscape talking. My father never told me the answer to the last question. Instead, whenever we stood outside in the approach of a storm, he would repeat, "What do you see the birds doing? What are they saying?"

This day I offered an answer: "Well, they look really busy."

He smiled, then asked me another question.

Many times before going back indoors, Dad would tell a story from his childhood in Newfoundland. His stories were tied to the weather and the land — passing along patterns, predictions, and sensory awareness.

These were relational moments, rooted in context, weaving my attention to his and to the natural world, just as his grandparents had done with him when he was a boy.

It was a ritual of looking, listening, smelling, and wondering together. I studied his movements — what he looked at, how he smelled, what he listened to, the quality of his energy, and the prediction he made about nature. Each story paired with observation created a web of context that connected weather, land, and relationships. We could call this relational parenting or even relational coaching.

Relational interactions awaken curiosity, increase attention, engage the senses, and invite neurological integration by giving meaning to an experience. It's the context in these moments that matter — the smell of the air, the feel of the wind, the behavior of the birds — each sense tying into a bigger story, while leaving room for mystery.

My father's predictions kept my curiosity alive, and when a storm he forecasted arrived, it created an integrative moment — linking his sensory habits of looking, smelling, and listening with the unfolding drama of the natural world. This multisensory connection left a lasting imprint. Even now, the sight of a nimbostratus cloud or the faint smell of rain sends my brain scanning the sky for a coming storm.

Today, more than forty years later, most days when I step outside, my eyes instinctively sweep the horizon. I notice if the birds are quiet and hunkered down, signaling a storm or predator, or if they are singing with the ease of a calm day. I feel for the direction of the wind — from the east or the west — and sense whether the air is moist or dry. These small acts of attention are not only about predicting the weather; they keep me balanced, grounded, and engaged — much like animals who remain attuned to shifts in their surroundings.

Just as my father taught me to read the wind and sky, my friend Jon shared how the San Bushmen teach their children to read their environment — because survival depends on paying attention. Among the San, every sense is tuned to the land. Children grow up noticing the shift in the air before a storm, the sudden silence of birds, the faint rustle of grass that means a large animal is near.

Jon shares a story from his time with the San people who, when asked about how they live among wild lions, the tribe tells this concise tale:

"A long, long time ago, the lions ate a lot of us. They ate a lot of us. The end."

Out of context, it sounds abrupt, even alarming. But within the San Bushmen's oral tradition, its meaning is clear. It is a sensory and relational teaching condensed into a single, unforgettable image. The story signals that people are safer now because they learned to read the signs, patterns, and cues in their environment that signal danger.

For San children, the story is another thread that, over time, weaves into a strong rope of survival knowledge. It reminds them to stay attuned to their surroundings — much like children who grow up near train tracks learn to sense the distant hum, the flash of lights, and the vibration underfoot long before a train arrives. The San learn to pair outer cues — the alarm calls of birds, the direction of the wind, the freshness of a track — with inner cues (interoception) like the tightening in their gut that warns of a predator.

For those of us living in suburbs, cities, or rural towns without lions, this brief story may seem difficult to relate to. But I can assure you, there are "lions" everywhere.

INVITATIONAL INSIGHT LANGUAGE

Our modern lions come in different shapes. They prowl as the endless scroll of a phone screen, the rush of a crowded schedule, the hum of constant noise. They hide in the subtle ways we are pulled away from each other, from ourselves and from the living world. My father's behavior at the door and the San people's story are reminders of how deeply our survival and belonging are shaped by attention to patterns and *shared connection*. People are growing up without those sensory roots, without a daily dialogue of land and life. How did we lose this way of being — and how can we find it again?

My generation often recalls our youth with nostalgia — the days we were sent outside and told not to come back until dinner. It's puzzling that a generation so fond of those memories has raised children who now spend, on average, 93% of their time indoors. If we truly cherish nature, why have we allowed our children to become estranged from it?

It's easy to blame media and technology, but those are only part of the story. The deeper issue lies in what's missing. Researcher Darcia Narvaez calls this absence "undercare," which she explains as a lack of positive, enriching experiences, a void where connective moments should be.[1]

Many children today move through repetitive, limited cycles of experience, with few genuine nature affordances. This loss stems from an intergenerational shift where adults themselves have grown distant from the grounding relationships with land and community that earlier generations relied upon. Without those roots, it's harder to pass along the habits of attention and connection that keep both people and place thriving.

Curiosity is the bridge back. It fuels engagement, connection, and learning. It softens judgment and opens the door to understanding meltdowns, resistance, sibling squabbles, and more. Yet when adults are weighed down by responsibilities or lingering trauma from their own early childhoods, curiosity can feel out of reach. But even a single moment of curiosity — one question, one pause to notice together — can begin to loosen that weight and bridge the gap of generational disconnection. Each small interaction is an opportunity to 'return the serve,' fostering shared meaning and rekindling connection. It might be as simple as asking, "Did you hear that bird?" or wondering aloud why the wind smells like rain — moments that invite both adult and child back into a shared conversation with the living world.

Good questions grow out of genuine curiosity. They invite us to look deeper, to wonder, and to connect the dots between what we see and what we feel.

Why does my 13-year-old daughter get so upset when her 7-year-old brother breaks the rules?

Why does my 7-year-old resist bedtime?

Why does my 3-year-old keep putting the ball in the sink?

For much of human history, sharing and listening to stories was an active process, fueled by this kind of wondering. A story was not something you simply received; it was something you helped unfold by asking questions, noticing details, and offering your own observations in return. Curiosity kept the conversation alive, and in doing so, it kept relationships alive.

In earlier generations, this back-and-forth happened naturally. Story exchanges brought sensory experiences into focus and gave shape to our understanding of the world. They are how we can reweave connection in our homes today.

When these connective moments go missing, disconnection takes root, and the habits that keep us attuned to each other slowly fade.

Simply being curious about one another's experience of life and their stories can change that. Even the smallest exchange can shift a household from one where undercare is the norm to one where interaction is the norm.

Stories help the brain make meaning of experience. Whether long, short, or unfolding daily, storytelling and story listening are integrative practices linking sound, touch, movement, internal sensation, and insight.

Megan Barrow, an occupational therapist and mother to six-year-old Anna and four-year-old Zoe, practices this art beautifully. A self-described bird nerd, Megan brought Anna on slow walks through parks and river trails as a baby, often stopping to imitate bird sounds or touch tree bark. "We did a lot of pointing," she recalls.

Much like Lindsay and her daughter, story exchange begins in these early serve-and-return moments — flying the baby toward wonder. Megan reported walking slowly, stopping frequently, and making many attempts to imitate new bird sounds. "I also let Anna touch bark on the side of trees, pick up feathers..."

As Anna grew, their nature walks turned into bike rides along a bird-rich river. Anna often spots the elusive green herons before Megan does. Her delighted cry — "Oh my gosh, a Green Heron!" — becomes more than a moment of excitement; it's an opening for a shared story. Megan pauses, meets her daughter's eyes, and steps into that space with curiosity.

Megan pedals and scans for traffic while Anna sits behind her listening and watching, relaxed and receptive. Anna's brain is interpreting environmental sensory stimuli like this —

My ears hear a specific sound, kuk-kuk-kuk-kuk. The kuk-kuk-kuk-kuk sound is one my brain hasn't yet matched with an image. But everyday along my bike ride I see a bird with a long neck, green feathers on the side, spear-like beak, who is usually near the river. The bird is silent and moves slowly before spearing a fish with its beak. We call it a Green Heron. But one day I hear kuk-kuk-kuk-kuk, and I turn my head to see something I've not seen before — Green Heron taking flight from the water in a burst of action.

Flying rapidly towards Green Heron is a bigger bird with a white head and white tail feathers. That is the bird we call, Eagle. Heron seems to be fleeing for her life as she shouts kuk-kuk-kuk-kuk-kuk. I determine that the kuk-kuk-kuk-kuk-kuk, is the alarm call of a Green Heron threatened by a Bald Eagle. Therefore, the specific sound kuk-kuk-kuk-kuk-kuk, now has meaning and can be organized in my brain as the Green Heron being preyed upon — It is integrated. Integration allows my brain to use less energy.

Megan doesn't rush to identify birds. Instead, she asks, "How did it move? Which way did it go? Show me how big. What colors did it have?" The exchange is about much more than birds. It's a way to build a shared experience and build connections. Each question invites Anna and Megan to notice more, remember more, and expand together.

These exchanges are the opposite of undercare. They are connective moments in action — curiosity meeting curiosity, weaving threads that strengthen the bond between parent, child, and place. Over time, these threads form the kind of sensory and relational rope that children can hold onto for life.

Imagine two different homecomings after outdoor play. In one, the child is greeted with warmth: "What did you see? What did you do?" The parent listens, asks, and expands the child's awareness. In another, the parent barely looks up from their device. One response invites connection. The other ends the exchange.

The difference often comes down to the kind of language we use. Some responses close the door — what I call deflective language. Others invite engagement — invitational language.

Deflective Example:
Child: Hey Mom/Dad?
Parent: Ah, hey. (Lacks Awakening — a response without a reciprocal interaction)
Child: Heads to room or other area of the house and opens a screen.
Parent: Scroll, scan, repeat.

Invitational Example:
Child: Hey Mom/Dad?
Parent: Ah, hey, what's up? (A response and invitation to reciprocal interaction)
Child: Nothing. I'm hungry.
Parent: What did you do outside? (Awaken attention)
Child: I don't know. Nothing.
Parent hands child food: So what did you see? (Engage the senses)
Child: Nothing, we just made a fort.
Parent: With what? (Expands the child's awareness of environment)
Child: You know that grass that grows over by the woodpile?
Parent: The stuff that cuts your hand if you pull it out wrong?
Child: No, the other stuff, the softer grass. The one that's easy to pull out at the bottom.
Parent: Oh, yeah, I think I know that. It grows where the ground stays kind of wet? (Child may not have noticed but likely will next time, expanding awareness again)

Child: Ah, I guess, well, we got a whole bunch of that stuff to make a soft bed inside the fort. Then we climbed in there and got really quiet and that's when the scrub jays started making all this noise so we followed them and found a nest!

Parent: A nest? Where is it?

Child: It's in the oak tree right next to the house! Can you believe it!

Parent: I can't believe they led you to their nest! Why would they do that? I wonder why they weren't quiet. Were there babies? (An Invitation to Integrate)

Child: Yeah, it was awesome!

Parent: How many babies?

Child: I don't know; we couldn't tell. Like, maybe 3?

This concept of invitational language — along with the examples of parent and child, Megan and Anna, and myself and my father looking at the horizon — shows the potential in every interaction to enrich curiosity and connection. These small exchanges remind us that the most meaningful discoveries can transform the mundane into relational magic.

For new parents navigating the joys and challenges of parenthood, these narratives offer a simple yet profound blueprint: Be present, listen deeply, and treasure the stories our children bring to us, for these are the threads that weave the fabric of lifelong learning and connection.

PAUSE: Take a moment, and consider: In the hustle of daily life, what small wonder of nature can you share with your child today? How might you turn a simple sound, a mere kuk-kuk-kuk-kuk-kuk, into a thread that connects your child to the world's grand relational web?

Try This

Story catching with Nature

Here's how you can begin practicing story catching with your own child — or with yourself:

Tune in like a birdwatcher. The next time you're outside, let your child take the lead. Follow their gaze, gestures, or footsteps. Where are they drawn? What catches their attention?

☐ Listen together. Pause and listen for sounds — bird calls, rustling leaves, distant water. Imitate them together or ask, "What do you think made that sound?"

☐ Name textures and sensations. Invite touch. Bark, grass, rocks, feathers — ask, "What does it feel like in your hands?"

☐ Ask curious questions. Instead of giving answers, try asking: "What do you think it's doing?" or "I wonder why it's here?"

☐ Catch the story. At the end of their time outside, ask your child to tell you the story of what they saw and did. Listen fully, reflect it back, and build on it with more questions.

☐ Let wonder lead. Resist the urge to correct or explain everything. Allow mystery. Stay in the "I wonder..." as long as possible.

Every moment you follow their lead, ask curious questions, and reflect their observations back, you're strengthening their sensory system, curiosity, and capacity for meaning-making.

Wild Reflection

In your early life, did the adults catch and follow your curiosity, or did they direct it?

What sensory memory stands out most from your own childhood nature play?

How could you catch the stories your child is trying to tell — whether in words, gestures, or sounds?

If your child had a "Green Heron moment" today, what would it be?

12

SENSORY ANCHORS

ROOTING INTO NATURE FOR REGULATION

> Emotions are not reactions to the world; they are your constructions of the world.
>
> Lisa Feldman Barrett, How Emotions Are Made

It may seem simple, but small rituals of noticing nature can help calm a child in the middle of a nervous system meltdown.

Mikey's story shows how brief connections, repeated over time, build the skills for regulation.

By the time I met Mikey, he was eight, and he'd already lived through more upheaval than many adults. Removed from his birth family as a toddler, and later adopted by his foster mom after his foster parents divorced, Mikey's early years were filled with disruptions and uncertainty. He towered over his peers in both height and weight, yet inside carried the fragility of a much younger child. He went through cycles of anger with meltdowns that involved crying, yelling, and throwing and breaking things.

Mikey's school had tried everything: behavior charts, sticker rewards, time-outs, small toys, pieces of candy. They had an iPad wrapped in a rubber case to keep him busy and a bin of fidget toys to occupy his hands.

His teacher whispered to me, "I'm afraid of him. I don't want to get hurt." I glanced at the behavior plan taped to the wall, full of goals about compliance and staying seated.

"Do you think any of these things are meaningful to him?" I asked gently.

Her eyes filled with tears. "No. But what else can I do?"

I saw Mikey once a week, taking him to the school garden, a small patch of green with a few raised planter beds and an old forgotten mulberry tree. A chain-link fence and a locked gate surrounded it. On the way to the garden with Mikey, I sang:

"When the red, red robin comes bob, bob bobbin' along…"

I'd pause and ask, "Do you think we will hear the beautiful song of the robin today?"

For weeks, Mikey and I visited the garden.

On our fourth visit, Mikey ping-ponged around, turning over stones and wood boards. He tugged at a low branch of the mulberry tree, and I whispered, "Oh, be careful with my limbs. I like to keep my leaves and give you shade on hot days."

He looked at me and smiled. "You said that!"

"Maybe," I teased.

He walked to a kale sprig and placed two fingers on a leaf as if to pull it. He turned and looked at me with a smile. I said, "Oh, Mikey. Please hold me softer than that. I want to keep growing so I can give you food."

He giggled, and we moved around the whole garden playing this charade. Towards the end of our mere twenty minutes together, a robin landed on a branch of the mulberry tree and sang "Chula-leep-Chula-loo!" I tapped Mikey on the shoulder and pointed to the robin.

"What does he say?" Mikey asked.

In a sing-songy robin voice, I said, "Oh Mikey, it was lovely to see you today. I'm so glad I could sing you my song and help your body calm down!"

"Yes! You DID! Thank you, Red Red Robin!"

A week later, I was called to his classroom.

He'd had a meltdown: thrown books, overturned chairs, ripped paper. The teacher and aides had evacuated the class.

When I entered, Mikey stood in the center of the chaos. His breathing was ragged; his face red with frustration.

"Hey, Mikey," I said softly.

He looked at me, walked past me toward the door, and shouted over his shoulder:

"Are we going to see the red red robin?"

A couple of months later, I arrived at Mikey's school for his annual meeting to update his services. As I walked toward the office, I saw his adoptive mom get out of her car. She walked with a tired lilt. Her clothes hung wrinkled, and her shoes were worn.

When she entered the meeting room, I offered her a window-facing seat with a view of an ornamental cherry tree. I pointed to the tree and said, "Sometimes a robin sits in that tree and sings."

She turned sharply toward me and half shouted. "Oh. So you're the bird lady!"

I laughed a little, and she did too, holding out her hand to shake mine. "Well. Then I guess I've got you to thank."

I raised my eyebrows. "Oh?"

She shook her head, blinking back tears. "Yeah. You see... all these people keep telling me my boy is a nightmare, that I should put him in his room, give him time-outs, take things away, you know, discipline him more. But none of those things ever work. He just gets even madder. The school says I need to give him medication. And then one day, he comes home, and I won't let him play his video game — I think it's bad for him — and I wait for it, for the tantrum. But this day, he does something different. This day, I watch his poor little face get beet red like always. He clenches his hands into fists and starts to tighten his whole body. But instead of screaming or throwing himself on the floor, he stops and says to me, *Mama... I'm going to look for the red red robin*."

My jaw slackened, and I held my hand to my heart. Her eyes welled up, and she shook her head, spouting, "Who would've guessed the damn birds would be the thing!?"

The robin's song had taken root. Mikey's brain filed it under *familiar, safe, and calming sounds*.

Mikey needed to thread his healing with positive and joyful inputs.

The threads of healing can be many things: a pause, a tone of voice, a birdcall, a star in the night sky. Each one is a small offer of safety. Mikey's threads began with a trusted caregiver and a robin.

It might be different for your child — a breeze, a tree, a scent, a backyard with a trusted pet.

A recent study shows that even ten minutes outside can calm an anxious mind and support both emotional and physiological reset. Few sounds are as soothing to the human nervous system as birdsong. Again and again, people name it above all other natural sounds as the one that helps them recover from stress and return to focus.

The focus on behavioral compliance distracts caregivers from staying curious about a child's underlying skill deficits behind their behavior.

Mikey needed to feel safe. He needed to be allowed small healthy risks, such as climbing on a rock, or exploring a forgotten garden, to help him reprogram and refine the way his brain was predicting. And most important, he needed to find a familiar and accessible way to calm his brain's response to unexpected stimuli. For him, that meant birds.

If your child's behavior confuses you, or you're not sure what to do to help them, keep it simple. Show up, listen, look, smell, and be curious together.

REBUILDING OUR SENSES

The robin's song became like an anchor to steady Mikey when his emotions got overwhelming.

We all need anchors, and we need landmarks for our senses — those familiar cues that help us find our way back. Without them, the world can feel disorienting. I've felt that disorientation in my own body, and I've seen it in children whose sensory systems never had the chance to fully develop.

I learned the importance of those anchors in a deeply personal way when, without warning, my own body lost its primary landmark for balance.

The doctor was a blur as he looked at me and said, "This may be permanent."

I was only 23. Far too young, I thought, to have my life sidelined by a debilitating disorder that had come on overnight. One moment I was a full-time college student who ran five to seven miles a day and worked two part-time jobs. The next, I was crawling from my bed to the bathroom, holding on to walls so I wouldn't fall.

My stomach churned constantly. I had lost my vestibular sense — my balance. I couldn't stand, drive, read, or even see straight. The third specialist echoed the others: "We have no idea why this is happening. There is no cure."

Then came the words that landed like a stone: "This may be permanent."

Scott McCredie, author of Balance, writes, "No other sense is as critical to survival as the vestibular sense. To lose one's sense of up and down, one's position on the planet, is to undergo one of the most profound disturbances a human can experience."

He was right. I couldn't eat. Couldn't think. Couldn't sleep. Talking took effort. My thoughts scattered. I was depressed and afraid. I slept on the floor for fear of falling out of bed.

And then — two and a half weeks later, just as suddenly as it had come, it lifted. My balance returned. No one could explain it. But I never forgot the disorientation of living without the anchors my senses had always provided.

Others have not been as lucky as I. For some, those anchors never return on their own. The landmarks stay blurred with the inner compass adrift. And for many children, this disorientation is not sudden like mine — it's the only world they have ever known. That's what I saw when I met Chad.

Up until third grade, Chad had been labeled hyperactive and a poor learner, but he'd generally been well-behaved. Things shifted during third and fourth grades. By November of his fourth-grade year, I got a call for help.

"We have a boy who's becoming a behavioral nightmare."

"What does that look like?" I asked.

"He's totally defiant."

"But what does that mean? Can you describe his behavior?"

"Well, he refuses to look at the teacher. He puts his head on his desk and covers it. Sometimes he pretends to fall out of his chair and then lays on the floor. Other times he turns his desk backwards. He rips up his assignments, doesn't do homework, and now he's having multiple outbursts every day."

"Any problems at home?"

"Not as far as we know. He seems to have a loving mother and a stable home."

"Is he violent?"

"Not yet, but I'm worried it will get there soon."

"Hmmm. OK, I'll come check him out."

When I walked into his classroom, Chad was easy to find. Hoodie pulled low over his face, hands gripping the edge of the fabric like armor, he sat tucked under his desk.

I crouched beside him and whispered, "Hey. You want to get out of here for a while?"

He moved the hoodie to look at me, nodded, and followed me out, bumping into the doorjam on the way.

Outside, he asked, "So, where are we going?"

"Well, I'm Ms. K, and my job is to help make school easier for kids who are having a hard time. Sounds like you might be having a hard time?"

"Ah. It's fine. So where we going?" His voice was flat, eyes on the ground, hoodie still shadowing most of his face.

"I thought we'd take a little walk before heading to my office. Get some fresh air. Have a break."

He shrugged and walked in a zigzag line, tripping over a curb. He didn't seem angry. He didn't seem anything at all. His lack of expression told me he wasn't in fight or flight. He was in freeze.

Freeze is the hardest place to start from. When a child is fighting or fleeing, they're still reaching toward the world in some way, even if chaotically. But freeze means the reach has stopped. The threads have gone slack.

I decided to see what his senses might still be reaching for.

"Hey, Chad. Can you point to the nearest bird you hear?"

We stopped near an ornamental cherry tree where I counted five noisy starlings. He pushed his hoodie back, tilted one ear toward the sky, then the other, pulled the hoodie down again, and kept walking.

"There are no birds," he said.

Wow, I thought. He really tried to listen.

"OK... how about pointing to the nearest bird you *see*?"

He stopped again, lifted his hoodie, looked skyward like someone searching for constellations, turned in a full circle and lost his balance. I caught him before he fell. He pulled the hoodie back on and started walking.

"There are no birds," he repeated.

"Okay. Chad. Can I take a look at something with your eyes?"

He shrugs and we stop walking.

"All you have to do is stand still and look at me. Don't move your head. Just move your eyes and follow my finger with only your eyes."

He nods. I hold my finger in front of him. His eyes land on my finger when it is still, but as soon as I move it, his eyes dart in different directions. I move my pointer finger from left to right, right to left, up to down. I repeat the test three times, and each time get the same result. Chad rubs his eyes vigorously.

"Are your eyes hurting?"

"Not really. They're just annoying and make me dizzy sometimes. It's no big deal."

But it was a big deal.

Chad couldn't see or hear the birds. He had no anchors or landmarks. His vestibular system hadn't had enough of a chance to practice and map his place in the world. Without that stabilizing force, his senses scattered. The centrifuge of balance — the system meant to hold everything together

— never had the chance to fully spin up. Every day at school was like navigating without a compass — exhausting, disorienting, and lonely.

He didn't need stricter rules or sharper consequences. He needed experiences that would give his senses something to hold onto. Movement, balance, vision, and sound woven together through play, practice, and nature.

We started small. Outside. Balancing on curbs. Jumping from one sidewalk square to the next. Walking like bears, then crabs, then tiptoeing across imaginary bridges. We spun in slow circles, played follow-the-leader, and scrambled over playground rocks. We turned "I Spy" into a game of tracking — finding the cloud shaped like a bird, the tree with a leaning trunk, the bird calling from the far fence. Each game offered his eyes and ears a new coordinate to chart, a new point of reference in his sensory map.

At home, his mother began weaving in movement before homework: climbing on the couch cushions, hopping from rug to rug, balancing on the curb while walking to the mailbox. There was no fancy equipment. No expensive program (other than the skilled guidance from an OT). Just everyday movement and exploration — the kind that had been an ordinary part of childhood not so long ago.

Week by week, his teacher reported fewer meltdowns. Fewer torn assignments. His reading began to improve. His mood began to lift. By the end of the year, Chad had gone from hiding under his desk to spotting birds on the playground — and naming them.

One spring morning, he ran toward me, hoodie down, face tipped to the sky. "Look Ms. K! A starling!"

Chad's behavior was a consequence of his undeveloped sensory system. This lack of basic development had gone undetected until fourth grade, when he could no longer hide his deficits. His vestibular system did not function properly to coordinate the rest of his senses with each other. The muscles of his eyes were one of the more obvious challenges.

How had this happened?

Chad's life was relatively sedentary; he lacked access to multi-dimensional affordances. Using our eyes doesn't happen automatically. There are many unseen skills the body and brain must build for vision to work. The following are just a few:

Eye-teaming — both eyes working in coordination to create a single, clear image

Eye-convergence — the ability of both eyes to turn inward together to focus on a close object

Visual-spatial awareness — the ability to perceive and understand where objects are in relation to where you are

Form constancy — recognizing an object as the same, even when it looks different in size, color, or position, and being able to remember it when it's out of sight

Near and far vision — the ability to clearly see objects both up close and at a distance, and to shift focus between the two

Tracking — smoothly following a moving object with your eyes, or moving your eyes accurately from one point to another

Imagine trying to watch and understand a lecturer without being able to coordinate your eyes. How would you compensate for this deficit? Maybe you would put your head down and rest your eyes? Maybe you would cover them and try to listen without being distracted by movement? Maybe you would feel depressed and give up hope?

Maybe you would look and act like Chad.

It's easy to forget in our modern lives that our senses are born ready but not fully developed until they are used over and over. Before screens or tightly scheduled days, children naturally built their senses by freely climbing trees, spinning in fields, balancing on logs, chasing shadows. That was the daily work of building a nervous system.

Today, we have to choose that work with intention. Because sensory deprivation doesn't always look like tragedy. It can look like a child who's "lazy," "defiant," "unmotivated," or "behind," — when, in reality, they're simply missing the practice their body needs to feel steady and oriented.

I still remember the fear of losing my own balance, the way it stripped away my sense of safety. And I remember Chad, walking beside me that spring day, hoodie off, listening for birds, spotting a starling.

Every child deserves the chance to feel the centrifuge gather scattered pieces into place so they can feel at home in their body and on the earth. We can't always change the world they are growing up in. But we can offer them small moments that build their capacity to meet it.

Moments that restore balance. Invite regulation. Strengthen connection.

And it can begin with a bird. A sound. And one caring adult.

Each one a thread, waiting to be woven into a rope. A way home.

Try This

Step outside your front or back door.

☐ Close your eyes and listen.

☐ Do you hear a bird?

☐ What's it saying? What message might it carry for you today?

Wild Reflection

Think of a recent moment when your child felt overwhelmed. If you could gently place a bird, a tree, a cloud, or a breeze inside that moment — what would you choose? How might nature offer a thread, a rope, a way back?

Think of a time your child seemed overwhelmed or disconnected.

What small sensory invitation could you offer?

A walk outside? A moment of balancing on a curb? A game of "I Spy" with the birds or clouds?

13

HOW ANIMALS TEACH

LEARNING TO READ WITH NATURE

Recognizing how we share our habitat — not only the physical world, but in what I call the habitat of the heart — is about the future children of all species. Each animal we encounter has the potential to become part of us or part of who we could become. If we meet them halfway.

Richard Louv, Our Wild Calling

Like other children I'd worked with, when Max's mother called me about his sudden "defiance," I suspected there was more to the story. His turning point began with a local wild animal.

I could hear the ache in her voice. "It's like he's not here anymore. He's not our Max."

Ten-year-old Max had gone from a silly, playful kid to a child who refused to do homework, lashed out in class, and got into playground scuffles. He came home daily with dreaded red cards — lost recesses, warnings, disciplinary slips.

"He's never been like this before," his parents told me. "He's always struggled a little with reading, but now he's falling apart." Doctors floated diagnoses: ADHD. Oppositional Defiant Disorder. Maybe an emotional disorder. Maybe parenting (ugh!).

They pulled him out of school while trying to figure out what to do. That's when they called me. "I heard about your nature program," his mom said. "We're an outdoorsy family. We hike, we camp, we watch animal shows together. We don't know what else to try."

When I first met Max, his eyes barely lifted from the ground. His shoulders slumped. His feet dragged. I asked if he was looking forward to the day, he shrugged.

By the third day of our program, we arrived at the sandy bank of a local river. His posture lifted ever so slightly when he saw the river. A flicker in his eyes. His voice showed a tiny spark of excitement. For the first time in months, Max wasn't the boy with red cards. He wasn't the boy who couldn't stay in his seat. He wasn't the boy who melted down over homework.

He was just a boy again — curious, engaged, alive.

We stood together at the river's edge, gazing at the ground. Beneath us lay the clearest set of coyote tracks I'd seen in days. Obvious to me. Invisible to him.

"Max — whoa! Look at this!" I said with a wide smile, inviting him closer. Max glanced at the ground, his gaze scanning around. He looked vaguely in the area but missed the track completely. His eyes drifted, landing on a patch of dirt a few feet off.

"Uh... cool," he said flatly.

But he didn't see it.

I bent down, cupping my hands around the track to help frame it visually.

"Try looking right here."

He stepped closer. His breath deepened. His weight rocked from foot to foot. His hands fidgeted in his pockets. I slowed my breath, knowing he was reading my body for cues.

I traced the track slowly with my finger.

"One... two... three... four toes," I counted aloud.

He leaned closer, brow furrowed, bending stiffly at the hips. Then, suddenly he blurted:

"OH! OH! I see it! Yeah! Yeah! I see it!"

Relief flooded me.

"Awesome. Want to count them again with me?"

"Yeah!"

We counted together:

"One, two, three, four."

I tapped in front of the claw marks.

"Do you see the claws here?"

He nodded eagerly.

I smiled.

"Hmm... so, it has four toes, claws showing... what kind of animal do you think made this track?"

After an uncomfortably long pause and with utter sincerity, Max shouted:

"AN ELEPHANT?"

I blinked. An elephant. In California.

It wasn't funny. It was revealing, and in that moment, although I continued, I saw what Max had been trying to communicate through red cards and lost recesses.

"Hmm. What makes you think elephant?" I asked gently.

"The toes," he said confidently.

Max wasn't just struggling with reading books. He was struggling to read the world. He couldn't visually locate the track until I guided him. And even then, his brain pulled from a library of disconnected information: a TV image unrelated to his local landscape, unrelated to the size or context of the track in front of him.

He wasn't defiant. He wasn't lazy. He didn't have attention deficit disorder. He literally hadn't developed the skill of seeing the world and connecting what he saw with what it meant.

This wasn't about knowing what a coyote is. It was about a brain that hadn't been practicing depth perception, size relationships, spatial reasoning, dimensionality.

When we think of "vision," we tend to think of whether a child can see an eye chart. But vision is so much more than that, as we saw with Chad. The ability to *perceive* what we see is not guaranteed just because a child's eyes function at birth.

Visual nuance needs to be honed and developed through daily multi-dimensional experiences: noticing the curve of a leaf, the shadow beneath a stone, the way tracks fade into dirt. Without that practice, a child's brain struggles to *interpret* what it sees. Screens and flat images don't provide the same input; they are two-dimensional experiences for a multi-dimensional brain.

That struggle shows up in the classroom:

Difficulty copying from the board.

Skipping lines when reading.

Losing their place on a page.

Flipping letters with writing.

Misinterpreting written instructions.

When visual processing breaks down, children rarely say, "I can't see it." They show overwhelm, avoidance, or struggle. It can appear socially too — missing body language, spatial cues, gestures, subtle expressions. Eventually it gets labeled as "behavior," when really it's a brain working overtime to make sense of fragments.

Max didn't need more flashcards. He didn't need another sticker chart. He needed chances to *practice seeing*. To see letters, he first needed to see shapes, patterns, shadows, textures, and relationships between objects. He needed to shift focus — near to far, far to near — to spot a bird in a tree, then notice tracks underfoot. He needed nature's multi-dimensional, ever-changing classroom.

In Max's time with us on the nature program, we never practiced reading words on a page. Instead, we awakened his sense of ecoception. We engaged him with the world, using curiosity and letting nature lead. He created threads to ropes all around him — bird language, mapping, moving across uneven ground. Although we never sat with letters, he grew skilled at reading marks in the dirt.

Then came the day we saw the coyote itself. Max had been practicing following tracks for weeks when, up ahead, a coyote appeared — loping across the riverbank, wild and alive. Max's gaze followed it, then dropped to the prints it left behind. In that instant, track and animal fused in his mind. It was a fully integrative moment, a bridge between the abstract and the real. What had once been invisible to him became whole: movement, mark, meaning.

By the time Max returned to school for fifth grade, he was reading words on a page too.

Does your child struggle with reading? Do they seem clumsy, distracted, or spacey?

Maybe they get frustrated over homework or give up before they start. Maybe you've been told it's defiance, laziness, or lack of effort.

But what if their brain just hasn't had enough practice reading the world in dimensions?

What if they need more real, multisensory experiences — walking in the woods, following tracks, noticing bird calls, balancing on logs?

These moments are practice. For the eyes, for the brain, for attention, for interpretation. And the beautiful thing? You don't need to be an expert tracker to guide them. But you do need to slow down. Wonder aloud. Ask curious questions. Invite their gaze to join yours.

Every track is a story. Every shape is a clue. Every shared moment of noticing is a thread weaving their brain toward deeper understanding.

Tracking signs and patterns — an ancient form of reading — is a skill as old as humans themselves; in this case, we were tracking animals. When looking at marks in the dirt, a tracker knows they form a story. Tracks tell who, what, where, when, and why. They tell us if the animal was walking easily, trotting joyfully, or running for its life — or its dinner. Tracks were once so important to our survival as a species that looking at them, and other features of the landscape — such as the red glow of the horizon or the brittle cracks of dryness in the earth — shaped human neurology. Deciphering and interpreting signs left behind by other creatures, following a sequence of them, and recognizing patterns stimulates cognitive processes crucial for navigation and finding food, water, shelter, and each other. The cognitive processes honed through tracking animals laid the groundwork for our brain's capacity to understand written symbols, recognize patterns in text, and comprehend sequences of information, like reading this sentence.

Psychologist Karin James, from the Action and Cognition Lab at Indiana University, has explored how our movements connect with how we think. Imagine walking through unfamiliar landscapes and spotting animal tracks in the dirt — it's like a puzzle for our brains. Observing those tracks involves not just our eyes but also how we move and feel. Multidimensional experience helps our brain and body — our motor skills and cognitive processes — work in a coordinated way.

For children like Max, whose visual processing, depth perception, and spatial awareness haven't yet been fully developed, tracking serves as more than just a fun activity; By learning to slow down, notice details, follow patterns, and make meaning from what they see, children strengthen their ability to interpret the world around them. This practice builds the foundational skills needed for interpreting written words on a page. And it's fun.

We tend to separate outdoor exploration from academic skills, but they are more connected than people realize. Helping our children read the land, read tracks, and read signs *is helping them learn to read.* Nature offers a multidimensional classroom where these skills can develop naturally through movement, attention, and wonder.

How Animals Facilitate Perception

> One sees the environment not with the eyes but with the
> eyes-in-the-head-on-the-body-resting-on-the-ground.
> James J. Gibson, Ecological Approach to Visual Perception

Max's journey reminds us that seeing the world clearly takes practice with our sensory orchestra, and the moments children spend interacting with their environment shape their vision, both literally and figuratively. But perception is more than visual processing. It's how we come to know the wholeness of the world and sometimes, we get it hilariously wrong before we get it right.

There's a moment in the 1998 movie City of Angels that has always stayed with me. Nicolas Cage's character, Seth — an angel — asks Meg Ryan's character, Dr. Maggie Rice, "What does that peach taste like?"

Maggie laughs. "You know what a peach tastes like!"

Seth replies softly,

"I don't know what a peach tastes like ——— *to you.*"

That line always lands and reminds me that perception is never one-size-fits-all. Each of us interprets the world in our own way, shaped by our senses, our experiences, and the meanings we attach to them. A peach isn't just a peach — it's *your* peach. The same is true for the way a child perceives a bird, a dog, or a parent's facial expression.

You might remember from an earlier chapter the concept of an affordance: how the world invites interaction, and how those invitations shape a child's development. A child has to engage — reach, touch, explore — to really form a concept of something. A tree isn't a tree until they've felt the bark beneath their hands, seen the way the leaves tremble in the wind, smelled the earthy scent beneath its canopy.

The more early interactions one has, the more accurate perceptions and predictions they might make. Sometimes the learning comes from accurate predictions, and sometimes they come from inaccurate predictions, like one that happened when I was in seventh grade.

I delivered newspapers before school. One freezing morning in Toronto, it was still dark out, and I focused on the icy steps beneath my boots. I rushed up onto the porch to tuck the paper behind the screen door. Just as I reached the top step, I surprised a cornered black cat, who hissed at me. "Here kitty, kitty," I whispered, trying to calm it.

The "cat" raised its tail, planted its front feet, and — wham! — from three feet away, a burning, sticky wetness sprayed my face. It turns out that "cat" was a skunk. I carried that smell with me for days, and the lesson still today.

I've never mistaken the silhouette or movement of a skunk for a cat again. My brain updated its prediction file. That's how perception works: it's built moment by moment, often through mistakes.

Another story stands out from my early years of parenting. We'd just moved from the East Coast to sunny California. My younger daughter, barely two, wanted to help us paint our new living room. We gave her a little paintbrush and outlined a square of primer on the wall for her to fill in. She painted with surprising concentration, utterly absorbed.

When she finished, she set down her brush and stood back next to her dad, admiring her work. Her head tilted thoughtfully. He was crouched, painting a lower section of the wall, his shirt riding up to reveal a pale patch of skin. I turned to the kitchen when I suddenly heard: "OWWWWW!" her dad yelled, leaping up.

I spun around to see our daughter standing behind him, mouth open, looking confused. She'd bitten him — hard — on the exposed skin above his waistband. Her dad stared at her, incredulous. "KIRA! WHAT did you do THAT for?"

Without hesitation, in her sweet, earnest voice, she answered: "But Dada... You looked like an egg."

And she was right, in her own way. From her vantage point — two feet tall, seeing that round pale curve between shirt and shorts — his flesh did resemble an egg.

Her brain made a prediction: "Looks like an egg." She tested it the way toddlers test many things: with her mouth.

Her innocent explanation turned confusion into delight, and we all burst out laughing — my husband, myself, even her big sister.

That moment, and the moment with the skunk, taught me what Lisa Feldman Barrett, calls a prediction error: when the brain expects one outcome, and the world delivers another. It's how we all learn. Our brain continually updates its "file" with new information. My daughter learned, very effectively, that her dad's back wasn't an egg, and she never bit him again. And I never encouraged a skunk with, *Here, Kitty Kitty,* again.

These moments, whether startling or funny, are how children build perception. Through trial, error, interaction, and correction, they learn what things are, how those things behave, and what to expect.

But perception doesn't develop in isolation. It needs a relationship — between things, or someone to guide attention, to ask questions, to gently narrate. As we explored with Max and the coyote track, sometimes a child needs help learning *where* and *how* to look in order to truly *see*.

Perception is seeing with the whole body. Seeing with the head-on-the-body-standing-on-the-ground, feeling the sun, sensing the space. It's movement and touch and smell and sound, all working together.

When we slow down with our children, when we let them point and lead, when we honor their "but it looked like an egg" moments instead of seeing it as naughty behavior or correcting too quickly, we give them room to practice perception. We allow their brains to update gently, rather than through shame or fear.

It's the same whether they're learning the sensation of tree bark or deciphering a facial expression from a parent or figuring out how big an animal might have been by the tracks it left in the dirt. Every interaction is shaping not just what they know, but *how* they come to know.

As parents, it's important to trust that the learning often comes from making the mistake, not in us correcting it. We must remember to smile, stay curious, laugh together, and keep exploring together as our children test the world with their senses.

Try This

The next time you're outside with your child, slow your pace.

□ Pause at something simple — a rock, a tree, a track in the dirt — crouch low and invite your child to notice it with you. Instead of telling them what it is, ask questions that spark their curiosity:

□ "What do you see here?"

□ "How does it feel?"

□ "What could have made this?"

□ "How do you think it moves?"

If their answer surprises you, or seems wildly inaccurate, try staying curious instead of correcting right away. Ask follow-up questions. Give their idea space. See if you can gently guide them toward noticing more, without shutting down their excitement.

Each time you do this, you're helping them practice perception: connecting their senses, their body, and their thinking into a more integrated understanding of the world.

Wild Reflection

Think of a moment when your child made a "mistake" in interpreting what they saw, heard, or felt. How did you respond? How might you approach it differently, knowing what you know now?

14

How Nature Nurtures Babies

Opportunities Outside Your Door

And remember that nature programs entirely for success.

Joseph Chilton Pearce

Before a child ever struggles to read words or navigate a busy class-room, before the challenges of school-age life take shape, they are busy weaving the threads of their foundation — one sensory interaction at a time, searching for patterns and connections that will help them grow.

Yet more and more children — like Chad, Jose, and Max — are showing early signs of what I've come to call *disconnection disorders*. These signs often take root in the first years of life, quietly shaping a child's capacity for learning and relating, sometimes going unnoticed until the academic demands of third or fourth grade begin to unravel them.

That was the risk with Jenna.

Jenna was just nine months old when I met her. Her pediatrician had referred her to early intervention, where occupational therapists assess how babies are moving, interacting, nursing, and functioning — in other words, how well their development is progressing. Development, after all, is the occupation of babies.

Jenna's pediatrician had noticed she wasn't holding eye contact for long, wasn't lifting her head well, and wasn't engaging in the responsive exchanges of serve and return that helps babies build healthy brains.

When I first arrived at Jenna's home, she sat in an infant carrier placed on the floor, batting at a dangling mobile. The TV played in the background. Her four-year-old brother, Peter, sat a few feet away with an iPad, eyes locked on the screen. Mom sat on the floor near Jenna with a laptop.

"I'd get up, but honestly, I'm too tired," she said with a forced laugh.

"I totally get it. Having a baby and a four-year-old is exhausting!" I said.

She told me Jenna was "easy," sleeping through the night, and that her pediatrician was probably overreacting. "Look how she loves that mobile," she said, pointing. "And she's obsessed with Baby Einstein."

Jenna fussed. Her mom quickly reached for a binky and dangled it in front of her face. "This I could do in my sleep." She said popping the binky in Jenna's mouth. "But this—" she nodded toward her computer—"ugh!"

Her love for her children was clear. But babies aren't passive receivers of sensory input. They are shaped by every small, real-world interaction. In homes like Jenna's, I see the quiet trade-off between convenience for taxed parents, and the fading rhythms of developmental engagement.

Across playgrounds, waiting rooms, grocery stores, I see the same thing: babies and toddlers tuned out of the tangible world, tuned into flashing, pinging objects. It's not that parents aren't trying — it's that our culture tells us toys and gadgets will help our kids develop, and that nature and human connection are optional extras.

I leaned toward Jenna and sang softly, "Helloooo, Jenna!" Her body wiggled at my voice, though her eyes stayed fixed forward. Babies are wired to notice lilting, sing-songy tones the same way our ancestors first noted the nuanced sounds of bird "language."

A sing-songy voice still works today because it cues the brain: "Hey. Pay attention! Something new is happening. "

I clapped behind her. No reaction. Next to her. Still nothing.

"Could we turn the TV off?" I asked. Mom clicked the remote.

"And who's this over here?" I asked of Peter.

Peter stared at his iPad, swiping at the screen periodically. I walked a little closer to him and said, "Hi Peeettterrr, it's nice to meeeeet you!" with a higher lilt in my voice. His head bobbled, and he gave me a sideways look. Upon seeing me, his head jerked, his eyes opened wider, and a smile spread across his face.

"Heyyyy! What you doing here?"

"Well Peter. I'm here to play with your sister!"

"She a baby. Babies don't play."

"I bet when you were a baby, you played."

"I cried all the time."

"All the time?"

"I play with you!" Peter offers.

"Okay. Maybe I can show you how babies play?"

"Will Sister play with me?"

"I bet she will, but not the same way four-year-old's play."

"Yeah. She play like a baby."

Helping someone younger can awaken capacities in a child that might not surface through adult-directed tasks.

I turned to Jenna's mom. "Is it okay if I take her out of the carrier?"

"Of course. Whatever you need."

As I lifted Jenna, lowering the mobile she'd been fixated on, her face scrunched in confusion. Her limbs flailed, her lips trembled. The world she'd been watching suddenly disappeared.

"Jennnnaaa?" I called softly.

Her movement paused. Her head wobbled; her eyes darted but didn't settle.

"Jennnnaaa?" I tried again.

Peter knelt beside me. "Jennnnaaa," he echoed, then laughed.

"Jeennnnaaaaa?" He imitates me again, staring intently at his sister. This time, her head wobbles and turns toward Peter. When her eyes land on him, her whole-body wiggles, as if it's smiling. Peter laughs. I laugh at Peter's laugh. Peter looks at me and says again, "Jennnnaaaaaa." This time Jenna laughs a bubbly gurgle. Peter shouts, "Hey! She laughing!"

Mom looked up from her computer and smiled.

In that simple moment — a voice, a turn, a giggle — a relational cycle was happening. A moment of mutual attention, a serve and return between siblings. That small but vital thread.

We repeated this interaction a few more times. Each time Jenna responded, Peter's excitement grew. "She playing with me!"

"She's lucky to have such a good big brother." I told him.

Peter stood taller. "She can play with my Legos!"

"Well, remember how I said she doesn't play like a four-year-old?"

"Oh." He says, deflated.

"Do you have any soft, cuddly toys?"

"Oh. Yeah." Peter jumps up and runs out of the room. I take the opportunity to lay a blanket on the floor and place Jenna on her belly. Jenna's arms and legs flail, find the ground, and push — lifting her shoulders. She briefly holds a seal position and then releases. Peter comes running back with an armful of stuffed animals.

"Perfect! Good job, Peter! Can I have this one?" I ask, pointing to a stuffed Great Horned Owl. He shoves it in my direction, almost knocking me in the face. "Your body seems very excited. Thank you, Peter's hand, for going slower so you don't bump my face," I say, and wink at Peter.

"Yeah. Thank you hand for not bumping...uhm...what's your name?"

"Ms. Kathleen."

"Yeah. Thank you hand for not bumping Ms. Kathleen!"

Together we practice saying, "Hoo Hoo Hoo Hoooo." Then I ask Peter to hold Hooty Owl about five feet in front of his sister and wiggle it around while remaining quiet. He's a perfect helper. Jenna is smooshing her face into the blanket and moving her head back and forth.

I ask Peter to move a bit closer. He does. Jenna doesn't see him. She pushes her torso an inch off the floor with her forearms. Once more I tell Peter to move a little closer to be about three feet in front of his sister. She's starting to get frustrated. I say, "Okay, Peter. Make the Hooty Owl sound."

"Hoooo! Hoooo!" he calls.

Jenna freezes. Then pushes harder. And then, slowly, she lifts her head.

"She see me!" Peter beamed.

"She's working so hard," I said, smiling at them both.

On my second visit I took Jenna and Peter outside.

We began simply. I sat with Jenna on my lap outside their back door, under a few trees. "Peter. I need your help. There's a bird hiding from me. We have to be very quiet and still, so we don't scare it away. Can you help me?"

Peter's face lit up with purpose. He sat beside me, watching. A woodpecker called from a tree: "Kleer! Kleer!" I widened my eyes, cupped my ear, and pointed. Jenna looked at me. Peter copied me. Each bird call was not only a sound to notice but an invitation for Jenna's brain to sync with ours.

We didn't talk much. We just sat, waiting. Listening. Every time a bird called, I pointed again. Sometimes I added a little vocalization to mimic the sound. Peter watched. Jenna watched.

At first, the activity only lasted a couple of minutes before they got wiggly or bored. But at each visit, Jenna lifted her head a little longer. Each time, Peter listened a little more closely.

And a beautiful developmental dance began to unfold.

One day, Peter met me at the door before I could even knock. "Come on!" he said excitedly, pulling me to a table covered in paper with colorful scribbles. "I been making birds!" he explained proudly. Then he ran to his sister and in four-year-old excitement, hugged her tightly, saying, "Yeah. And my sister talk Bird!"

"She talks bird?" I asked.

"Yeah." He looked at his mom. "Tell her! Tell her what sister says!"

"You're not going to believe this..."

Mom shared that she had taken the kids outside the day before, and a bird (she didn't know what kind) was making clear one-syllable sounds. "It was very loud."

Mom was certain that Jenna was mimicking the vocalization of the bird — as if Jenna and the bird were talking back and forth. Mom got a big smile on her face and said, "And this morning, Jenna pointed at the front door and made this little sound, kind of like the bird she heard yesterday. I think... she was asking me to take her outside."

That's the magic of nature, and of small moments repeated with love and reciprocal attention.

Babies don't just "absorb" the world. They interact *with it*. And we can notice *with* them. By pointing things out, being quiet together, and listening together, we invite their senses to wake up, practice, and relate. It's the same serve-and-return process we've talked about before: a loop of communication, of curiosity, of responding to the world.

Those simple moments are building the roots from which your child's wild, thriving life can grow.

Try This

Tomorrow, take five minutes to go outside with your child.

- ☐ Sit quietly.
- ☐ Listen together.
- ☐ Point to a sound.
- ☐ Let them show you what they notice.

You're not "teaching," you're sharing an experience. Let nature lead.

Wild Reflection

Think back to your own early memories of nature. Was there a tree, a bird, a plant, a sound, or a place that called your attention?

How did it make you feel?

Now, imagine your child lying on their belly or sitting in your lap, soaking up their first impressions of the world.

What's one simple, beautiful thing outside your door you'd like to introduce them to this week?

Let it be small. Let it be ordinary. Let it be enough.

15

The Attributes of a Good Human

Developing Character

How wonderful it is that nobody need wait a single moment
before starting to improve the world.

Anne Frank

The small exchanges we've witnessed — between caregiver and child
and between a child and nature, are roots for the deeper qualities of
becoming a good human.

The question becomes not only, What will my child be able to *do?* But
who will they *become?* Beyond skills and milestones, beyond the walls of
our homes, what qualities will help them craft a life that leaves the world
better by being alive?

When I was a young mother, no one asked me what kind of people I
hoped my babies would grow into. Yet, it was a question that I sat with
from the moment I became a mother.

It wasn't until that workshop back in 2003 with Jon and Paul, as we
learned about bird vocalizations and animal behavior, that answers to
questions I had carried took shape. During the workshop, Jon shared a

list that he'd co-created with Gilbert Walking Bull, an elder of the Lakota people. They called it the "Attributes of Connection."[1] It named qualities I longed to nurture in my own children, and in myself.

That same gathering offered another gift. Paul spoke about elderhood, inviting us to reflect on our own childhoods: Who were the elders whose presence you cherished? And if you did not have such a person, what qualities would you have wished for? Then came his invitation: Aim to become that person for others.

I've carried both teachings ever since. For more than twenty years, I've returned to those attributes, letting them guide me as a parent, a mentor, and a human still growing. Over time, I've gently adapted the list, adding language to reflect developmental language, and renamed it, The Attributes of Habilitation.

I share them with you now as an invitation.

Below is my light adaptation of the original attributes.

The Attributes Of Habilitation

VITALITY

A person with a brightness about them. They have an excitement for life, and when you are near them you feel this excitement and energy in their being. This person has the vitality to engage with people and situations in a way that is helpful to others.

CHILD-LIKE CURIOSITY

A person who explores and is interested in all aspects of life. They ask questions, are humble in their pursuit and do not interpret questions or challenges personally.

ATTENTION AND FOCUS

A person who has developed the ability to focus and pay attention in a meaningful, functional, and contextual (integrated) way.

COURAGE

A person who engages thoughtfully, and with an open but clear heart — even when fear arises or when interacting with challenging people, experiences, or situations. This person demonstrates courage in the face of adversity.

GRATITUDE
Demonstrates a natural and unforced gratitude for life. Feels and expresses gratitude even in difficult moments and situations. Celebrates life.

MEANING
Participates in life through meaningful activity and experiences. Creates meaningful connections with nature, family, and community.

LOVE, EMPATHY, AND FORGIVENESS
Demonstrates respect and care for all living things. Communicates kindly and effectively. Finds forgiveness for self and others. This person has found inner peace among hardship, offense, or injustice. This person embodies and lives with unconditional love and a forgiving heart. Demonstrates a generous spirit.

STILLNESS
A person who can quiet their body and mind in order to sense what is unfolding within and around them. They attune to the sensory symphony of life — the hush of wind, the weight of silence, the stirrings of others — and respond with presence rather than urgency. Even in moments of unrest, they carry a grounded calm that invites peace in others. This stillness is not passivity, but an active form of listening. Think of Ghandi, or the hush of a winter forest — alive with subtle signals, yet deeply at rest.

Imagine a world where every elder embodied these "attributes."

Imagine a world where every child — anywhere on the spectrum of neurodiversity — is encouraged to grow toward these attributes in their own unique way.

Imagine if education aimed not just for academic milestones, but for nurturing deep, meaningful connections with life itself.

Nurturing the Attributes of Habilitation in Children

The version of the attributes that follows is a child-centered interpretation. It offers parents a way to recognize what these attributes might look like as they begin to take shape in daily life. These are not traits to push for or measure. Instead, they can serve as gentle guideposts, helping us notice, nurture, and support what is naturally unfolding.

You will find each attribute paired with simple ideas that connect these qualities to ordinary moments. Through nature, play, and relationships, children build their capacity for vitality, stillness, attention, empathy, and more.

VITALITY

A child with vitality shows a spark for life. They light up when they discover something new, and their energy can be felt by those around them. You might see it in their excited storytelling or the way they jump into play. When we give them space to move, express, and explore, we help them grow that brightness into a steady, joyful presence in the world.

CHILD-LIKE CURIOSITY

Curiosity is alive in a child who wants to know why and how. They turn over rocks, ask questions, and experiment with everything from mud to ideas. They're not afraid of being wrong — they are learning how to wonder. By slowing down and wondering with them, we help that spark grow into a lifelong openness to learning.

ATTENTION AND FOCUS

When a child is developing attention and focus, they are learning how to stay with something. Attention and focus are first built through things the child is interested in or cares about — a story, a sound, a task, a bug on the sidewalk. Focus may begin as short moments and grow over time. When we honor their pace and support them in following their interests, their ability to tune in gets stronger, both with things of interest and with unpreferred things.

COURAGE

Courage in children shows up when they try something new, speak up for themselves, or stay in a situation that feels hard. It may not look big or loud — often it's quiet and personal. We help build courage when we support them to stretch without pressure, stay present when they feel unsure, and celebrate their efforts more than the outcome. When we say, "I believe in you," courage grows.

GRATITUDE

Gratitude grows when a child notices something beautiful or meaningful and feels glad. It can sound like "thank you," but also shows in how they care for a rock they found, a friend who helped, or a flower they love. We nurture this by modeling appreciation, speaking aloud our own thanks, and noticing life's small gifts together.

MEANING

A child begins to find meaning when they feel they matter — when their role in the family, their bond with a place, or their care for an animal gives them purpose. You'll see it in the pride they take in helping, in the stories they tell, and in the rituals they return to. Meaning is built through belonging, shared purpose, and time spent in connection.

LOVE, EMPATHY, AND FORGIVENESS

Love and empathy show up when a child cares for a pet, comforts a friend, or notices when someone else is hurting. Forgiveness begins when they learn that making mistakes doesn't mean love is taken away. When we respond with warmth, name feelings, repair after ruptures, and model kindness, we help them grow into people who can connect with others from a generous, open heart.

Try This

Bring the attributes of habilitation into the rhythm of your everyday routines by practicing them in small, natural ways.

☐ Choose one attribute to notice this week. For example, if you want to nurture curiosity, make a point of pausing when your child asks, "Why?" Instead of rushing past, join them in wondering, even if you don't have the answer.

☐ Turn ordinary moments into practice grounds. At the grocery store, on a walk, or before bedtime, invite your child to engage one of the attributes: patience while waiting in line, gratitude for the food you're preparing, care for a bug on the sidewalk.

☐ Model what you want to see. When you show kindness to a neighbor, perseverance in a frustrating task, or humility when you make a mistake, name the quality out loud: "That took patience," or "I'm practicing being gentle." Your child learns not only through imitation but also through hearing the values you live.

☐ End the day with a story or memory. Share a simple tale from your own life (or a family story) that highlights one attribute. Children absorb values most deeply through story and example.

Wild Reflection

Take a moment to reflect on the qualities you hope to nurture in your child.

What traits matter most to you?

Where did those values come from?

How do you model those qualities in your daily life?

If you imagine your child grown, looking back on their childhood, what would you hope they say they learned from you?

Write down three of the qualities you hope your child carries into adulthood and ask yourself: What small, every day practices might help those qualities take root?

16

AN ACE'S EPIDEMIC

HOW STRESS SHAPES THE BRAIN

> Most people wouldn't suspect that what happens to them in
> childhood has anything to do with stroke or heart disease or
> cancer.
>
> Nadine Burke Harris, The Deepest Well

As my children grew, I returned again and again to my questions: What does habilitation really mean? How does it happen? Is it possible to recover missing or misaligned developmental pieces? And what does nature have to do with raising skillful humans?

Those questions followed me through my early years of motherhood and professional life, through hardship and heartbreak, through joys and so many losses I never imagined I'd face. They stayed with me all the way to a conference room in 2015, more than twenty years after I first began asking them.

While preparing for my first presentation at the California Occupational Therapy Association's annual conference, I came across something that stopped me in my tracks: the Adverse Childhood Experiences (ACEs) study.

Suddenly, the puzzle pieces of my life, my work, and my deepest questions clicked together.

The study showed that the struggles we carry from childhood are more than emotional — they're biological. What happens to us early in life literally shapes the architecture of our brain and body, our stress responses, our current and future health, and our habits.

The night before my presentation, in my hotel room, slides finished, laptop glowing in the dark, I clicked on a TED Talk by Dr. Nadine Burke Harris: How Childhood Trauma Affects Health Across a Lifetime. Those next 15 minutes would once again change the way I saw myself, my children, my work, and every child and parent I've worked with since.

Dr. Harris described how researchers in the 1990s uncovered a powerful link between childhood adversity and lifelong health issues — things like heart disease, depression, addiction, autoimmune conditions, and life expectancy. It wasn't just that hard childhoods made life emotionally tougher. They taught brains to brace instead of breathe.

Dr. Elizabeth Stanley explains in her book *Widen the Window*, that early adversity conditions the brain to predict threat even when none exists. The body does more than remember the past — it prepares us based on it.

It made so much sense to me.

The compelling science didn't stay abstract for long. I opened the questionnaire, expecting more curiosity. What I found hit much harder. The original ACE survey asked ten simple questions about different kinds of adversity experienced before age eighteen. Each "yes" adds one point to your score — and the higher the score, the higher the risk for serious health problems later in life.

I counted my score.

One. Two. Three... Six. I stopped counting.

Six.

As identified in the study, an ACE score of four or more raised risks for serious health issues. Six isn't good news. But here I was — still standing. Still loving. Still growing. Still happy to be alive.

And yet, as I read more about how early life adversity sets us up for a hard adult life, I found some powerful research showing that it doesn't have to define us. Our patterns are not set in stone. Just as a tree can find a new direction toward light after a storm clears the canopy above it, we can heal, we can grow, and we can compost our own childhoods into more enriching soil for ourselves and our children.

Dr. Harris' talk cracked me open.

And I knew from that night forward, the conversation wouldn't be complete without ACEs.

You may have heard of ACEs before, or maybe this is your first introduction. The study identified ten categories of adversity and has added to those in the years since:

Physical abuse

Emotional abuse

Sexual abuse

Physical neglect

Emotional neglect

Witnessing domestic violence

Living with someone with mental illness

Living with someone with substance use problems

Parental separation or divorce

Having a household member incarcerated

Chronic poverty or housing insecurity

Racial or cultural discrimination

Being a refugee or displaced by war

Exposure to community violence

Chronic bullying

Natural disasters

Parental military deployment

Each of these experiences adds weight to a child's developing system. And yet...

Your child is not their ACE score. And neither are you.

And if you are coming to this information early in your parenting journey, you can significantly reduce your child's ACE score. YOU can restructure your brain and body to expect safety and reduce your future health challenges.

If you are coming to it later in your parenting journey and your child has been through a lot, you can provide restorative experiences and improve their long-term health.

Seeing my ACE score was sobering, but it only felt like part of the story. If certain experiences could harm, perhaps other experiences could help?

Yes, I'd had adversity. But I'd also had protections — moments of wonder, awe, connection, and grounding. There had been many hints of light in the darkness. Looking back, I could see them like bright threads running through the harder years:

Wild places that offered solace.

Birdsong that said I belonged.

Wind that reminded me I was alive.

A well-placed smile or word of encouragement from a friend, family member or even a stranger.

Trees I climbed or lay under, holding me when people couldn't.

Trails I wandered barefoot, softening my anger.

Grandparents, who I now understand, offered moments of gentleness when and where they could.

All these seemingly small moments were seeds that bloomed later in life. Developmental science has a name for them: Protective and Compensatory Experiences — PACEs.

PACEs help tilt the scale back in a positive direction.

Even one seed, one stable, loving, responsive relationship — one person or place — can buffer a child from the harshest effects of adversity.

For your child, that person might be you.

For yourself, it might be the tree you sat under at the end of each day.

It might be a teacher, a grandparent, a coach, a mentor, a neighbor. It can be one stable parent in a difficult divorce. It can be nature itself offering moments of wonder, regulation, and hope.

As Stanley and others remind us, healing doesn't happen in a single leap. It happens in small, repeated cycles of safety. Each time our nervous system learns, "I'm okay right now," we slowly widen our window of tolerance — rewriting the brain's predictions from fear to calm, from danger to possibility.

Adversity shapes us, but it doesn't have to break us. ACEs point to patterns, and the hopeful thing about patterns is that once we see them, we can interrupt and change them — like placing your hand in an eddy of water breaks the circling and sends it flowing into the downhill stream again. Sitting there in the hotel room, counting my checked boxes, I felt a wave of recognition, a rush of grief, and then a determined fierceness.

PACES don't erase what happened, but they can change how these experiences metabolze in the body. They weave helpful threads into the nervous system, forming neural grooves of holistic potential. Over time, these positive experiences can become the brain's new reference points —

steady, safe moments the nervous system can return to. PACEs become the evidence the brain uses to rewrite its predictions, helping our nervous system learn to trust that not all moments are dangerous.

Safe relationships are a PACE.

Belonging is a PACE.

Connection with nature is a powerful PACE.

I'd seen it in myself. In my children. And I was seeing it again and again in the new generation. Children like Mikey, Max, Chad, Jenna and others. Children whose nervous systems were bracing, defending, searching, surviving. And yet, after being re-awakened to nature, with a robin's song, a breeze catching their cheek, a squirrel darting past, their bodies softened, their eyes lit up, their attention stretched outward again and they found joy.

Nature extended its hand, and they took it.

That's why this work isn't just about sensory input or developmental milestones. It's about the birthright of connection. And it's why, no matter what your child's story — or your own — you are never too late, too fractured, or too far behind to start threading protective and compensatory experiences.

Nature can help rebuild what disconnection tried to erode, or was never built to begin with.

It can begin with something simple like the presence of at least one caring adult who invites a child to return nature's "serves" and weaves those moments into a rope of connection. Because when that trusted adult can no longer be there, nature can.

Science confirms what we've seen and felt:

A 2015 Stanford study showed that even a 90-minute walk in nature calms the parts of the brain that spiral with worry and self-criticism.

A 2019 review found that spending time in green spaces lowers stress hormones, improves heart health, and boosts attention.

A 2022 study found that children who have more regular contact with nature show fewer behavioral and emotional difficulties — and bounce back from stress more easily.

Most powerful of all: nature connection in childhood doesn't just help in the moment — it predicts better well-being into adulthood.

Nature connection is a protective experience. And when adversity has already shaped a child's story, nature can offer compensation — restoring what was lost or building what was never gained.

The best news? It doesn't have to be a Grand Canyon adventure or a week-long camping trip. You can start right where you are:

Point out a bird to your child.

Pause to listen together for a frog, an owl, or the rustle of leaves in the wind.

Notice a drifting cloud, a floating leaf, or wonder together at a tiny ant crossing the sidewalk.

These micro-moments, when strung together over time, become ropes of connection. They support your child's development and help restore your own.

No matter how strong the storms have been, no matter what patterns you inherited, you can begin weaving a new story.

Not every child's story is shaped by obvious storms. Some carry an invisible kind of adversity — not from what happened, but from what didn't. This quieter absence can leave marks and it, too, calls for repair.

While children with high ACE scores often carry the weight of visible adversity — loss, family instability, community violence — I wondered about the other children I was seeing. Their lives didn't appear chaotic. There was no clear event or injury. And yet, their nervous systems told stories of overwhelm. Their symptoms — difficulty focusing, anxiety, meltdowns, withdrawal, social isolation — were not unlike those of children with more recognizable trauma histories.

Could there be another kind of adversity at play?

I thought of Gabor Maté's words: *trauma is not just the bad things that happen to us, but also the good things that don't.*

What happens when the foundational ingredients of development — presence, play, shared joy, relational-regulation, supported curiosity, healthy communication — are missing? Not all adversity comes from crisis. Sometimes, what's missing leaves just as deep a mark as what's overwhelming.

Sophie was in fourth grade when I met her. Her parents were concerned because she struggled to keep friends. She came from what most would describe as a "good" home — a stable neighborhood, parents together since before she was born, steady jobs, and the same house since she and her older sister were born.

In school, she was a good student — compliant and independent. She completed her homework without argument and didn't stand out. Although she tapped her pencil, looked around the room, and wiggled in her seat, so did many of her peers. Initially, she blended right in. She raised her hand quickly and worked quietly at her desk. On the surface, nothing seemed unusual.

But recess told a different story.

When the bell rang, she bounced from group to group: first kickball, then a circle of girls sitting on the blacktop, then the swings, and finally wandering alone. She didn't actually join in — she didn't kick the ball or sit with the girls. She stood at the edges, arms crossed, watching.

As I observed her more, then worked with her one-on-one, the picture became clearer. Sophie didn't know *how* to interact with other kids. She spoke rapidly and at length about a TV series she loved, imitating the characters and barely pausing when I responded. She struggled to read my cues or shift to a topic I introduced.

She attempted the physical games I introduced, like hopscotch and jumping jacks, but she struggled to coordinate her body. Her movements were disorganized and hesitant. After a few tries, she gave up and returned to talking about her TV shows.

At first glance, some might wonder about attention differences or autism spectrum traits. But I've seen how quickly those labels can be applied in ways that overlook the deeper story for some children. The body and brain learn to coordinate together. Movement and conversation both rely on timing, turn-taking, and rhythm. The ability to engage with peers and respond appropriately grows through repeated opportunities to practice those interactions over time. Sophie simply hadn't had enough of those opportunities.

Her family was steady and well-resourced, but not consistently emotionally or physically available in the ways she needed. Between career demands, social commitments, and the pull of technology, Sophie spent many hours with shows that modeled sarcastic, snarky communication between kids. She hadn't had enough real-life, relational, or sensory-motor experiences to anchor her in the give-and-take of conversation or the flow of dynamic play.

When caregivers are stretched thin, overwhelmed, or distracted, it can be harder to model the back-and-forth of conversation, the rhythm of shared play, or the simple joy of noticing the world together. The absence is often unintentional — born of stress, not a lack of love — but the impact on development can still be significant.

Without regular moments of shared attention, physical play, and sensory exploration, a child's body adapts to a world that feels less predictable. The brain works harder to sort through unfiltered input, scanning for what matters, often bracing for the unknown. Over time, this can create a low-grade, chronic stress state — a kind of internal disorganization that has nowhere to go.

Screens can temporarily quiet that uncertainty, giving the brain something steady to focus on. But the relief doesn't last, and re-entry into the unpredictable pace of real life can heighten stress even more.

You've probably noticed this in your own child. They appear focused while absorbed in a screen, only to become jumpy, annoyed, or unable to settle down once they step away.

Researchers have a nickname for what happens when kids spend a lot of time on fast-moving screens — they call it *popcorn brain*. It's when the brain gets used to quick, nonstop bursts of information and starts to expect that pace all the time. Then, when life slows down — like during dinner, homework, or a walk outside — it can actually feel uncomfortable or even stressful, simply because it's so different from what their brain has been practicing.

A Danish study found that just two weeks of reduced screen time improved children's peer interactions and emotional well-being, underscoring how digital immersion can dampen real-world social engagement. In

Sophie's case, long hours of screen time primed her for rapid, scripted dialogue — not the unpredictable rhythms of playground conversation and play.

Research from a Finnish cohort found that high screen time in childhood correlates with increased stress and depressive symptoms in adolescence, while regular physical activity offers protection against these effects.

This quiet erosion of skill-building opportunities is a form of developmental deprivation — a kind of sensory starvation and connection disruption caused by the absence of experiences children need to grow.

Developmental deprivation can shape the nervous system in similar ways to ACEs.

It's important to say: this is not the same as surviving acute trauma. The pain is different. But the impact can still run deep.

When movement, nature, and connection are replaced by sitting and swiping, the brain is left hungry for the sensory-motor nourishment it was built to receive. The dance of back-and-forth exchanges — with people, with trees, with wind and water — goes unlearned. And without that practice, we see behaviors that were once the rare storms of childhood — meltdowns, shutdowns, anxiety, trouble focusing, withdrawal — become regular weather patterns.

In nature, wind shapes trees and grows strong roots — but too much wind without rest weakens rather than strengthens. Children's nervous systems respond in the same way. A steady breeze of challenge can build resilience. A relentless storm can wear a child down.

Dr. Elizabeth Stanley reminds us that when the nervous system faces stress without enough recovery, it begins to perceive the world as unsafe by default. The brain stops distinguishing between real threat and simple uncertainty. Without enough restoration, the stress response stays switched on, slowly exhausting the body, and making it harder to learn, feel joy, or connect.

The Harvard Center on the Developing Child describes three kinds of stress:

Positive
Tolerable
Toxic

Positive stress is like a small gust of wind. It's the challenge of learning to walk, of climbing a tree, of trying something new. It temporarily raises the heart rate, sharpens focus, and — especially with a supportive adult nearby — helps a child grow braver, stronger, and more confident.

Tolerable stress is a sudden storm. It might be the loss of a grandparent, moving to a new town, facing a scary illness, or even a community catastrophe like a flood or fire. It can also be a short period of family hardship, such as a parent losing a job or a temporary separation due to work or travel. But with steady, loving adults nearby, or a community working together for recovery, the child's nervous system bends and sways without breaking. Given time and support, it recovers and can even emerge stronger.

Toxic stress is the hurricane that won't let up. It's stress that lasts too long, comes too hard, or arrives without enough protection. It can come from constant tension, unpredictability, and chaos, such as ongoing exposure to violence, living with untreated mental illness or substance use in the household, or repeated housing instability. It can also come from a quieter source: the absence of what's needed. This might mean growing up without consistent warmth, movement, nature, shared joy, or responsive care — the very ingredients that help a child's nervous system feel safe enough to grow.

Whether born of overwhelm or absence, unpredictability or emotional distance, toxic stress wires a nervous system for survival, not curiosity — for scanning for danger, not soaking in wonder. Safety, like danger, is learned. And when safety is absent for too long, the search for it becomes relentless.

That relentless searching brain is a stressed brain.

A brain wired by toxic stress is like a pinball — bouncing, ricocheting, always scanning, never settling. And the ripple effect doesn't stop with the child. One stressed nervous system can stir up stress in everyone nearby. Researchers call this stress contagion — the invisible transmission of tension from one person to another.

If you've ever felt your own heart rate spike when your child is upset, you've experienced stress contagion. One person's dysregulation can ripple through a room, activating the nervous systems of everyone nearby. Just as a baby's cry on an airplane can raise the collective pulse of passengers, a stressed child can stir up tension in parents, teachers, siblings, and peers.

And our children are swimming in that current every day.

One in three parents report feeling at a breaking point. That stress spills into homes, schools, and communities. And our schools, the places where children spend so much of their waking hours, are filled with adults under chronic strain.

Research shows that three out of four teachers experience significant daily stress. Not occasional pressure but *daily overload!* Chronic stress is toxic, and it takes the same toll on long-term health as a high ACE score.

Think about what that means in a real classroom: if most of the adults are operating from a stressed or depleted state, how many genuine moments of attunement, patience, and safety can consistently happen? How often can the back-and-forth exchange of connection — the very foundation of learning — take root?

I don't share this to discourage you, and it's certainly not our teachers' fault. I share it because it's the water our children are swimming in. And we can't change what we don't see. Even if your child isn't experiencing adversity at home, they're spending their days in systems shaped by toxic stress.

And yet, there's hope.

The same forces that transmit stress can also transmit calm. A regulated nervous system offers others a rope back to safety. And nature, reliably and without judgment, can help us find our footing so we can offer that rope.

Even micro-moments of connection — with people and with nature — make a difference.

Nature isn't a nice "extra" for when the weather's delightful or the schedule's clear. It's a powerful protective factor for us all. Spending time in nature reduces cortisol (the "stress" hormone). It boosts attention, lowers anxiety, and improves mood. It calms the "fight or flight" parts of the brain. It restores.

Everyday sensory moments — listening to birdsong, touching a tree, breathing the air after it rains — recalibrate a nervous system shaped by stress. Your child's, yours, and their teachers.

When you or your child's teacher is stressed, your child's system absorbs that stress and needs a way to release it. Alternatively, when you or your child's teacher is regulated, you offer their system a rope to regulation.

You might be wondering where to begin?

The good news is that strong roots grow from small gestures over time. Offer your child — and yourself — small, steady moments of sanctuary by being present and noticing nature together.

These moments build in buffers against toxic stress, providing relief and restoration. It's a reliable and rooted place to begin.

Micro-moments of shared stillness, of attuned noticing, are the small, reparative loops that help a child's brain — and yours — revise its prediction system. Over time, with enough safe moments, even when the ripple of someone else's stress hits, the brain can learn to predict it is safe even amid another's storm.

Stanley calls this the work of *widening the window* — expanding the capacity to predict safety instead of being pulled into stress contagion and reacting to potential threats. And you can widen the window for your own nervous system as you help your child widen theirs.

We can't control every storm. But we can deepen our roots, plant our feet in the grass, turn our faces to the sun, and keep weaving small moments of sanctuary. It's in those moments — over days, weeks, months, seasons, and generations — that healing takes root and lasting change happens.

17

UNBURDENING OUR CHILDREN

THE COST OF ADAPTABILITY

...when you allow your heart to speak, the burdens it carries diminish, a new lightness enters your body, and relief floods the heart.

John O'Donahue

I f a baseline is built on a foundation of ACEs without the chance for restoration, even small stressors can eventually cause it to collapse. By the time I understood the long-term effects ACEs could have, my own body was beginning to break under their weight — and that's when I realized adaptability and resilience are not the same thing.

Adaptability means *adjusting* to new or difficult conditions.

Resilience means *recovering* from new or difficult conditions.

I'd always prided myself on being adaptable — able to pivot, push through, adjust to whatever life threw my way. I could survive nearly anything, or so I thought. But what I've come to understand through the work of Elizabeth Stanley and others is that without real recovery, without "widening my window," adaptability can look more like chronic exhaustion dressed up as strength.

And I was tired.

Even after years of helping other people navigate stress, the signals my own body sent didn't quite register. I dismissed the tightness in my chest, the headaches, the fatigue that clung to me like a second skin.

I kept telling myself I was fine — until one day, I wasn't.

Stanley writes that our culture often mistakes high functioning for resilience, as if holding it all together means we're strong. But resilience isn't surviving with a smile. It's the body slowly building a baseline of the felt sense of safety through cycles of rest and recovery.

ACEs were my baseline.

And I'm not alone. At least one in eight people has four or more ACEs — the threshold associated with significantly higher risk for depression, addiction, chronic illness, and a shorter life span. One in three children today is at risk for toxic stress. It's far from rare. It's epidemic.

For someone who's experienced four or more ACEs, our life expectancy is twenty years less. Twenty years! We should all be alarmed.

I witness these numbers in children and families every day. Like Jake's.

Around the time I learned about ACEs, I was working with a seven-year-old boy we'll call Jake. From the first day, I felt the pull of instant affection I have for all the kids I work with. He was bright-eyed, curious, smart, and incredibly impulsive. On more than one occasion, Jake's impulsivity got him in trouble at school.

When Jake poked another child with a pin, the school called a team meeting. His teacher, the principal, specialists, and Jake's parents attended.

I'd had many conversations with Jake's teacher, and she always seemed at a loss about how to support his learning. She had tried having him sit next to her, giving him extra time to play, sending him on "errands" like taking a note to the office so he could get a break, setting up behavior charts and rewards, assigning him less homework — and so on. The teacher undertook all this while working with several other students who needed extra support, and a class of thirty. More than once, she told me plainly, "I'm stressed all the time."

When I spent one-on-one time with Jake, he was caring, cooperative, and very talkative; his intelligence shone. He had a wealth of knowledge — and he was scattered. Left to his own initiative, he jumped from one thing to another in my office, never spending more than a few moments on any one task. He appeared clumsy, often knocking things over or breaking them. He was always apologetic when that happened and would ask, "Am I gonna get in trouble now?"

The team meeting began with introductions, and the facts that had made this gathering necessary. Rachel had tears in her eyes. She held and rocked an infant of about five months old. "Jake's a really good boy. He really is. It's just... it's just that he never sits still, and he is so impulsive. I'm exhausted."

As I listened to Jake's mother, my heart quivered. Something felt incredibly familiar. Just as I began to speak and share my findings with the team, Jake's father blew through the door. He closed it hard behind him, saying, "Oh, jeez, sorry I'm late. The guy who was supposed to fill in for me was late."

The baby in Rachel's arms began to cry, and Rachel bounced her up and down. The team paused while Jake Sr. clambered into his seat. He leaned over, gave the crying baby a kiss, and put his arm around Rachel. She looked relieved to have him by her side.

The principal attempted to talk while the baby cried. I interrupted: "Maybe we should take a five-minute break and let mom and baby get settled?"

The team looked uncomfortable. Teachers and administrators were, as usual, fitting a long day into short hours. Everyone agreed to the break.

Out in the hallway, it was clear that both Jake's parents were invested in the well-being of their children. Dad took the crying baby, bounced her, and sang softly. The lines in Mom's face smoothed, the baby calmed, and everyone returned to the meeting room.

At the meeting, we decided on a new plan for Jake. My mind, however, went somewhere else. I understood what Jake and his family were experiencing — and that whatever plan was put in place at school, Jake's family needed something else, first and foremost: someone to see them and what they were struggling with — toxic stress.

Giving them a handout listing resources would be entirely ineffective.

When a family is living with toxic stress, even using offered resources is a skill — one that has to be built. And building it takes more than good intentions. It takes recognizing you need help, having the time and guidance to navigate systems, and often, having the financial resources to make it possible. They need someone to take them by the hand and say, "Here, let me help you. I'll do this with you."

For me, Jake wasn't "just a boy who couldn't sit still." He was a child in a web bound together with his parents' exhaustion, his teacher's strain, and the school's limited capacity to meet everyone's needs. And running through that web was a thread of toxic stress.

The meeting sat in my chest like a stone as I drove home. When I got home, the weight of the stress I'd been carrying for decades released an unexpected memory.

I was about ten years old, and my family had recently moved from a small rural town in Connecticut to the inner city of Toronto. Dad struggled to find steady work, so he formed a music duo and began touring to make a living. He had a beautiful tenor voice and could teach himself to play any instrument. When he played guitar and sang — whether at home or around a campfire — he was happy. Mom was happy too. And when they were happy, I felt safe.

With this newest endeavor, I believed we would soon live the music dream and our financial worries would disappear.

In 1980 there were no answering machines or cell phones yet, so my parents paid for an old-fashioned answering service to take messages for potential music gigs. The way it worked was you had to call the service and ask them to turn it on or off.

The duo had been playing gigs for a month or two, often on the road for a week at a time. One day, Dad was scheduled to return home in the evening. My mother's stress was palpable that morning as she rushed around, cleaning the house while getting herself ready for work and my youngest brother ready for day care. As she ran out the door, she called over her shoulder, "Don't forget. Before you leave for school, turn on the answering service so we don't miss a call for new bookings."

I got myself and my seven-year-old brother breakfast, walked him to his school, then went to mine.

At the end of the day, I picked up my brother and walked us home. That's when I realized I had forgotten to turn the answering service on.

I ran upstairs, locked myself in the bathroom, and sobbed for what felt like hours. At some point my father returned and rapped on the door, his voice sharp: "What the hell's going on in there?"

Without opening the door, bracing for anger, I stammered, "I... I... forgot to turn the answering service... on."

My parents' chronic stress had seeped into my nervous system. In that moment, I believed the entire music dream — and our chance at stability — would collapse because of this one small mistake. I waited for my father's rage, but after a long silence, he said casually, "Oh. Is that all?" And he walked away.

It should have been a relief. But instead, I felt like a fool. Like my emotions were too big, too much, and somehow wrong.

Something shifted in me that day. I stopped trusting my own feelings. I began ignoring my body's signals but became even more attuned to other people's moods. I adapted.

It is my first big memory of not being able to calm myself down. In hindsight, it's the kind of neural confusion that can turn into depression. I was ten.

The dysregulation I felt on that bathroom floor is common for children who live with chronic stress and ACEs. Spilled milk becomes the expletive, expletive, expletive, end-of-the-world, voices-raised disaster. These children develop watchful minds that focus on certain details but don't even see others. Most of their energy is spent on minimizing feelings of stress. When the brain is constantly predicting that something negative is about to happen, it uses all its resources to find the quickest route to safety.

When the brain doesn't have a chance to discharge stress for recovery, it may become brilliant at adapting, but it doesn't build regulation or resilience.

Without discharge, stress builds up, and the brain shifts into energy-saving mode. It starts to pull away from what's causing the stress, which can look like sadness, loss of interest, worry, trouble remembering things, constant fidgeting, difficulty focusing, impulsivity, or feeling unmotivated. And maybe most importantly, it stops paying attention to the body's signals — unless those signals are screaming that something is immediately threatening.

This pattern of toxic stress, so common in my students, began to hit me viscerally. About a month after the music fiasco memory, another child added a crushing weight to the stone in my chest — Kevin.

During a school meeting with Kevin's parents, I look over to see sheer exhaustion, confusion, hopelessness. His father looks down at the stack of reports placed on the table, while his mother's eyes well up and spill over. Topics shift from reports to behaviors to goals and how to get ten-year-old Kevin to interact with his peers at recess and stop isolating himself.

At this point in the meeting, I realize something is very wrong. Everyone is looking at me. I am doing my best to make words begin, but my mouth just won't work. I'm dizzy. I'm thinking about my interaction with Kevin yesterday.

I'd met him at our usual place, by the outdoor lunch tables. As always, we quickly moved to a large black oak tree off to the side. There, Kevin walks a well-worn path around the base of the oak, following the bark with his hand as if reading braille. Now and then he stops, and stares directly at the tree, looks up, cocks his head to the side, then continues walking and talking as if responding to a question I can't hear. A small group of girls snicker in his direction, and he quickens his pace. When the bell rings and the yard clears, his frenetic movements calm, his pacing slows, he kneels at the base of the tree and mumbles, as if talking directly to it. He stands up again and walks between this oak and the next and back again. I half whisper, "So, what is it about this tree that makes you want to stay here?"

He halts, turns his entire body in my direction, and throws his arms out to the sides. His eyes widen, and he stammers, "Because... BECAUSE... I just LOVE this TREE. I love IT. I love it SO MUCH!"

Kevin is often the subject of cruel jokes and subtle bullying. My thoughts jumped to memories of my older brother and the relentless bullying he endured at every new school we attended. I felt the stress of my recesses spent scanning the playground, on alert for the aggressive body language that meant trouble was heading his way. My heart ached.

The team was still waiting. The principal's eyes searched mine. It felt as if I'd been injected with the numbing agent at the dentist's office and I couldn't form words. I had spoken up for countless kids in these meetings before, and usually the team is receptive, empathetic even. But this time, I couldn't find my voice.

When I've said things like, "We are designed to connect first and learn second," light flickers behind their eyes. Hope glimmers when I share that "nature is the best sensory support we can offer children, and it's free and right outside the door." But meetings end, teachers return to numbers of students that make even basic safety management near impossible. Administrators dive into stacks of papers so high they might as well sleep at their desks, and service providers wring their hands, push papers and pencils, and resort to process instead of connection.

Apathy returns, and the lions eat a lot of us.

The room grew hotter. The team shifted in their seats, imploring me with their eyes: *Say something*. My hands press into the table, but the words stay lodged in my chest, blocked by the image of Kevin clinging to his oak tree... and by the memory of my brother's scared face on the playground.

I push my chair back, stand, and walk to the nurse's office. She wraps the blood pressure cuff around my arm and frowns.

"Girl," she says, "you're going to the ER."

At the hospital, a doctor flings the curtain open. He glides up next to my bed on a rolling black leather stool. "Are you under any stress?" he asks casually.

He is young, fit, and seems really put together. I do a quick present life-scan: stable job, a roof over our heads, the chaos of post-divorce custody mayhem is behind us. We've buried Mac — my best friend, the man I fell in love with three years after the divorce — and the tangle of debt left by cancer, divorce and bankruptcy has finally settled. "No. I think right now... I'm OK... maybe in the past... but right now..."

I wasn't having a heart attack. I was having a delayed reckoning.

All the stress I had adapted to, tucked away, and pushed through to survive had accumulated, and my body finally said, enough!

The doctor's concern about my symptoms is apparent as he watches the blood pressure monitor rise and fall, and it occurs to me that his eyes can't see the faces of the children I see. He can't see their parents' worry when they are told something is wrong with their kid. He can't see the forlorn little bodies with the energy of gazelles and lemurs being reprimanded for leaping and running in the courtyard, the teenagers with empty eyes hiding out in the bathroom and counting minutes till the bell rings, the social butterflies who have to sit alone in the corner of class. Does he know about the number of prescription medications my coworkers take just to get through the day? Or the number of kids medicated into compliance? He can't see Kevin's light dim when he is told to leave his tree. He can't see the irreparable hole in my heart from the time when in sixth grade, despite my vigilance, I failed to see trouble brewing at recess, so that my brother was attacked, the perpetrators carrying him, his legs splayed open, and slamming him into a metal pole.

The doctor said, "How about I write you a note? Take a couple of days off work... since they made you come here after all." He winks and adds, "Make an appointment with your doctor. I'll be right back with a form."

As he stepped out, I lay there and finally allowed my mind to understand why I was so tired.

Not just from the day, but from decades. I'd adapted until I couldn't anymore.

When we carry a baseline of toxic stress, it weaves itself into our nervous system. It shapes how we predict, react, and relate. It's like living in a house of cards: one more gust and the whole thing might collapse.

I saw it in Jake's restless energy and his parents' weary eyes.

I felt it in the ten-year-old version of me, locked in the bathroom and convinced one mistake could bring the whole house down.

I saw it again in Kevin, circling the oak tree that offered more safety than the surrounding humans.

The hopeful thing I've learned through research, practice, and lived experience is that it's never too late to build new foundations. We can strengthen the frame, add support beams, lay down fresh neural pathways, and root ourselves into deeper, more life-giving soil.

If we can spot signals of stress in our children, change can happen quickly — sometimes in ways that seem almost miraculous. It takes a little more undoing and a bit more intention for adults, but it's worth every ounce of effort.

Although it can feel miraculous, recovery isn't one dramatic swoop. It's small, steady updates in the nervous system. One safe moment layered on another: a child seeing delight in your eyes when they were bracing for a harsh word; a soft curve across your lips at a robin's song; a shared breath at dusk when they expected you to be elsewhere; the warmth of the sun on your skin when you might have rushed past it. These are the micro-moments that slowly shift the brain's architecture from chaos toward a calm coherence.

Whether survival has shaped your nervous system or you're simply worn thin by the relentlessness of parenting in a disconnected world, there is more available to you — and to your child — than mere adaptation.

There is repair.

Regulation.

Recovery.

Resilience.

Try This

The next time you notice your stress rising — whether it's your child whining, a mess on the floor, or a moment of protest, and it feels like too much — pause before you respond.

☐ Step outside if you can, even just to your porch or a patch of sidewalk.
☐ Take one slow breath. Then, look for one small, living thing: a bird, a tree, a weed breaking through a crack.

Say to yourself, *Life is reaching for us. I can reach back differently.* Let that pause be the beginning of a new neural pattern — for both of you.

Wild Reflection

Recall a time when you were a child and felt overwhelmed, but didn't have the support to make sense of it. What did you need in that moment?

Now, think of a recent time when your child was overwhelmed. How might you become the person you needed back then — for them, and for yourself?

Alternatively, if you remember a time when you felt overwhelmed, and *you did* have the support to make sense of it, what did you receive in that moment that helped?

18

REWIRING FOR RESILIENCE

MOVING PAST THE LEGACY OF TOXIC STRESS

The research literature has identified three factors that universally lead to stress: uncertainty, the lack of information and the loss of control.

Gabor Maté, When the Body Says No

I didn't always believe there was more available to me. For years, I thought my exhaustion was a personal flaw and that if I worked harder, pushed harder, and did more, I could do better. But the more I learned about how adversity wires a nervous system, the more I began to see my symptoms not as failures, but as the body's way of trying to slow me down and protect me.

That realization came into sharp focus the day I followed up on the ER recommendation to see my doctor. Sitting in the exam room, I peered over the doctor's shoulder and read one word in my chart: dysthymia.

A quick google search told me that dysthymia was a type of long-term depression. *What?! Depressed?!* I didn't feel depressed. I felt bone-tired and deeply sad, which made perfect sense given the recent years.

She ordered a litany of blood tests. She didn't know about ACEs. She was unaware that my brain had been wired to stay on high alert, and that hypervigilance had long been my baseline.

She couldn't see that symptoms like fatigue, anxiety, and brain fog weren't signs of weakness — they were the body's protection at work.

What I needed most was for someone to say, "This makes sense." That my exhaustion was a natural outcome of living in survival mode for too long.

And most of all, that none of it was my fault.

To a nervous system patterned by adversity, even help can feel like a threat. A brain like that doesn't distinguish between danger and overwhelm — it simply says: this is too much.

I stuffed the lab order into the glove compartment of my car. Making appointments with strangers in clinical spaces felt impossible. Instead, I returned to something I'd practiced over and over:

nature — my relational-regulator. My neural anchor. My place to breathe.

In nature, I paid attention and looked for clues about building resilience. I found trees that, although broken, stood strong, sending out new shoots. I watched rivers flow. I sat with a plant called the Wooly Starflower and wondered how, despite almost no rain for an entire year, it bloomed. I learned lessons from our neighborhood birds, like when the grosbeaks rebuilt a nest and started again after the first had been plundered. Nature doesn't shame what has been damaged, or get stuck on what's already happened. Nature works with what remains, finding new routes to life.

Watching how nature persisted taught me to listen to my own body: its signals, its scorecard, and its desire for change.

The signs had been there for years. My first bout of vertigo came around age ten. I fainted in church around eleven. My older brother and I shared jokes, saying, "going blind, going deaf, going blind, going deaf," referring to the sensation of passing out. We shared other jokes too — the one where we couldn't breathe, or the one where we made fists and pounded our chests over our hearts, exclaiming, "Heart attack! Heart attack!" Our humor masked the truth: our bodies were overloaded and our sensory signals disorganized.

By high school, I was hiding in stairwells with stabbing abdominal pain. I'd crouch, wait for the pain to pass, then move on with my day. In hindsight, each strange symptom was a signal of body distress.

From migraines to menstrual pain, peripheral neuropathy to chronic fatigue, my symptoms became part of daily life. I often felt like I'd done something wrong, which brought about feelings of shame and silence.

If you've felt ashamed of your symptoms and believed they are your fault or your weakness, know that the science says otherwise. These may be protective adaptations in response to a life that has asked more from you than your neurology was equipped to handle.

From my early twenties on, I worked hard to be healthy. I ran. I ate well. I spent time outside. But I did it with blind discipline, not with compassion. I didn't yet understand how deeply adverse experiences could shape a body.

By forty, my physical house of cards began to wobble. I looked energetic, optimistic, outgoing — but my nervous system was frayed. I was both adaptable and unraveling.

Reading Van Der Kolk's *The Body Keeps the Score* raised new questions. Was my early menopause another entry on my body's scorecard? I'd always known how to push through, but I couldn't push any harder.

Lisa Feldman Barrett teaches that the brain doesn't passively react to life. It predicts it. Based on past experience, the brain makes guesses: safe or unsafe? Opportunity or threat? In childhood, we learn what to expect. If the world feels rushed, chaotic, or painful, the brain predicts more of the same. The costliest prediction? Uncertainty.

For a child living with chronic unpredictability, uncertainty isn't an abstract concept — it's a felt sense that keeps the body braced, even when nothing dangerous is happening in the moment.

Elizabeth Stanley builds on this understanding with a simple but profound truth: when a nervous system is patterned on threat, the body doesn't relax — *because it can't*. Safety isn't a known sensation. It must be learned through repeated experiences that contradict the brain's alarm and gradually replace it with safety.

This is why we return to nature. To relational-regulation. To repetitions of safe engagement.

To stop pushing so hard, we must rewire the brain's expectations and build what was likely never built in the first place.

Neuroplasticity offers a hopeful path. As Norman Doidge explains in *The Brain That Changes Itself,* our brains can keep changing throughout life. One story he tells is about scientist Paul Bach-y-Rita, whose father lost much of his ability to move and speak after a stroke. Through daily practice and creative exercises, his father's brain found new pathways that allowed him to regain many of those lost abilities. The same principle applies to everyday life: when we create and repeat small, positive moments — especially with people we care about — we build and strengthen new pathways. Each time we do this, we're helping our kids and ourselves grow stronger and more resilient.

By actively cultivating positive moments, creating a nurturing atmosphere, and learning to navigate emotions together, we're fostering generational resilience.

And yet, knowing the brain can change also means reckoning with what we are trying to change. Many of the patterns we face are not of our own

211

making — they are the well-worn ways of thinking, feeling, and responding that have been passed down through our families, often without question.

I think of parents I've worked with who try to bring more calm into their homes, yet find themselves reacting in the same ways they once feared from their own caregivers. These are not failures of willpower. They are the echoes of old patterns etched deep into the nervous system. This is where Dr. Nadine Burke Harris's work becomes vital.

Dr. Harris followed up her ACEs TED Talk with a book, *The Deepest Well*. In it, she states: "ACEs and toxic stress thrive on secrecy and shame, both at the individual level and at the societal level. We can't treat what we refuse to see."

I carried my own silent stressors: my father's rage rooted in the years he suffered horrific childhood abuse by clergy; my mother's crushing depression after the devastating loss of her younger sister in childhood. Both grieved in silence during an era that denied children's pain. What my brothers and I inherited was not their trauma itself, but the ways they had learned to carry it — the silence, the guardedness, the bursts of anger.

While secrecy often begins in shame, it's upheld by silence — and by systems that ignore the impact on families. If our medical and educational institutions refuse to acknowledge how toxic stress derails learning and health, why would those of us who've suffered want to speak up?

Research shows that health declines further when a person is alone with the events of toxic stress. When we keep that weight hidden, the patterns stay in motion — undischarged — because they have been rehearsed for generations.

Undischarged stress eventually metabolizes into real illness with symptoms like exhaustion, pain, and a nervous system that simply cannot keep up.

I was doing okay. I was. And then Mac died.

Two years after my divorce, I fell in love with my best friend. He'd already been diagnosed with melanoma. He was young, strong and symptomless at his diagnosis. We believed he would beat it. We were wrong.

After he died, I experienced something I'd never felt before: apathy. It was as if my feelings had been unplugged.

In hindsight, it was nervous system collapse — a full-body freeze when my system ran out of ways to respond. It was the body falling back on its most ancient form of protection. When the pain becomes too much, the nervous system sometimes chooses numbness over overwhelm. Not out of weakness, but to protect us.

When Mac died, I had no savings, no family help, and returned to work six days later. Prior to his death, I'd left the non-profit I so dearly loved and taken contract work as an occupational therapist in nursing homes to pay the rising medical bills and have a flexible schedule for his appointments and my daughters' needs. A month after he died, I took a full-time job at a local school.

Most mornings, before waking the kids, I sat in the backyard, going through the motions of my well-practiced "sunrise sit," listening to birds. I didn't feel connected at first, but I kept going. Eventually, it helped me come back to myself.

The practices I'd built long before — sitting outside, listening to birds, breathing, waiting — were the deepest source of healing.

I hadn't realized I'd been laying down neural trails to restoration all along.

Those well-worn nature practices had become my nervous system's refuge. Without knowing it, I'd been creating the pathways that let me survive the reckoning.

It wasn't too late. And it still isn't.

Learning about ACEs helped me make sense of life through a lens of compassion. I'd long thought life was hard because I wasn't trying hard enough. But it wasn't a lack of effort. It was the ripple effect of patterns my nervous system had learned long before I could choose differently.

The choices I once blamed myself for had roots. Understanding those roots allowed me to transform them. That's why I'm sharing these vulnerable pieces of my story: so you might fortify the soil of your child's becoming, and find a little more ease in the unfolding of your story — and your child's.

If you have a high ACE score, you can alchemize your challenges too. It starts with recognizing which of your behaviors are survival strategies. Then, using conscious effort and nature-connective practices, you can begin to reshape your nervous system — and your life.

You can find more resources at kathleenlockyer.com

19

THE CIRCLE GAME

GRIEVING, GROWING, AND COMING BACK TO LIFE

Fear keeps us focused on the past or worried about the future. If we can acknowledge our fear, we can realize that right now we are okay. Right now, today, we are still alive, and our bodies are working marvelously. Our eyes can still see the beautiful sky. Our ears can still hear the voices of our loved ones.

Thich Nhat Hanh

R ecovery is more like a breath than a finish line — an inhale of possi-
bility, an exhale of release, and periodically long pauses in between. I was in the pause. My body was slowly finding steadier rhythms.

The financial stress from divorce, illness, and homeownership had taken its toll. About a year after Mac died, our house went into foreclosure, and the only affordable rental that would keep my daughters in the same school was a log cabin tucked deep in a canyon.

We lived and rested there for two years. Like so many single parents navigating hard seasons, I juggled grief, parenting, and work. On weekends,

I wandered the canyon for hours with our German shepherd, Shadow. Those walks didn't erase the grief, but they gave my nervous system space to breathe. I'd return home calmer, steadier, and with a growing sense that maybe — eventually — it would all be okay.

In the canyon, my brain and body exhaled.

I started running again. I climbed the steep fire road behind our home each morning and again after school pickup. On many days, one or both of the girls joined me. We'd huff and puff up the hill, pause to catch our breath at the top, then walk home as shadows lengthened across the dirt road.

We slept. A lot.

We sat. A lot.

Outside on the porch, under the wide arch of a live oak tree, we watched waves of juncos cross the yard and listened to the evening songbird chorus. We learned the habits of our non-human neighbors: who nested where, how the fox's piercing scream alerted us to its trail through the gully, the feeling of tension in the landscape that signaled mountain lion presence, and how the sun rose and set painting the canyon walls.

Nature didn't erase our sadness, but it gave us a different reference point. It gave us a sensory thread we could weave into our nervous systems, allowing our brains to predict peace instead of panic. When so much had been chaotic, these moments brought coherence. For you, it might be as simple as a park bench on your way home from the subway, a tree in your yard, leaving your window cracked to listen to the rain, or the daily sight of the sky changing color at sunset.

We were rewiring for more than survival. We were listening. Slowing. Returning. And in doing so, we were replacing inherited patterns of urgency and vigilance with calmer comfort — giving our nervous systems the

216

thing they most needed: time to discharge and recover. Time to learn new patterns.

We laughed again. We cried too. But above all, we felt safe.

And we had nature.

And kind, stable landlords.

And time.

And each other.

Can you feel my exhale?

From that place of calm, I reflected on the parts of my childhood that would be called PACEs. Recall that PACEs are the counterweights to ACEs.

PACEs come in two forms: supportive relationships and enriching environments.

And nature, especially when shared, offers both.

Thousands of studies show that nature supports learning and mental health. But in 2020, researchers Touloumakos and Barrable confirmed what many of us already knew: nature connection is a PACE.

Nature buffers adversity. It builds resilience.

It rewires the brain toward awe and joy.

Where might you have had a PACE in your life, or provided one for your child? Was there a grandparent who listened? A neighbor whose presence offered safety? A tree you climbed so often it felt like your best friend? An aunt or uncle who took you camping?

Where might you have provided a PACE for your child? Have you spent time sitting on park swings side by side? Do you take walks together after dinner? Do you have moments of pure silliness that end in laughter?

Those moments matter.

Or maybe your childhood was steady, and so is your child's, free of major adversity, charmed. Even so, if you're overwhelmed now, you are not alone. Today's parenting landscape is full of pressure. And chronic stress, even without a high ACE score, can take a toll. All nervous systems need restoration. Our need for nourishment is universal.

You don't have to live in a canyon to access healing. You can begin right where you are — with moments that matter. Because as Dr. Stanley's work reminds us, healing happens through small, repeated cycles of safety.

Each time your child stops to watch raindrops make circles in a puddle...
Each time you pause to observe the clouds together...
Each time you sit beside a tree and exhale...
You are restoring your body's scorecard to a healthier, calmer baseline.

You are saying: this moment is safe.
You are laying a foundation that will carry you and your child through life's harder seasons.

Re-Membering

Our children's development is a dynamic, ever-moving experience, like the seasons. We may find that we've finally learned how to work with a behavior or help them resolve a challenge, only to have another one present itself. We may go to bed thinking, Oh my goodness, I've completely screwed this parenting thing up, only to wake and discover our child greeting us with a day of laughter and joy. Growth is like seasons, moving in and out the way spirals swirl. Some feel so close we can touch them, while others seem lost forever.

I'd been watching my young daughters grieve, and there were days I worried the joy of their earlier years would never return. But spring always returns after a long winter. That's how it felt when a rare summer rain descended on the canyon — and how quickly a single moment could carry me between the present and the past. As the rain fell, I was suddenly back at my younger daughter's third birthday, the year she first fell in love with Joni Mitchell's song, *The Circle Game*.

The song traces the way life ripples across the seasons and years, capturing the wonder of childhood, the ache of change, and the inevitability of time. She begged me to play it again and again, the way children beg repeatedly for their favorite stories. But instead of feeling annoyed at her persistence, I felt a lump rise in my throat. Three felt enormous.

Each time I restarted the song, tears filled my eyes.

Mitchell's lyrics felt like a foreshadowing. I worried that the sacredness of her third year and the innocence of this child would one day ripple away.

I remember wondering if the spark I saw in her could last.

Would she still chase dragonflies? Still sing herself to sleep? Still find joy in puddles and pinecones?

219

I grieved preemptively, fearing that her pure, in the moment, and un-abashed joy for life might fade. That life would change the child I saw fully alive, the brightness in her would dim with time, with loss, with life. I wanted to protect her from that.

Have you felt that ache too? The longing to preserve your child's magic, to keep the world from dulling the light in their eyes?

Or perhaps you've felt the pull to find your own light again — that unexplainable bliss when nothing else exists but you and that caterpillar, tree, frog, or cloud.

Can you remember a moment from your early years when you were in communion with something pure and vital? How long has it been since you felt that way? Has the path back become overgrown with time and responsibilities?

Seven years after Mitchell's song filled our house on repeat, and we were living deep in the canyon. Another drought year had settled over California, echoing the thirst and longing we carried in our own lives.

In her ten short years, my daughter had already weathered so much heartache and upheaval. She was no longer the wide-eyed toddler dancing barefoot through the garden.

Some days, she carried a heaviness I couldn't reach, expressing anger and sadness often. I worried my earlier fears had come true.

Would the spark I once saw in her return? Would she have another season of awe, joy and wonder?

Or had the weight of life already dimmed her light?

My heart ached wondering if I'd ever see that free-spirited girl again.

Then, one afternoon, thunder cracked overhead.

"RAIN! RAIN! IT'S RAINING!" she shouted.

Before I could respond, she threw open the front door and leapt barefoot into the yard, singing and giggling with her clear umbrella twirling above. She danced under the downpour like she'd been waiting her whole life for that one moment. And just like that, the child I'd worried was lost was before me.

Nature has a way of washing off the road dust, cycling us back to wholeness, and reminding us that life is always reaching for us.

When we say yes to life, the seasons of joy return.

Watching her that day helped me understand why rain had always lifted *my* spirit. The twirl of her umbrella brought me back to a moment at my grandmother's house when I was a girl. She'd given me a clear umbrella, almost identical to the one my daughter danced with.

I would take it outside and sit under it, endlessly watching the rain drip, splat, and roll down the sides.

I remember my bare, cold, muddy feet. I remember being wet and feeling wild. I remember the relief. The release.

I also remember being witnessed.

My grandmother sitting on the porch, watching me.

Celebrating me.

At home, my mother's smile when I came in the door, soaking wet.

They didn't redirect me.

They didn't chastise me for dirty feet.

They didn't call it too messy.

They said yes.

And in that yes, they gave me a lifelong PACE. A permission I now passed to my daughter.

When she twirled in the rain, she reclaimed her joy and she set down, even if for a moment, the weight of the worry and sadness she had learned to carry. And my fears, if even for that moment, were washed away.

The circle game played on.

Even amid messiness and inconvenience, when we say yes to our children's joy, we plant seeds. Those seeds may lie dormant, waiting for the season to shift, for the rains to return.

Parents ask me how they can help their child come back to life or how to reawaken curiosity. The answer isn't always complicated. It can begin with an invitation. A little freedom. And the willingness to witness.

Helping our children come back to life can start with remembering what we were given — or what we needed — and offering it now.

Transformation comes in many forms.
Some seeds wait for water.
Others require fire.

The Wisdom of Fire Seeds

The rain was a brief respite from the drought, and later that summer, a wildfire crept over the hills near the canyon, forcing us to evacuate.

As smoke filled the sky, I thought of another fire years earlier.

I was nineteen, visiting Yellowstone National Park not long after the historic fire that burned nearly 800,000 acres.

Blackened hills stretched for miles.

But out of the charred earth, an astonishing sight emerged: brilliant green grasses, crimson and golden wildflowers, flocks of birds calling, flitting, surviving.

It was a stunning contrast between destruction and renewal.

It was there I learned about fire seeds.

Fire seeds lie dormant for years, sometimes centuries, waiting for the heat and pressure of fire to crack them open. The landscape of Yellowstone with its color and contrast radiated a fierce will to live — a will that belongs to all living things, including us. The color contrast from that fire became a touchstone for me.

Its lessons rooted deep in my psyche: sometimes it takes fire to awaken the most vibrant blooms.

In 2023, researchers studying ancient 2,000 - year-old coast redwoods discovered that after a fire, some of these trees release seeds that have waited a thousand years to grow.

A thousand years.

That is how long some seeds hold on, waiting for the right conditions.

Waiting for the right disturbance.

> Fire seeds embody the profound re-
> silience of nature. And because we are
> nature, they reflect our resilience, too.

Have you had a season of fire?

A divorce. A diagnosis. A loss. A burnout so deep you weren't sure you'd come back.

Fire seeds remind us that some parts of us can only bloom after a burn. Even if a way of living or a part of ourselves has gone quiet, it may simply be waiting for the right moment to grow again.

As we nurture our children's development, their resilience, and their sense of safety, we also nurture our own. We can choose to release what no longer serves us.

To say yes to rain.

To rebuild from scorched ground.

To remember what seeds we carry, even if they've been buried a long, long time.

We can become the next generation of compassionate, skilled, and nature-rooted stewards — guiding our children forward while restoring ourselves along the way.

Just as the canyon walks and summer rain rewired my nervous system toward safety, fire seeds remind us that nature holds the cues and conditions we need to re-pattern — and those cues are available to us in small, everyday ways. These moments are sensory restoration, the foundation of our habilitation and, when needed, our rehabilitation.

Try This

Reawaken a Dormant Seed

Over the next few days, carve out a small moment — ten minutes, even — to step outside and engage one of your senses on purpose.

☐ Let your child lead if you can. If you're alone, let curiosity lead.
☐ Touch the texture of bark. Smell the air before it rains. Lie on your back and look up at the sky. Follow the sound of a bird until you see it.
☐ Don't "teach" anything. Just notice.
☐ Do you breathe differently? Does your body settle?

Each time you say yes to a small sensory moment like this, you're watering a new pathway in yourself and in your child.

Wild Reflection

What sensory experiences lit you up as a child?
    The smell of pine needles?
    The patter of rain on the roof?
    The feel of mud between your toes?
    Which of those sparks has gone dormant inside you — and might still be waiting to rise again?
    Write down one memory from a time when you felt wild and alive. Now ask yourself: how can I say "yes" to something like that again? For my child and for myself?

20

SPEAKING BELONGING

LANGUAGE AS A BRIDGE TO NATURE

The pleading eyes of a child can speak a thousand words.

Jamie Sams, Earth Medicine

When I began working as an occupational therapist, most children still felt like children — silly, curious, playful. They rode bikes, climbed trees, dug holes, played tag and hide-and-seek. Special education was reserved for those with significant developmental differences.

That's no longer the case. Schools across the country are witnessing a surge of children needing additional support, not only for academics but also for emotional, social, and behavioral development. Many 'support teams' now work in almost every classroom.

Even with intervention, the number of kids struggling continues to rise.

This isn't a random crisis. It's relational.

When I walk down school hallways, I don't see lazy kids. I see disconnected ones.

Children who don't make eye contact. Children who've stopped asking questions.

Children whose nervous systems are signaling distress.

What I see locally is a problem nationally. Between 2008 and 2019, rates of chronic hopelessness among U.S. teens rose by 65%. That means for kids born between 1994 and 2005, sadness and disconnection weren't rare. They were normal. For this group, hopelessness became an epidemic.

And now, this generation is becoming the next generation of parents.

Although parental depression lives in the adult, it echoes in the child. A dimmed inner world makes relational attunement difficult. And when enough caregivers are surviving instead of thriving, the effects ripple out into our collective nervous system.

Rachel Carson understood this kind of ripple. In her seminal work, *Silent Spring,* she wrote about birds dying and about what their silence foretold.

One of Carson's questions haunts me:

"How do we tell the children the birds are dying?"

Today, a more chilling question emerges:

What if the children don't even notice they're gone?

When I ask children to point out birds in the local landscape, more than half report that there are none.

The birds aren't gone.

Children can't see them.

This is an indicator that our connection to the natural world and our appreciation for it, is deteriorating rapidly. And children are not responsible for this disconnection.

Despite the many scientific studies detailing that children require hours of movement and exploration each day to develop their sensory perceptions, we place them in environments that rob them of essential experiences — physically and linguistically.

They are compelled to sit still, remain silent, and comply with adult priorities, even as their nervous systems beg them to move, explore, and relate.

They learn that assisting one another is equivalent to cheating.

Peer interactions are restricted for much of the day, but we worry when a child is not social enough.

We ask children to override the wisdom of their bodies, then punish them for the behaviors that override creates.

Those who resist these hazardous expectations are labeled defiant or naughty.

Those who comply too easily run the risk of depression, anxiety, and disconnection.

Because many of us grew up with the same expectations, we often mistake them for normal — regardless of their origins.

> *...too often, school is a polite form of incarceration...*
> — Richard Louv, Last Child in the Woods

Like Louv, I don't believe the problem lies within the child.

It lies in the environments that fail to reflect their biology.

It lies in the systems that deny their senses a context to develop and integrate.

And it lies in the stories we unconsciously tell through our words.

Because the language we use in our environments matters.

In Carson's writing, birds function as sentinel species — biological indicators of ecosystem health. They respond quickly to pollution, imbalance, or disruption.

Children are similar.

They too respond to toxicity in their environment.

Their dysregulation, shutdowns, and emotional volatility are signals — not of failure or pathology, but of feedback.

Remember Chad, the boy who couldn't hear birdsong? Or Jose, who fled from the sounds of the bathroom? Their behaviors weren't irrational. They were responses to systems that overwhelmed their senses and failed to recognize their alarm signals.

When I say their distress was ecosystem feedback, I mean it literally.

They were, like birds, trying to survive.

And they were trying to tell us something.

When the sensory environment is too loud, too fast, too still, or too disconnected, children respond with dysregulation. But the way adults interpret those behaviors — through our words, tone, and stories — becomes part of the child's inner world. This means that behavior is not only shaped by sensory conditions, but also by linguistic ones.

The words we speak to, about, and around children become the internal messages they carry forward. Words can reinforce disconnection, or they can spark belonging.

They can build a bridge or widen the gap.

Recall from an earlier chapter the week I spent collecting nature-negative language — the offhand comments children and adults say without realizing the damage they do.

"Ugh, there's dirt on my hands."

"Don't touch that, it's gross."

"Get away from that bug, it might bite."

"Why are you just staring at the clouds? Get moving!"

"Stay out of the rain or you'll get sick."

"That's just a weed."

Language, too, is a sentinel. It alerts us to how we are relating to the world, whether through control or through connection. Each of the above phrases subtly communicates that nature is something to fear, avoid, or control. Over time, those messages don't stay external. They settle into the child's nervous system. They shape perception. And eventually, identity.

These are cognitive and sensory messages — the tone of a reprimand, the repetition of avoidance language, the urgency in our voice — these are processed by the child's nervous system and sculpt their worldview. Over time, these impressions form a perceptual bias: nature is unsafe, the body is wrong, curiosity is dangerous.

The same week that I noted nature-negative language, I visited another school. A place where the mentors had taken a NatureLed™[1] training.

At Weaving Earth, an outdoor program in Northern California, I recorded the spontaneous, reverent, and relational language I heard from both mentors and students.

Some of their words from the earlier list:

From the mentors:

"Wow, feel how rough that is."

"Let's walk softly through the grass."

"Remember to thank the bees."

"Have three points of contact when you're climbing."

"Did you see any hawks on the way here?"

From the children:

"Can I eat it?"
"I think I saw a robin."
"It feels soft."
"Let's roll down the hill."
"Birds are so cool."
"Don't step on it. It lives here."
"Nature loves me."

These simple statements were attunement moments.

Each one affirming a child's right to be curious, to be sensory and to be in relationship with the world around them.

Simple changes in our language build nature-positive foundations. Each one affirms a relational presence. It shifts focus from control to connection, from fear to wonder and from an isolated view of oneself as separate from nature, to being in relationship with nature. The power of nature-positive language is that it turns everyday moments into sacred ground for becoming part of the larger world.

And the best part? You don't need to be in an outdoor program to begin. You can begin at home in your backyard, in car rides, morning routines, on a sidewalk, or even from a window. When your child points out a snail, a puddle, or even a crack in the concrete where something other than human is growing, you have a moment. That moment is an invitation to respond with language that says: I see what you see. I value what you notice. Let's return nature's serve.

These micro-shifts lay a foundation for trust and shared meaning between parent and child, and between human and nature, body and world.

This is what nature-positive language does.

It reframes the human-nature relationship from one of dominance to one of dialogue.

It shifts the script:

From "Don't touch that." → to "What does it feel like?"

From "It's dirty." → to "That's alive."

From "Be careful!" → to "How will you move through this?"

And perhaps most importantly, it says:

You belong here.

You're not a stranger to the wild.

You are part of it.

Language may seem like a small shift. But in a child's nervous system, a word can become a root. And a root, once planted, can grow toward trust.

When we shift our language, we do more than change the mood. We change the ecology. Language is how we give weight to what's worthy of attention and how we decide what belongs. When our words reflect reverence, curiosity, and relationship, they invite a child's nervous system into coherence. Language, then, becomes a bridge to nature and to wholeness.

Try This

Speak the World into Belonging

Over the next few days, try shifting the way you narrate the world around your child.

□ Start with the next walk, car ride, or glance out the window.

□ Instead of naming or labeling things, try speaking relationally. Express curiosity.

You might say:

□ "Who do you think lives in that tree?"

□ "Let's see how this rock feels in our hand."

□ "That flower looks like it's reaching for the sun."

□ "Thank you, wind, for cleaning the air."

□ "Where's the nearest bird?"

It may feel simple. Even silly. But it's also neurological.

These small, sensory-rich comments help your child's brain build meaning.

They teach the nervous system that the world is worth noticing, and that they are allowed to be part of it.

Try one new phrase a week. You might be surprised by what your child begins to notice, or what they help you notice.

Wild Reflection

Think back to a moment in childhood when someone used words that made you feel small, silly, or separate.

What was said?

How did it land in your body?

Did you carry it with you?

Now think of a moment when someone's words made you feel seen.

What was different?

What if language could be a place of repair for your child, and for you?

Consider this:

How do you speak about rain, mud, bugs, and birds?

What do your words suggest about the body, about risk, about wonder?

What might change if you began to speak nature into belonging?

Write one phrase you want your child to remember about their relational life.

Something like:

"Your eyes are good at seeing beauty."

"You belong here."

"That bird might be telling us a story."

"The world is full of things worth noticing, and you're one of them."

Then try saying it aloud tomorrow.

21

ECHOES IN THE BACKYARD

HOW BIRDS HELP US LISTEN, HEAL, AND BELONG

Gather the birds to your breast; they are your kin, feathered
fragments of your longing for the sky.

Hilda Doolittle, Sea Garden.

When our words invite belonging, they do more than shape a child's
sense of self — they sharpen the senses that keep them connected
to the living world. And once those senses are awake, the world begins to
speak back.

Before our ancestors spoke, they listened to the nuances of sound. They
learned to live by attuning to the voices of the wild.

In nature, perhaps no voice is more consistently available or more neurologically meaningful than the voice of birds. Bird "language" has accompa-
nied us for millennia, threading across cultures and through generations.
Birds have helped humans know how to respond to their environment.
They've taught us when to be still, when to move, when to soften our
breath, or lift our eyes. In their calls and rhythms, we've found guidance
— for survival, and to realign with our place when we're out of sync.

Learning to listen to the subtle trills of juncos, the sharp cries of scrub jays, or the low murmur of mourning doves is what our nervous systems expect. As I wrote in earlier chapters about ecoception and auditory patterning, the ability to orient to sound in meaningful ways helps build a cohesive experience for the brain. That cohesion supports regulation, and regulation makes space for healing.

Bird language offers children and adults a naturally occurring system of prediction, safety signaling, and shared regulation — all vital forms of sensory restoration.

But getting back in sync is a process and, like the zigzag pattern of a nighthawk, or the refrain of a Joni Mitchell song, healing rarely happens in a straight line.

For my daughters and I, the voices of the birds stitched us together across time, transitions, and the work of healing.

Even before the canyon, before the rain dances and wildfire evacuations, there were lessons with birds.

Bird wisdom surrounded us, and in 2004, during the first year of our outdoor preschool program, I saw my children weren't the only ones who responded to birds. All the children in our program met birds with natural ease and openness, reminding me that kids arrive eco-receptive — already primed to connect — to these kinds of experiences.

One of those lessons unfolded during an ordinary moment with a puddle.

The moment happened when the mothers and toddlers arrived on a wet morning. I asked the group rhetorically if we should go outside in the rain. They all responded with a forlorn, "Noooo." So, kicked off my rain boots and socks, and invited the mothers and their children to join me. We stepped into the drizzle together, the cold water soaking our feet as we jumped in puddles. One of the little girls noticed a bird splashing in a puddle and stood quietly, watching. She studied every movement as the bird dipped its head, let the water roll down its back, then gave a full-bodied shake before flying away. Without prompting, the girl stepped into the puddle and mimicked the bird's actions. She splashed, shook, and embodied each gesture with joyful precision.

The girl was doing more than mimicking. She was responding to the rhythm and energy of another being, attuning to something outside herself. That brief, easily overlooked moment showcased ecoception, alloception, and interoception at work in the preschooler's body.

The group noticed, and the moment rippled outward. From then on, when a child in the group became dysregulated, someone would suggest, "Let's be like the bird! Let the water roll off our backs." And we would all move through the motions of the bird from the puddle. Remarkably, it worked. Again and again, it helped calm the kids and their parents.

About twelve years later, I shared a different, simple bird story with author Richard Louv. When he was gathering stories for his book *Our Wild Calling: How Connecting with Animals Can Transform Our Lives and Save Theirs*, he asked me, "Do you have one about a child connecting with an animal?"

He'd already received powerful stories from around the world about larger-than-life interactions between humans and wild animals. One involved an octopus who enveloped a man, then floated him to the ocean's surface and released him. Another told of a man who learned everything he needed to know about business by observing the playful life of elephants.

With stories like that, it surprised me to learn that Rich opened chapter eight with a simple moment between my daughter and me in our backyard, listening to a common bird.

When I first told him the story, I explained how I often introduced children and their parents to birds. He asked me, *"But why birds?"*

I could have spouted a list of scientific reasons — research from the Max Planck Institute showing that listening to birdsong reduces anxiety and improves overall health, or the ways it supports a child's ability to process sound — but for me, the science was only part of the answer.

His question lingered. Birds had always brought comfort. And since learning about bird "language" they'd become connectors, developmental allies, and therapeutic interventions. But how could I explain the totality of their importance? I thought long and hard about "why birds."

My younger daughter, Kira, was born three and a half years after her sister. She emerged in my bedroom, windows open, just before the dawn chorus of birds sang us into a new day. I remember hearing birdsong shortly after she arrived. It's curious how I've always thought of her as a bit birdlike. She loves being in trees and carries a unique freeness about her.

I'd felt more prepared for Kira's birth than I had for her sister's, but things hadn't gone as expected. Though it's a story for another time, I nearly died afterward. What I didn't realize then was how much the relationship I'd built with our backyard birds — their steady calls and seasonal rhythms — helped me recover.

Soon after, we moved from Connecticut to the central coast of California, just before Kira turned two.

Back in Connecticut, Kira and her older sister would often press their faces to the sliding glass door. Even at ages one and four, they could stand still long enough for birds to hop close to the feeder just outside. When a cardinal came within six inches, they'd hold their breath, then squeal with glee when it flew away. We left behind three pairs of beautiful cardinals who visited our feeder daily.

The girls were teary-eyed leaving "their birds" and our human neighbors — friends, grandparents, uncles, and an aunt. I was sad too. We had a reserved excitement for the adventure ahead.

Still, after we relocated, I found myself feeling lost. There are no cardinals on the central coast of California. The new landscape differed from anything I'd known in my thirty-three years. I wasn't familiar with the local birds, or plants, or the rhythm of seasons. I didn't know anyone in our new town. Everything felt foreign.

But slowly, through birds, sensory threads began to weave new patterns.

To reorient myself, I rose before dawn each morning and sat outside on the patio. Our new yard was much smaller than the acre we'd left behind, but it faced east, and the sky was open. I could witness the sunrise most days.

The first morning I woke in our new home, I stepped outside with a blanket and a cup of coffee. Kira toddled quietly behind me and backed her body into my lap as I sat cross-legged on the ground.

The world was quiet. We were still. It became our ritual.

Each morning before dawn, we listened for a sound that would pierce the silence and announce a new day in one shrill, echoing note. My toddler would point in the bird's direction and whisper, "Mama," then turn to look at me.

"Yes," I'd reply. We'd smile at each other, and she'd snuggle deeper into me.

When we walked in the neighborhood, hiked the hills, or even strolled downtown, the girls repeated bird sounds. My favorite was when Kira shouted, "Mama! It's the Bo-Bo-Wee bird!"—her name for the call of the resident redwing blackbirds.

They talked to birds the way I did, saying hello to ground robins, chanting the mnemonic "Chi-ca-go, Chi-ca-go" to our neighborhood quail. These small exchanges were threads of sensory connection, weaving familiarity into our days. Being in conversation with the birds gave us joy, a sense of community, and helped us feel less lost.

There was deep learning in those moments too. The kind of learning that forms neural structure and prepares a brain for things like reading, writing, math, and regulation — all of it built on a foundation of sensory development. Processing bird sound, shape, behavior, color, detail, and pattern recognition became daily practice without feeling like "lessons."

Three years after the move, their father and I divorced. Our bird interactions wove through the heaviness of our new reality.

Sometimes, I'd find Kira curled in the fabric swing under the ash tree in our back yard.

"What are you doing out here?" I'd ask.

"Just listening to birds, Mama," she'd say.

The memory of hearing those words still unclenches pockets of leftover sadness from that time.

The story Richard Louv included in *Our Wild Calling* happened during that transitional time. Kira and I were in the backyard. She was cracking acorns, pulling out the nuts, and pulverizing them into meal with a stone mortar and pestle. I sat nearby, lost in paperwork for my job.

"Mama! What's he saying?!?" she asked.

I looked up from my papers, scanned the yard. No one. A small flutter of confusion rose in me. I listened again. Still no one.

"Who?" I asked.

"Him. That guy," she said, not looking up.

I walked to one side of the house. Then the other. No one.

"Who are you hearing?" I asked. She stopped pounding and, as condescendingly as only a seven-year-old can, said,

"That guy. Liisssten!"

I cupped my ears and stood still.

"That guy!" she repeated, motioning behind her with the stone in her hand. Then, finally she said: "That bird!!"

My body softened. Relief and recognition washed through me. My ears adjusted. "Oh... yeah. Now I hear him." I exhaled. How did I miss that bird alarm?

"Sooo... What's he saying?" she asked.

This time, I closed my eyes and turned my ear toward the sound. Through a leaf blower's whine, road noise, an airplane hum, and the daycare chatter across the street, I finally heard it: the steady cheep, cheep, cheep of a California towhee.

It was the same bird species we used to listen to in the early morning stillness after our cross-country move.

"Mammaaaaa?" she said imploringly. The bird's call rang like a metronome.

"I don't know what he's upset about," I said. "Let's go find out."

For us, that question, and the act of listening for the answer, was everything.

Birds were more than background noise. They helped Kira and her sister organize their senses, anchor their attention, and feel the steadiness of something ancient when so much around them was uncertain. That alarm call, like others before it, worked almost like a filter. It helped the girls tune out adult stress, emotional static, and the heaviness of unspoken grief. The towhee became a PACE (Protective And Compensatory Experience), buffering their nervous systems during a time of upheaval.

This kind of listening is more than skill. It's a biological inheritance. Human beings evolved in close relationship with birds. Our language, our awareness, and our sense of belonging are shaped by our long history in the presence of birds.

When Kira asked, "What's he saying?" her curiosity was looking for a pattern to find a thread of coherence in a chaotic world.

Her brain couldn't ignore that alarm because it offered a chance to confirm that what she heard and felt made sense. Did it have a source and a reason?

When we investigated, we discovered that the towhee's alarm was an attempt to protect its nest from a raiding squirrel. That moment gave her nervous system a flash of sensory integration — a feeling occupational therapists recognize as the brain and body coming into alignment. Integration is when the sensory orchestra makes beautiful music.

This is what development expects: repeated moments where perception lines up with reality. Those moments lay the foundation for trusting our gut sense — our interoception — later in life when the stakes may be far greater.

Bird sounds are nuanced. When children notice and interpret them, they are practicing emotional intelligence, spatial awareness, sensory integration, pattern recognition, belonging, and discernment.

Discernment is learned, for example, when that same towhee gives a different alarm call that signals a snake up ahead. You hear it, slow down as you approach the corner, and stop with plenty of time to avoid stepping on the snake in the middle of the trail. Recognizing the differences in bird's calls becomes a powerful lesson in awareness and trust.

What Kira and I shared in our backyard wasn't new. It was ancestral. For hundreds of thousands of years, humans have listened to birds for survival — for food, for safety, and even land orientation. Elders passed this knowing to children by modeling presence, sharing attention, and telling stories that wove in the birds.

And the lions stopped eating so many of us.

When Kira asked, "What's he saying?" She was doing what children have always done. She was weaving herself back into the web of things. Becoming a listener. A feeler. A meaning-maker. A part of the landscape.

Thousands of bird moments throughout my daughters' lives add up to more than sweet memories. They are PACE moments that lay the ground-work to pull on threads of connection in times of stress and change.

Letting Rich's question linger helped me understand *why birds.* In a world flooded with random, human-made input, birds offer a multisen-sory, accessible way to learn trust in the world and in ourselves.

Whether you're seven or seventy, raising children or trying to stay grounded in a scattered world, birds can be wise reminders that there is color after the burn. Sound after silence. A thread of connection, even when our ropes have been frayed.

Bird language can build a solid foundation for our children's nervous systems to feel safe, to trust, and to belong. And for us as parents, it's an opportunity to lift our house and remodel our foundations.

□ PAUSE

What bird is your closest neighbor?

Do you recognize its call?

What might it be saying—right now, outside your door?

Take a moment to listen. Resist the urge to identify or name the bird. Just look and listen. Get to know it. Consider its chit-chat call, song, or alarm and invitation to make a connection.

Try This

Tune in to the Bird Language of Your Life

For two to three days, take ten minutes — alone or with your child — and listen for birds with full attention.

☐ Don't try to identify them.
Just notice:
☐ Where are they?
☐ When you hear their sounds, what does it feel like in your body?
☐ Do their calls change depending on who or what moves nearby?

Then try one or more of the following:

☐ Imitate one bird's call together. Let your child lead if they want.
☐ Sit quietly until you hear five different bird sounds. Try to tell them apart.
☐ Make a simple map or drawing of where you heard birds and what they were doing.
☐ Keep a shared "bird journal" for one week. Record the time, place, and sound. Write what you think the birds might be communicating.

These small practices build attention, curiosity, regulation, and relational rhythm. And each time your child hears a familiar bird and says, "That's our bird!"— you'll know they are stitching threads to the world.

Wild Reflection

Was there a time when birds were part of your life?

Maybe it was a nest near your window.
Or the coo of doves as you fell asleep.
Or the silence after a bird's sudden flight?

Did anyone ever point birds out to you? Did you discover them on your own?
What would change if we treated our backyard birds as neighbors?

Now reflect on your child:

Have they ever stopped to notice a bird's sound or flight?
Could you imagine their curiosity about a robin or hawk or pigeon as the beginning of a lifelong sensory conversation?

What might shift if, instead of tuning out birdsong, you treated it like an invitation:
to connect,
to notice,
to belong?

22

TWO LIFELINES

WHAT ADOLESCENCE REVEALS ABOUT BELONGING

Those who have a why can bare almost any how.

Victor Frankl

B irdsong, trees, wind, and the cacophony of wild spaces can carry us for a long time. Nature gives us a place to grow and connect, and it offers us millions of years of wisdom. It can compensate for loss, lack of nurturing, loneliness, and even trauma. With our hearts and hands, we can find abundant, meaningful ways to be with nature that return us to our pure, unfiltered selves — the part we inherited to belong.

But even in our most rooted belonging with nature, we are still human. Nature can give us much, but it cannot replace our need for deep, trusted connection with other people. At some point in our nature-connection journey — and perhaps even more importantly, to help our children feel whole — we need to reweave the rope to human relationship. Especially if our hands once put it down when the pain of broken trust became too much to bear.

The day I walked in the door after school and found my father on the couch, cigarette between his index and middle finger, with smoke encircling his head, was the day I felt the truth of his tattered rope. I'd seen him like this before, but this time, his eyes held an unfamiliar hollowness. His hands were cracked and bleeding from worsening psoriatic arthritis.

These were the same hands shaped by Newfoundland's rugged coastline — hands that had mended nets, hauled cod from icy waters, built boats, fixed engines, cradled babies, and strummed guitars. His hands were his dignity. His belonging.

Those hands had helped him grip the last thin threads of connection, lifelines that kept some semblance of control within reach. They had picked berries and skipped stones when his mother moved the family from their small coastal town in hopes of keeping her young children together. But that move was the first fraying of his lifeline to a world that made sense. Into that fray crept deeper wounds: betrayal by those who were supposed to protect him. Abandoned by his father, then emotionally, physically, and sexually abused by clergy, his trust was severed not only in people, but in belonging itself. His secrecy and shame created more exile, leaving him alone in the pain of what had happened — and feeling the three things Elizabeth Stanley tells us create trauma: helplessness, powerlessness, and lack of control.

His trauma from clergy lasted from age seven until 14, when his mother, desperate to find work and feed her six children, moved them again — this time from St. John's, Newfoundland to the big city of Toronto, further isolating him from all the nature he had known and taken solace in.

That loss of place, combined with the violation of sacred trust, left a fracture in him — a gap he would spend the rest of his life trying to fill. Without people or place to ground him, he became unmoored from belonging itself. His sense of alloception — his rope to others — had been severely frayed. In his search for safety, that rope became too messy, too heavy to carry. So, he put it down.

It took many years for me to realize that where I was handed one rope, there should have been two: a rope to nature and a rope to people.

It's no coincidence that I was 14 when I came home that day and found him with his hands painfully defeated. The ache of his defeat rippled forward and met me, as many inherited wounds do, in adolescence.

We had moved only weeks before and transferred schools — again. Until then, I'd accepted our moves, seeing them as big adventures, but this one landed differently. At my last school, the academic crowd had welcomed me, and a sense of belonging was taking root: after-school float-building for homecoming, invitations to lunch tables, weekend hangouts.

Then we left.

I remember sobbing and throwing things in my room the night my parents told us we were moving. On the day of the parade, I went back to see the float. But something had changed. I was once again the outsider. No one was unkind, but I didn't belong to the group anymore.

It was the first time I became aware of the ache of not belonging — the echo of my father's wound repeating in my own life.

Most fourteen-year-olds don't have someone to talk with about belonging or developmental rupture. They simply know it hurts not to belong. Research affirms what we often sense instinctively: meaning, purpose, and connection are powerful buffers. Especially in adolescence, the need to belong is as real as the need for food or shelter, and it can reduce depression, anxiety, loneliness, addictions, and other struggles. A study by Lambert et al. confirmed what Frankl wrote so long ago: those with a "why" can bear almost any how.

Maybe you've had a moment like that too — when it felt like your whole world disappeared in front of you. Perhaps you have recognized the ache of your parent's longing in yourself, or seen it in your child.

Have you ever felt something was missing, and caught slight glimmers of it in a stranger's kindness, a beautiful slant of light, an unexpected invitation, the surprise of a hummingbird? Maybe your fracture is in your ecoception, interoception, or alloception — in the world, in your body, or with others.

Healing begins with understanding the original rupture. It grows with the courage to forgive its source, and it takes root when we find the will to write a new story. That courage can offer a generational leap forward — releasing our children from the burden of disconnection.

The most consistent thread my father was able to provide for me was my PACE of nature. It was the only thing that hadn't let him down or broken his trust. But he never found a way to stitch what he had learned in nature back into his human-connection experience. He never re-braided that rope of belonging to people. I don't know where he would have been without nature. It was his lifeline — and eventually, it became mine.

In nature, nothing is wasted. Even what appears broken becomes part of renewal. A fallen tree becomes a nurse log, hosting moss, fungi, insects, and seedlings — supporting a whole new generation of life. What's scattered can become a pattern. Murmurations of starlings — thousands of birds moving in apparent chaos — form breathtaking expressions of coherence and unity. What's severed can regrow roots. A willow branch, snapped off and placed in water or soil, will sprout new roots and grow again.

I've found that when teens are given the space to be courageous, these truths of nature are also truths of adolescence. Teens demonstrate the courage to forgive, to grow, to love, and to connect through great difficulties. And courage helps them find purpose. And purpose protects.

Like the nurse log or the willow branch, we can root again — sometimes in the very place where we were cut down. A sense of meaning — whether from joining a nature club, building something with your hands, or being part of a float crew at school — can increase longevity, reduce illness, and fortify us against toxic stress and trauma.

Looking back, I can see that my own 14-year-old self was already living the story I would later witness in so many teens — standing on the bridge between childhood and adulthood, with one rope to nature firmly in hand, and the other to human connection frayed but waiting to be rewoven.

Try This

Reclaim a Sense of Belonging Through Nature

This week, take one small action that helps you reclaim place — in your body, your family line, or in the land around you.

You might choose to:

☐ Sit quietly under a tree you pass each day. Let yourself notice its shape, its rough bark, its rootedness.

☐ Visit a place from your childhood where you once felt alive, safe, or free — or find a new place that offers that feeling now.

☐ Choose a simple, sensory ritual you can repeat daily: putting your bare feet on the ground, greeting the morning sky, or whispering "thank you" to a patch of moss, a bird, or at sunrise or sunset.

As you do, breathe into this idea:

Even if you've inherited disconnection, you can still choose to re-root. You are not exiled from belonging.

You are invited — again and again — by your wild insides to come back home.

Wild Reflection

Think back to a time in your life when connection felt ruptured — a move, a betrayal, a sudden change that pulled you away from a meaningful relationship.

What did you lose in that moment? A place? A person? A sense of who you were becoming?

How did your body respond — with sadness, anger, numbness, searching?

What, if anything, helped you begin to trust in safety?

Now reflect on this:

What have you passed down — knowingly or unknowingly — from your own story of disconnection?

What might healing that rupture look like in your family, your brain and body, or your daily rhythms?

And finally, what if you trusted that, like a nurse log or a broken branch, the very place of the fracture could become a site of new and abundant life?

What if you don't need to 'find' meaning and connection — and believe it can be created right now where you are?

23

THE TROUBLE WITH TEENS THESE DAYS

CHANGING THE NARRATIVE OF THE TROUBLED TEEN

> How strange that the young should always think the world
> is against them — when in fact that is the only time it is *for*
> them.
>
> Mignon McLaughlin, The Neurotic's Notebook

Adolescence is meant to be a bridge, a daring, thrilling passage from childhood into adulthood. A time for bold risks, deep connections, and discovering one's place in the larger story we all belong to. But in the modern era, we've all but burned the bridge.

We've stranded teens in an artificial world that stifles their natural drives to explore, connect, and practice being courageous. We've raised a generation that, for the first time in human history, may never have fully inhabited their own senses. So, when the inevitable pressures of family, school, or society bear down, where do they turn? Who can they trust if they can't even trust their own bodies?

Think about that for a moment. Many of today's teens have never felt the cold sting of rain soaking their skin because they were shielded from harsh weather. They've never heard the chorus of birds welcoming dawn because their mornings are spent indoors with earbuds in, rushing through rigid schedules. They've never climbed high into the canopy of a tree or marveled at the crunch of frost underfoot on a winter morning. They've never run so far and so fast through the woods that they felt their heart pound with both exhaustion and exhilaration. And it's no coincidence that this same generation is experiencing an epidemic of anxiety, depression, and chronic hopelessness.

We've severed them from the relationships that matter most — with themselves, each other, and with the natural world. When teens are deprived of these connections, their emotional and mental health collapses under the weight of their isolation. The rise in mental health challenges among adolescents is more than alarming. It's predictable.

Gail Whiteford's work on "occupational deprivation" speaks directly to this. When humans are denied the chance to engage in meaningful activities that match their innate capacities and evolutionary design, they suffer. And yet, the bridge to a solution is often right outside the door.

Molly

Molly was twelve when she swaggered into nature school, eye-rolling and unimpressed. "I don't. Like. *Do* nature," she announced, daring anyone to challenge her. Beneath her bravado was a child still hurting from her parents' divorce. She was fiercely independent and aching for connection. She was a self-described lone wolf.

I didn't argue with her that day. Instead, I challenged her. "Prove it," I said with a smirk. To prove me wrong, she enrolled. At first, Molly stayed guarded and skeptical. She communicated with sarcasm and kept a veil of

'I'm untouchable' up. But nature called her bluff. Little by little, it chipped away at her defenses. She couldn't resist the pull of it.

Soon, Molly was the first to leap into cold waters, the first to smear mud on her face for camouflage, the first to notice the tracks of coyotes. By the end of the season, she had transformed from a cynic into a leader — carrying younger kids on her back when they got tired, helping build fires that kept us warm and telling jokes that made us all laugh until we cried.

Molly's transformation came from the space to challenge herself, the courage to connect with others, and the new experience of belonging to a place.

A 2023 study explored how nature-based therapy affected young people recovering from abuse. Participants reported that time in nature helped them reconnect with their bodies, feel safe in their environment, and re-frame negative self-perceptions. Nature acted as a nonjudgmental pres-ence, providing a grounding experience that contrasted sharply with pre-vious chaotic or unsafe environments.[1]

Molly's story is not one of abuse, and it is not unique — but it is perva-sive. For many teens, their first meaningful experience in nature feels like stepping into a world they've longed for their whole life. It's as though a light is switched on inside of them. These are the same teens we've been dis-cussing since early childhood. Many grew up without natural sensory-rich, relational opportunities. Their caregivers may have been overwhelmed, fearful of risk, or misled by societal "shoulds." They missed foundational experiences that laid the structure for resilience and thriving. And now, as teens, they are lost in a culture that doesn't know how to help them build a bridge to themselves.

Their needs are timeless.

The drive for meaning and for habilitation is core to our humanity. And nowhere is it more active than in adolescence. Teens are wired to test boundaries, search for purpose, and figure out where they belong in the greater whole. When that search is thwarted, the results can be devastating.

Teens in the western world may not be experiencing the kind of extraordinary suffering of teens in war-torn countries, but their plight is far from harmless. The modern adolescent landscape is saturated with noise, pressure, and unending distractions, while lacking the grounding threads that give life direction. What our teens face today may not come with obvious scars, but it leaves them feeling empty and alone without understanding why[2].

Overstimulation without true connection. A culture of comparison with little room for agency. The pressure to perform without a place to rest. The accumulation of toxic stress, undischarged trauma, and the rapid pace of life. These forces erode the passion for which teens are historically known, undermining courage, curiosity, and care.

And in the absence of something meaningful to hold on to, many teens are scattered and adrift, disconnected from others, and from themselves.

In the case of teens these days, there isn't one obvious crisis sounding an alarm for society to pay attention to. It is more of a steady, pervasive absence of a sense of purpose, a place to belong, a reason to keep showing up.

People who view their lives as meaningful have greater emotional resilience, cognitive flexibility, and physical health[3]. Data shows that across the lifespan, those with a sense of purpose live longer and with far fewer health complications.

Adolescence is the developmental season when identity, values, a sense of meaning and the desire for purpose form.

Which makes me think of Jenny.

Jenny

Jenny came to our program after her mother withdrew her from school in sixth grade. Her mom was growing increasingly concerned about the mental health crisis among girls — disordered eating, bullying, risky behavior. Jenny's mother felt the traditional school environment was simply too toxic. Jenny had recently endured a traumatic experience that made national headlines. The attention from that experience only deepened her instinct to retreat.

When I first met Jenny, she struck me as a bright but deeply anxious girl. She was quiet and introspective, and while I could see a spark in her eyes, it was distant, almost unreachable. She apologized for everything, hesitated before speaking, and avoided eye contact. Any mention of the "incident" would make her shrug, brush it off with a nervous laugh, and quickly change the subject. "Yeah. That was pretty crazy," she'd say, before diverting the conversation elsewhere.

A couple of months into our time together, I wove a story inspired by the herbalist Rosemary Gladstar — a tale about the common dandelion, the resilient little plant dismissed as a weed. I shared how the dandelion withstands being trampled on, driven over, sprayed with chemicals, and even submerged in floods, yet still manages to pop up, bright and stubbornly alive. Jenny lay in the grass, her head resting on her forearms, listening intently. Now and then, she'd lift her eyes to catch my animated storytelling, a half-smile spreading across her lips.

The very next day, she came running down the hill towards our meeting place, her hair flying behind her, her face glowing with excitement. She was clutching something in her hands, and as she came closer, I saw it was a cereal bowl filled with dirt, greens spilling over the sides, and a single, bright yellow dandelion wilting in the center. Breathless, Jenny pushed the bowl toward me. "I found this in my yard and wanted to dig it up for you because you love dandelions so much!"

In that moment, it was as if the dandelion's fierce resilience had taken root in Jenny's heart. From that day forward, something shifted in her. She was lighter, quicker to laugh, and far more willing not just to be *in* the world, but to be *of* the world. The hesitation that had once marked her every movement seemed to fade, replaced by an eager curiosity that was both infectious and deeply moving.

Nature's wisdom did what no amount of talking could do. It met her where she was. It reflected back her strength and her light. Jenny didn't need lectures about resilience or discussions about her anxieties — she needed the chance to feel like she belonged to something real. She needed to see herself in the simple cycles of the resilient natural world, which helped her trust that life was calling for her. In adolescence, nature mirrors back the parts of us that are still whole, even when everything else feels fractured.

Our ecoceptive wiring is profoundly supportive of our mental health, and as her guide, I had to open the door for Jenny to step into that space. I had to trust that she would find her own answers among the weeds.

Jenny eventually returned to public school for high school, confident and eager with a conquer the world attitude. She earned early admission to a top university and often credits nature school for helping her become who she is — a mother now, rooted in confidence, curiosity and ready to help her daughter's light shine.

Jenny and Molly were lucky to have parents who saw their light dimming and could make a different choice. That kind of attention changes things. One person willing to walk slowly enough to match the pace of a teen's confused heart can be life-changing. Not all teens (or parents) have that opportunity. But when they do, nature provides a bridge we can walk across with them.

The bridge to nature was present throughout my young life. It helped me weather many upheavals, but as I entered the teenage years, I longed for a steady anchor. To be 'alone' as a teen without a lifeline to hold is dangerous territory. When those lifelines are cut and nothing healthy takes their place, hope drifts. Without hope, despair can turn to apathy or to grasping for connection in risky ways.

I know this from both sides — watching teens in my programs, and living it myself at fourteen and beyond.

Research shows that a strong sense of belonging is linked to greater resilience, lower rates of depression and anxiety, stronger problem-solving, and fewer addictions. Belonging gives life meaning, and it doesn't require a grand vision of the future — though that can help. Belonging can be found in small, vivid moments: the pride of building a homecoming float, the bowl of weeds dug up for someone you trust, the preschooler carried on your back, the leap into cold water, the feeling of being remembered, included, and seen.

That's why the stories of Molly, Jenny, and so many others matter. Nature gave them what their culture had forgotten how to offer: agency, the courage to act, and a place to belong — to both a group and the land.

It offered them *a why.*

And teens, more than perhaps any other age, are searching for that why — even if they can't articulate it yet.

Why should I care?

Why does this matter?

Why do I feel so alone?

Once a teen finds their "why," the rope to belonging with the land, themselves, and with others strengthens.

When we restore what's been blocked — stars overhead, dirt underfoot, a story passed around a fire — we are not romanticizing the past. We are restoring a biological sequence. We are reintroducing what our neurology is expecting with sensory nourishment, emotional reflection, and social anchoring. We are helping shape meaning from matter; the cold sting of river water, the caress of wind on skin, the memorable moments that come with the smell of spring or intentional campfire smoke. We are helping to reclaim awe.

Teens need an ecosystem that induces awe and allows purpose and belonging to emerge.

Adolescence isn't a problem to be managed or solved. It's a sacred passage to be honored. And nature is the oldest guide we have to shepherd us through it.

The Healing Power of Awe

Awe isn't just an emotional experience — it's a biological reset. Studies show that awe reduces proinflammatory markers linked to chronic stress, supports emotional regulation, and fosters greater connection to others. Awe shrinks the ego, quiets mental chatter, and reminds us we are part of something larger. Whether it's sparked by a towering redwood, a murmuration of birds, or the sudden hush before a storm, awe helps rewire the nervous system toward calm, resilience, and purpose.

Research confirms that awe is medicine.[4] Experiencing awe promotes kindness, generosity, and deepens one's sense of connection and purpose. In therapeutic settings, awe can help reorient teens toward resilience and possibility.

Try This

Teens may resist when you say, "Let's go for a hike." It can sound like work, or worse — your agenda. Instead, invite them to take a wander. A wander is different: it has no destination, no plan, no pressure.

☐ Pick a place that feels a little outside the ordinary — a creek, a patch of woods, an abandoned lot, or even a neighborhood trail. Somewhere with a hint of discovery. You can say something like, "Hey I heard about this cool place; let's check it out."

☐ Begin walking together without words. Don't explain, don't direct. Let your teen step into the lead.

☐ Notice what happens when they set the pace, choose the turns, or pause to look at something. Follow without correcting.

☐ See what comes up on its own. It might be silence, a question, a laugh, or even a complaint. Let it be whatever it is.

☐ When you return, resist the urge to process or evaluate the experience. Trust that the simple act of wandering — without judgment or agenda — is enough.

A wander hands the thread of agency back to your teen. It tells them: I trust you. I'll walk with you. I'll follow your lead. That quiet exchange can open doors to belonging and purpose in ways talking (which often feels like lecturing to teens) can't.

Wild Reflection

When you were a teenager...

What made you feel truly alive?

Who (or what) made you feel like you mattered?

Was there a place — a tree, a field, a park, a song — that helped you feel like you could breathe?

Now ask yourself:

What small, wild moment could you offer a teen today — even if they roll their eyes at first?

And what parts of you are still longing for meaning?

24

THE VILLAGE

NATURE AS A SHARED EXPERIENCE

Connection is a biological imperative, vital to our survival.

Stephen Porges

F or teens, feeling connected is especially urgent — because the village that once held them through the threshold to adulthood has grown thin. Nature can restore some of those missing strands.

Earlier in the book, we explored that many children today resist the outdoors because it is unfamiliar. Teens are no different. Much of their lives are spent indoors, but indoor experiences rarely induce the kind of awe that researchers show as growth inspiring or therapeutic.

This shift in brain *preference* for the indoors reveals a deeper cultural drift, showing how nature is treated as an activity rather than an identity.

One generational story illustrates this shift[1]. The story goes that in a certain village, each child's life is honored and guided with their unique song. When a woman learns she is pregnant, she walks intentionally into the wild alone. During her wander she is supported by others, but not disturbed. Her time is spent freely connecting with birds, plants, animals, water, and nature until she hears her child's song — a melody given by the land. When she returns to the village, she teaches the song to her community. After the child is born, her community surrounds mother and baby, singing their specific song to connect the child with human and non-human life. The child grows with the song as a touchstone of who they are. If the child makes an unskillful or uncaring choice or diminishes themselves or another, instead of punishing the child, the villagers sing the child's song back to them, helping them remember their true nature.

Our children's songs may not come to us in the same way, but the need for belonging is unchanged.

Most of us don't live in villages with this level of connection anymore, but we continually hear that it takes a village to raise a child. What does it actually mean to *be* a village?

Traditionally, a village was a local landscape full of shared experience: hands in soil, neighbors gathering food or firewood, stories told under the same stars.

Today, a single day might include a global news headline, a traffic jam, a podcast from a stranger, processed food from a delivery app, a conversation about fundraising for things no one really needs, and bedtime stories from a random stack of books. Those random experiences will be different for each individual. None of it is inherently bad, but it's scattered. Disconnected. And our brains are wired for coherence.

Coherence increases meaning at the neurological level and it requires context. That's why even the smallest points of shared experience matter. That's why strangers talk about the weather. Weather is one of the last shared environmental touchpoints, connecting people across backgrounds and beliefs.

By deepening a shared experience of nature, we can restore our sense of the village.

A simple example: a neighborhood bird check-in. "Hear that? That's our Merlin." I've seen birds connect complete strangers across language and geography. I've seen them inspire names for children — Phoebe, Robin, Hawk, Wren, Finch. I've watched kids from different cultures share in the imitation of bird songs, discover hidden nests, and track predators together.

Birds, like so much of nature, invite presence. Birds offer practice in the art of connecting with each other by watching how they call and respond to each other. The micro-moments, although fleeting, can be lasting in the psyche of our young ones. Moments like one evening when my older daughter was about six and her communication resembled the back and forth of birds that we listened to together.

Tensions were running high in our home. I was preparing dinner, and she sat on the floor nearby. She called out, "Mama?"

"Yes, honey," I answered. My eyes still on the counter.

"Mama?" she said again.

"Yes?" I replied, still not looking up.

"Mama?"

I finally put the knife down, knelt beside her, and said, "Yes. What do you need?"

Her eyes opened wider, and she said, "Nothing Mama. I just wanted you."

Connection doesn't always come in the form of questions, deep processing or even doing anything specific. Sometimes, as young ones and birds remind us, it's a moment of presence that says, I'm here. I see you. Let's belong to this moment, together.

Moments of presence linger. Opportunities for these moments show up in seemingly mundane daily interactions, like the story of a little girl next door.

My neighbor's five-year-old asked if I'd like to hear her story. I said yes, and she read me the following story she wrote:

Once upon a time, there are birds.
Once upon a time, there are trees.
Once upon a time, there are flowers.
And finally, with a proud beam:
Once upon a time, there are birds in trees.

Her mother whispered that she had almost corrected her with — "there *were* birds" — before realizing her daughter was right. Birds aren't a thing of the past. There *are* birds. And trees. And stories. And time to notice.

When we help kids notice nature, we open the gates to a village of support for them.

In our first meeting, eight-year-old Riley insisted that there were no birds, "and anyways, birds don't matter."

"Well, they matter to me," I told her, and waited to see if she would say more. She didn't

The next time I saw her, she asked, "Why do you like birds anyway?"

"They help my ears learn how to listen."

She looked down. "My ears have a hard time listening."

"Maybe the birds can help?" I offered.

The next time I saw Riley, she began a conversation with an exuberance that she hadn't shown before. "Hey Kathleen! Guess what! I saw a bird!" My heart jumped, and then she said, "Right in my yard!

Riley's mom told me her daughter was following directions more and paying attention better. I wasn't surprised. Bird language supports sound processing, attention, and sensory integration. But more than that — it gave Riley a non-threatening path to connection. A bridge to belonging.

In our final conversation, Riley said, "Hey. Kathleen. Actually. You know. I think maybe I kinda like birds now."

Recontextualizing your life with nature can begin with something as small as a bird question or a moment of noticing. It can grow into something bigger: a conscious NatureLed™ community with an outdoor storytelling night, a community garden, a shared community bird map, or a group of families who walk together once a week just to notice nature.

Nature is not an endpoint. It is a biological imperative and a relational opportunity — the context that binds your child to their place, their people, and their self.

Try This

The next time you're with a child and doing something you do daily — walking to the car, making tea, or standing on the front porch — pause. Take a breath. Then choose a nature neighbor to connect with and say something like:

☐ Where do you think the closest wild animal lives?

☐ Point to where you think the closest bird nest is.

☐ Where is the bird who is making that sound?

Ask it once a day for three days.

Then watch what happens on the fourth day.

You don't have to explain or insist. Even if they don't respond, go through the motions. You are modelling your relationship with place and how you care about nature. You are demonstrating that noticing nature is as natural as asking, How was your day?

Wild Reflection

When was the last time you shared a moment of wonder?

What are the most familiar natural elements in your daily life — the ones you could name without thinking?

Are there any that have disappeared?

Now consider:

What would it mean to be the one in your family who starts reweaving nature into daily life?

What song, sound, or story from nature feels like it is part of you?

How could you begin sharing it as a thread of connection?

Write down one small practice you could begin this week that says, "Nature is us — and we are it."

And then ask:

Who might join me if I begin assembling a village?

25

WHEN THE WORLD PAUSED

LETTING NATURE LEAD

I n 2020, the hum of daily life stopped on a global scale. The world went still. The pandemic arrived and rearranged everything — our routines, our expectations, and the ways we connected. In the stillness, the birds kept calling.

When the world went into lockdown, my daughters were nineteen and twenty-two. We had already logged thousands of hours outside together, listening to birds, tracking animals, wandering, wildcrafting plants for medicine, nature-journaling, and playing.

Two weeks turned to three months, and the three of us were bumping elbows and emotions in our 900 square foot home. Like so many families, we had no idea what was coming, or how long it would last. Maniacal laughing and crying for no obvious reason were as abundant as the dishes piling up in our sink. Our previously slightly neglected dog became an over-loved emotional support hero, burying his head into one or another of our laps, as if to express sheer embarrassment at the amount of petting and cuddling we lavished on him daily.

Explosions of paintbrushes and paper, fabric and sewing machines, beads, books, and laptops covered every surface in our house. A guitar was perpetually in someone's hands. Zoom became a verb, and we finally made headway with the almost expired cans of beans, spaghetti sauce, and rice from the back of the kitchen cabinet.

One morning I sat in our backyard, under the silver-green leaves of a pineapple guava tree. Despite the fences that surrounded us and separated our yard from the neighbors', ours with the tall grass that we let grow for bird habitat felt like an oasis. Our nature landscape was modest, but alive.

I felt blessed yet worried.

While my boyfriend, an electrical contractor, was overworked with people enhancing their home spaces, my daughters and I had jobs on hold for an indefinite amount of time.

A house wren above me called for her mate, disrupting my worried mind. "Chit Chit?" *Are you there? Mate?* I stayed still, watching her.

Our house wrens were in constant communication with each other about the neighborhood cat, fox, Cooper's hawk, and many other constant threats. I listened more closely. The wren's companion returned her call. "Chit! Chit!" *Yes, I'm here.*

She cried again, "Here?"

Companion, "Here."

"Here?"

"Here. Right here."

Then my neighbor shouted from over the fence, "Hey?"

"Hey!" I responded.

"How's it going over there?"

"Well. We are all well. Feeling blessed to have this outdoor space. How about you?"

"Going a little crazy here all alone. Drinking too much. Playing a lot of guitar."

"Yeah. Us too!"

I thought about my good friend, who texted that morning: "Hi. I miss you."

"Oh. I miss you too."

"See you soon?"

"Soon. I hope!"

Like birds, we send our calls across relational space. And like birds, we need those calls returned.

Our human world isn't that different from the bird world. Birds call to each other to stay connected with each other and stay attuned to the environment. When one's call is unanswered, a tension grows.

"Chit?"

Silence.

"Chit? Hey, you there?"

More silence.

"Chit, chiit — hey you there? I'm freaking out over here, wondering if you are okay?"

"Chiit, Chitt, Chiit. Sorry. Yeah, I'm here. I was picking through leaves and looking for bugs and didn't hear you. Sorry. Didn't mean to worry you!"

It's this pattern — the call and return — that stabilizes connection. In the absence of a response, disconnection creeps in.

From the backyard, I could hear my daughters talking to each other in the kitchen. One asked the other,

"So. What are you doing today?"

The other one didn't answer — silence.

"Hey? The first one asked.

Silence again.

"Are. Are you okay?"

Finally, the second one responded, "I don't know."

"Wanna take a walk or something?"

"Yeah. I guess. You want me to make some food?"

"Uhm. Yeah. Thanks."

Their conversation with its back-and-forth mirrored a wider need I had been reading about — the growing crisis of adolescent disconnection. Researcher Robin Gurwitch wrote that "We see [increased] depression and anxiety in all age groups, but in adolescence, it's on steroids. When kids look into the future now, they're looking at one that wasn't what they envisioned before...[1]"

Besides our basic needs of shelter, water, and food, we need our companion calls returned. Lieberman tells us that social connection is so important to humans that "social pain activates the same neural circuitry as physical pain[2]."

The wrens continue to flit about my yard, singing, hunting insects, and calling to each other. They make it look so easy to stay connected. A simple chit back and forth keeps an invisible thread between them. They go about their business, getting things done, productive but not too busy to respond.

The wren moved closer to me and sat on the vine of a climbing rosebush. "Chiit," she said, in a whisper almost. I closed my eyes and waited.

A muted response, "Chit," came from another wren, which I could hear but couldn't see when I opened my eyes.

I wonder how many times my daughters may have called out to me, served me a "chit" that I hadn't noticed. When someone lobs a serve and no one returns it, the message to the brain is "not important" or, in a more personal interaction, "You are not important." But the brain will keep asking, Is this important? How about this? And more personally, how about me?

The pause in my backyard gave me space to consider how many times had I become frustrated with more insistent and demanding calls, MAMA!? How many times have I've missed a child, friend, partner, or parents' call — too busy, too overwhelmed with the predation of life, job, bills, debt, and so much more.

How often do we overlook a chance to connect, however briefly? A smile. A bird song. Wind on skin. These small moments matter more than we realize, and I've come to see them in the rhythm of my own relationships, too.

Did we learn this call and response from the birds a million years ago? Could our need for social interaction, for someone to answer our reach out, our calling, be from the need to know that maybe all is well in our bubble? That everything is right in our world? Or perhaps it is not all right, but that someone is with us, out there returning our call?

My dad, who lives alone since my mother died seven years ago, calls me almost every morning. Sometimes I don't answer, but I eventually call back. When I don't, my dad worries, has something happened? I get a message, "Hey. Yeah. Uhm, just give me a quick call and let me know everything's okay." So I do, but I make it quick. "Just letting you know all is good. I'm busy, so I'll call ya later."

When he doesn't call me, I worry too. Is everything okay? I call him. He doesn't always answer. Twice I have phoned one of my brothers, who then calls him also. Once I have phoned the police to check on him. He was okay.

I think about all the ways my partner calls to me — a hand on a hip or a knee, a glance across a room, a smile, a text. Sometimes when I am working on my computer, he walks by and slides his hand across my shoulders. I meet his gesture with a glance and a smile.

Lately, I've been asking myself: What are the ways my children call to me *now*? What calls have I returned, and which ones floated unanswered into the silence?

You might wonder too. How does your child reach out to you? How often do you return their call?

Sarah Pultorak, an occupational therapist, professor at the University of Wisconsin, and mother of a toddler, wrote me the following story.

My eighteen month old son will often say, "Want mama come over here." And when I do, he will often carry on playing by himself, but he'll add, "watch you" (meaning "watch me"). It's as if he does not necessarily need me to play with him, but he just wants me to be near, watching him, caring about what he cares about (which at this age, is every type of truck under the sun and digging, scooping, and dumping dirt and sand).

Humans companion call in many ways: giving a general nod, wave, or "hello" when passing someone on the sidewalk just to acknowledge that they are seen, a "hi, how are you," to the cashier at the grocery store, a "Thumbs Up" on social media (or for those who recall the early 2000s-era Facebook, a "poke"), etc.

My husband and I whistle 2 notes to one another (just like birds!) whenever we get home from being out or if we don't know where the other person is in the house. We listen for the other's whistle just to get a sense of where they are, and may or may not follow this up with a conversation. It's just a way to check in and say, "hey I'm home," or "where are you? oh, good, you're here somewhere."

My dad once sent me a text that said, "just a love text." And now he and I, or my mom and I, regularly text "love text!" to one another to say, "hey, I'm thinking of you, I care about you...even though I have nothing novel or interesting to say at the moment."

I love the idea that we possibly learned this from the birds many years ago. Or maybe all animals do this in some way, and we are less attuned to the messages of species who are less vocal, less omnipresent, or less audible to us.

Try This

When your child calls to you — with a word, a look, a gesture, or even a tantrum — pause and return the call.

□ Respond with a word, a touch, or your presence.

□ Notice how even the smallest "chit" back, steadies the space between you.

□ Practice this with your partner, friends, or parents too — a smile across the room, a text, a gentle hand. These small call-and-returns are threads of connection that weave belonging.

Wild Reflection

How does your child "call" to you? What form do their companion calls take?

Think of a time when you didn't return a call — what might have been the message your child received?

What are some ways you call to others — and how does it feel when your call is returned, or when it is met with silence?

How can you create more moments of companion calling in your family, like the wrens in the backyard?

26

IN THE HANDS OF OUR NEXT GENERATIONS

CROSSING THE BRIDGE TOGETHER

You are the bows from which your children as living arrows
are sent forth.

Kahlil Gibran

*Raising children who know how to find their way back to meaning
when life gets messy is among the greatest gifts we can give the future.
It is the hope that they will see themselves as part of something larger — woven
into the fabric of life, rooted in the earth, in each other, and in something wild
inside.*

In every small interaction — a hand on the shoulder, a murmured *I'm
here*, a shared sighting of a hawk — we offer one another the stability that
modern life too often strips away. We can't eliminate adversity, but we can
offer a compass through it. And nature can hold that compass when we've
lost our way.

I invite you to take a moment here and remember a time when you
were a child, and you felt joyful, excited, and alive! Now close your eyes
and picture the moment. Feel the moment. What were you doing? Would

you describe it as meaningful? If you could experience again what you felt during that moment, would you? What might allow you to do that?

Children find meaning in places adults often overlook or dismiss. When we allow them to follow nature's lead — even when it disrupts our plans — profoundly meaningful moments can unfold. I've had many such moments, but the one that follows left an imprint I will carry for the rest of my life. It began when I chose to sit beside my older daughter at a rusty water trough and let nature guide us.

She was eight. I'd been trying to persuade her to help me plant our garden. Unsuccessful, I loosened soil and planted seeds until she shouted, "MMAMMAA. COME OVER HERE!"

I looked to see her leaning over, almost into, the old trough.

I had been trying to motivate her to share in the work of our garden. "Come on, honey, we might find worms!" And "Won't it be fun when we can just walk out here and eat sugar peas!" I wanted to teach her about growing food and the cycles of life and death. I wanted to teach her about the interaction of insects and plants, about how different plants need different amounts of light and water and nutrients, and how the same plant will grow differently, depending on where it grows.

I'd given up cajoling her when she implored me again, "MMMAAA-MA!"

I put down my shovel and went to see what had her attention.

I sat down beside her. The wind tugged at the brim of my hat as a ray of sun penetrated green algae on the water's surface. Staring into the water, we watched as a dragonfly nymph emerged, dragging its tiny water-logged body to rest eight inches above the water's edge. There it began a slow and laborious process of shedding its muted grey shell.

My daughter and I huddled close in silence, as if attending a church sermon. Her body remained still, her eyes wide, her hair whipped and tangled around her face in the wind.

Every few moments she cast her eyes in my direction, beckoning me to stay with her — to be still and wait. I studied the face that so many say looks like mine. Her high freckled cheekbones, her blue eyes, her fine sandy colored hair. I'm often drawn in by her reverence for life, and now, by her attention to this dragonfly.

People who didn't really know my daughter said things like, "She's so sensitive!" As if sensitive is bad.

"She's a difficult child, isn't she?" As if to mean that easier is better.

"Wow, she is intense!" As if she should be more demure.

"Your daughter literally stared me down today!" As if curious eyes are threatening.

"I'm actually afraid of your daughter!" — a friend laughed as she said this.

It's true. People often saw my daughter in that way. When she was a toddler, she growled at people who got too close. She refused to talk to certain adults but was insanely chatty with others. She never wanted to sleep alone. Whenever we went on a trip, she threw up before we left. Her version of cuddling at night was frequently, *lie as close to me as you can but don't touch me,* and in her nursing years she was like a third appendage!

But there at a rusty water trough, she was confident, present, calm, wise. There, she was the curious, kind, wide-eyed observer I still had to force myself to stop looking at in amazement — so I could do something productive. And I wonder — when did being present for, and sitting with a child come to be seen as an unproductive waste of time?

That dragonfly "moment" lasted an entire hour as we kept our steady, quiet focus. When the creature finally freed itself from the hard, ugly shell keeping it alive underwater for the past five or so years, we made slack-jawed soft gasps. Long wobbly legs walked to the top edge of the metal trough. There it stood in stillness with its wings spread, waving them in slow motion, up and down — to feel the newness of sensation wings must give to a back.

Still trying to 'teach', I said, "Wow! No mother. No father. How does it know what to do?"

My daughter responded in a hushed tone, as if her heart was speaking out loud:

"Mama. Maybe. Just maybe. She dreams a dream her whole life, until one day, she wakes up and just knows what to do."

My response, "Maaaayyybeeee," came out thick and drawn, the way honey is pulled from a honeycomb.

The dragonfly stretched out its wings further, and my daughter straightened her backbone, mirroring the dragonfly's movement. When the insect seemed satisfied that its new skin was formed and dry, it lifted off for its first glorious flight. We held our breath.

In awe, my daughter looked as bright as the sun.

But the very moment the dragonfly launched into the air; a violent gust of wind slammed it back onto the surface of the water. Dismay and shock froze me, but not my daughter. Swiftly, she placed her hand underwater and lifted the dragonfly out. Using her body to shield it from the wind, she held her hand steady while the insect dried its new wings again. Thus fortified, the dragonfly lifted once more, this time successfully, into the spring wind.

Every child comes with a dream. Call it an internal compass, a spark of personality, a neural template formed by evolution. Their environment either activates or suppresses that dream.

Through ecoception — their sensory dialogue with the natural world — they can engage in ways that carry their development forward. We as caregivers can help or hinder that process. We can either make the soil fertile, or deny the roots what they need.

When well-meaning people told me my daughter needed to be "more independent," they couldn't see her bursting creativity or the way she busied herself for hours on a task that interested her. Many well-meaning friends suggested that I was too attentive, too gentle, too loving, but they couldn't feel her arms wrapped securely around them, returning that love. When she was younger and her arms reached for me, I picked her up, and people asked, "How will she ever learn to be independent?" My daughter growled in response. I kept holding her and walked away.

I've often thought about how easily that moment with the dragonfly could have passed us by.

It could have gone differently. My daughter could have been impatient and cut short the time she spent observing the dragonfly, missing the moment when the insect emerged and when it needed a hand. She could have reacted impulsively and just grabbed it, crushing it instead of helping it. She could have been worried it would bite her and not reached out to help, and watched the dragonfly flail and drown.

I could have gotten in her way and stopped her from touching the dragonfly. I could have insisted she come learn my lessons in the garden instead of her own. I could have listened to people who wanted me to do such things in the name of "independence."

Instead, we let nature lead us.

This is what I now hear from others about both my daughters:

"Your daughter is so talented!"

"Your daughter is so kind!"

"Your daughter is so smart!"

"Your daughter is such a joy!"

"Your daughter is a natural leader!"

"Your daughter is such a self-motivated learner!"

"Your daughter is so creative!"

Years have passed, but the lessons from that water trough live on. The girl by the water trough is now twenty-seven years old. Her younger sister, the one with the swing, and the birds, and the *you looked like an egg* moment, is twenty-four. They know when to emerge from dark waters to fly and when to wait and dry their wings a little longer. Sometimes they still need me to lend a hand and lift them, and sometimes they provide that for me. I look at them and reflect on the capable women they have become. I exhale and whisper, *Thank you, nature.*

The lessons don't end with our children. They echo forward into the landscape that holds all of us. Birdsong can call us back to wonder, and attention. Trees can show us much about life, the way they bend in the wind, rise to the light and even the way they break. Plants can teach us about growing in fertile soil or withering with too much sun, too much water or not enough of both. Bugs and butterflies can bring us to the edge of awe.

Nature gives us a sensory-rich context for becoming habilitated adults. But it can't provide for us one special thing that we humans need: each other. At some point, we need someone to return our call. To answer the question: "What's he saying?" We need someone to catch our stories. To be in relationship with.

Because the meaning we get from being in relationship with nature can't be the only rope we pass on. It must be woven together with threads of shared moments, glances, touches, smiles, and the intersection between these three things: ecoception, alloception, and interoception.

When we stop engaging with the world or each other — by choice, illness, trauma, or overwhelm — we lose the connections that have always given our species meaning. Like topsoil stripped bare by years of storms without the renewal of compost, the ground of our being can erode over time. When we lose our connections, we lose our way.

Nature offers healing, yes — but without others, without the stability of relationship, even the wild can't always call loud enough to reach us.

My father knew nature. He listened to birds, tracked storms and found connection in nature. That intimacy with the land carried him for years.

But he was missing something essential.

He kept moving. Turning away from intimacy. The betrayal of his childhood left shame in its place.

Nature gave him solace. But what he needed most was a bridge to bring the rhythms, reciprocity, and trust of the outdoors into his relationships.

I may never know why some find that bridge and others don't.

But I know this:

My parents got me partway there. They brought me to the edge of the bridge.

And I walked *my* daughters across it.

That's what we all long for. Two ropes woven into one bridge. And that is my bridge for you and your child — the one you can help them across.

AFTERWORD

I am the first generation of the last generation.

I, you who are reading this, we, are the bridge generations.

Both of my parents passed away while I was writing this book.

And though this book is not about them, their stories are part of it — threaded through every chapter, every choice I've made as a mother, a mentor, a meaning-maker.

I believe they each tried, in their own way, to raise their children differently. To protect us in the places they hadn't felt protected. To love us in ways they hadn't always received. To embody the best of the elders who had shown them tenderness, strength, or joy.

I've done the same.

Like many parents, mine were determined to do better on their own. And in many ways, they did. My brothers and I have built lives that are not only more resourced, but more connected than the ones they knew. That is a legacy I don't take lightly.

But none of us were meant to do this alone. We all need a village to lean on.

Raising a child — raising ourselves — requires a web of support. Mentors. Elders. Witnesses. People who can say, "I see you," and mean it.

I've been fortunate to find those people along the way. And if this book has offered even a sliver of that to you, then it has done its work.

This is how we change the world — not in sweeping declarations, but in the courageous and sometimes unskillful work of showing up differently for the next generation.

In the end, my parents had each other. Despite the struggles, despite the ruptures, they stayed. And though there were many things I had to unlearn, there were gifts they passed to me that I hold with fierce gratitude: Courage. Grit. Unconditional Love. And a Deep Connection to Nature.

The rest?

It has composted.

It has broken down in the soil of my becoming, feeding a more generous, more aware, more whole being. I believe this is what it means to heal — not to erase the past, but to transform it. To turn pain into wisdom. To turn patterns into possibility. To offer our children what we never received, and in doing so, receive it too.

If you're reading this, you are already part of that transformation.

Thank you for walking this path with me. May you continue to root, reach, and return — again and again — to your *Wild Inside.*

ACKNOWLEDGEMENTS

It's hard to know where to begin, and I am sure there will be those whom I unintentionally leave out — for that I am truly sorry.

For my maternal grandparents, David and Caroline Cronin. My paternal grandmother, Maisie Knox. My parents, Roch and Caroline Lockyer.

For Mac Stewart, (1967-2009) for your gentle heart and for reminding me of the beauty of this life and the love that is possible between two people.

May the ancestors rest in peace.

287

I send a gratitude to my non-human teachers: Earth, water, water beings, stone, moss, mycelium, fungi, insects, reptiles, amphibians, four-legged animals, low lying plants, trees, birds, winds, the orienting directions, storms, and the spirit that moves through all these things.

I send gratitude to the Chumash people, on whose stolen lands I live, and to the Haudenosaunee Nation and First Nations people, on whose lands I grew up on.

My greatest teachers are the young ones I've had the great privilege of working with, living with, and mentoring. And to those who've given me the honor of the names "Auntie" and "Mama K."

I am beyond amazed and grateful for all I've learned and shared, and continue to share with my fiercely beautiful and fun daughters, Veda and Kira. For the humans you have become, for your relational lives, your choice to stay open through the storms of your becoming, and for the insanely capable people you have become. Thank you for coming to me.

I have no words for the gratitude I hold for my love, Jim — for your generosity, kindness, honesty, patience, integrity and belief in me — without which I could not have finished *Wild Inside.* Thank you for being such an exceptional and loving human who rises with love even in the face of tremendous adversity and who chooses to keep showing up for all the people in his orbit, who keeps his door open for the lost but not forgotten, and who lives in relationship with the wild creatures and spaces.

For my bonus daughter Amber — your trust in life and your courage to love, and to keep loving, in the face of it all.

For Isabelle — Love is patient. Love is kind. You are loved.

For the editing and feedback of my lovely Havenista's who have spent countless hours helping to shape *Wild Inside*: Lauren Strach, Cathy Brigden and Cynthia Hamilton Urquhart. You are the best!

For Susanna Brougham's fine editing and feedback.

I am deeply grateful to my brother Peter for his encouragement, writing advice, editing and gentle nudging to get Wild Inside out into the world. And for sharing the middle child space with me!

To my brother Allan, who was my first motivation in life to be a better person. His big heart and resilience inspire me to believe.

To my sister-in-law, Melanie, for loving us, and for caring so deeply about children and others.

For my 'Irish twin' brother, Roch, and the shared moments of our young lives together.

For my mentors and teachers who held my hand or placed breadcrumbs along the way: Rosemary Gladstar, Jon Young, Paul Raphael, Alexis Henry, Joyce Thomson, Richard Louv.

For the women of La Leche League International who first taught me to trust my heart, my body, and my children.

To the first women who dared to step into a shared vision of a more connected developmental and educational experience for their children and leap into the non-profit that began as the Central Coast Village Center: Angela North, Lindsay Pera, Liz Ellis, Ann Osbaldeston, Marie McCree, Donna Helete, Susan Pendergast, Toni Van Rynn, Heidi Harmon, Kathy Wensloff, Judy Wensloff.

For my dearest friend Mimi Rutman Vincent, who asks me hard questions while holding my hand and heart gently.

To Laura Munson and Haven writing retreats for stirring the creative juices and loading the fire.

To my neurologist, Dr. David Yeh — the first and only doctor to say the words, *"It's not your fault."* Your words allowed me to exhale a breath I'd held for decades, and although it may have felt like nothing to you, it was everything to hear those words.

To the profession of occupational therapy: May we stay true to the meaning and connection that the future so desperately needs.

And for OtterPlay Publishing, who pushed this book into the wider world.

And last but not least, to you, Dear Reader, for your heart and willingness to journey with me in these pages. 10,000 Thank Yous.

xoxo

Kathleen

Forgiveness does not change the past, but it does enlarge the future.

ENDNOTES

The Cost of Survival

1. Roch, pronounced as Rock.

2. Mark S. Rosenfeld, *Wellness and Lifestyle Renewal: A Manual for Personal Change* (Rockville, MD: The American Occupational Therapy Association, 1993).

What To Expect When You Are Not Expecting

1. Jeffrey J. Wickens, et al., "Development of a Ground-Based Analog for Studying Sensorimotor Impairments After Spaceflight," Frontiers in Physiology 16 (2025): Article 1369788. https://www.frontiersin.org/journals/physiology/articles/10.3389/fphys.2024.1369788/full.

2. Center on the Developing Child at Harvard University, "Serve and Return," accessed November 17, 2025, https://developingchild.harvard.edu/key-concept/serve-and-return/

Composing Connection

1. Barrett, Lisa Feldman, and W. Kyle Simmons. "Interoceptive Predictions in the Brain." *Nature Reviews Neuroscience* 16 (2015): 419-429. https://doi.org/10.1038/nrn3950

Risks and Hazards

1. Heffler, K. F., Sienko, D. M., Subedi, K., McCann, K. A., & Bennett, D. S. (2024). *Early-life digital media experiences and development of atypical sensory processing in toddlers. JAMA Pediatrics, 178(3),* 266–273. https://doi.org/10.1001/jamapediatrics.2023.5923

2. Krasotkina, A., Götz, A., Höhle, B., & Schwarzer, G. (2018). *Perceptual narrowing in speech and face recognition: Evidence for intra-individual cross-domain relations. Frontiers in Psychology, 9,* Article 1711. https://doi.org/10.3389/fpsyg.2018.01711

3. U.S. Bureau of Labor Statistics. (2023). American Time Use Survey — 2022 results. U.S. Department of Labor. Retrieved from https://www.bls.gov/news.release/atus.nr0.htm

4. Larouche, R., Garriguet, D., Gunnell, K. E., Goldfield, G. S., & Tremblay, M. S. (2021). Outdoor time, physical activity, sedentary time, and health indicators at ages 3–12: A systematic review. International Journal of Behavioral Nutrition and Physical Activity, 18(1), Article 63. https://doi.org/10.1186/s12966-021-01097-9

5. World Health Organization. "Suicide." *World Health Organization.* Accessed [insert access date]. https://www.who.int/news-room/fact-sheets/detail/suicide

6. Centers for Disease Control and Prevention. "Suicide Trends Among Persons Aged 10–24 Years: United States, 1994–2012." *MMWR Morbidity and Mortality Weekly Report* 64, no. 8 (2015): 201–205. Accessed [insert access date]. https://www.cdc.gov/mmwr/preview/mmwrhtml/mm6408a1.htm.

7. Sheftall, Arielle H., Lisa Asti, Lisa M. Horowitz, Amanda Felts, Cynthia A. Fontanella, Jeffrey V. Campo, and John A. Bridge. "Suicide in Elementary School–Aged Children and Early Adolescents." *JAMA Network Open* 4, no. 8 (2021): e2119282. https://jamanetwork.com/journals/jamanetworkopen/fullarticle/2782417

8. Barrett, Lisa Feldman. *7½ Lessons About the Brain.* Houghton Mifflin Harcourt, 2020.

9. Stanley, Elizabeth A. *Widen the Window: Training Your Brain and Body to Thrive During Stress and Recover from Trauma.* Avery, 2019.

10. Grahn, Patrik. "Nature-Based Therapy in Individuals with Mental Health Disorders, with a Focus on Mental Well-Being and Connectedness to Nature." *International Journal of Environmental Research and Public Health* 20, no. 3 (2023): Article 2112. https://doi.org/10.3390/ijerph2003211

11. Ceunen, Elke, Johan W. S. Vlaeyen, and Ilse Van Diest. "On the Origin of Interoception." *Frontiers in Psychology* 7 (2016): Article 743. https://doi.org/10.3389/fpsyg.2016.00743.

12. Dodd, Helen F., Louise FitzGibbon, Ben E. Watson, and Jennifer L. Hudson. "Children Who Play Adventurously Have Better Mental Health: An Analysis of Data from Over 2,400 Parents in Great Britain." *Child Psychiatry and Human Development* (2021). https://link.springer.com/article/10.1007/s10578-021-01229-0

13. Dankiw, Kelly A., Michael D. Tsiros, Katherine L. Baldock, and Shona Kumar. "The Impacts of Unstructured Nature Play on Health in Early Childhood: A Systematic Review." *Early Childhood Research Quarterly* 51 (2020): 557–569. https://doi.org/10.1016/j.ecresq.2019.02.006

14. Brussoni, Mariana, Lise L. Olsen, Ian Pike, and David A. Sleet. 2012. "Risky Play and Children's Safety: Balancing Priorities for Optimal Child Development." *International Journal of Environmental Research and Public Health* 9 (9): 3134–48.

15. Sandseter, Ellen Beate Hansen. "Categorizing Risky Play—How Can We Identify Risk-Taking in Children's Play?" *European Early Childhood Education Research Journal* 15, no. 2 (2007): 237–252.

16. National Institute for Play. *The Power of Play: Losing and Finding Ourselves Through Everyday Play.* National Institute for Play, 2024.

17. Kleppe, R., Sandseter, E. B. H., Sando, O. J., & Brussoni, M. (2024). *Children's dynamic risk management – a comprehensive approach to children's risk willingness, risk assessment, and risk handling. International Journal of Play,* 13(4), 395–409. https://doi.org/10.1080/21594937.2024.2425539

18. Hansen Sandseter, E. B., Kleppe, R., & Ottesen Kennair, L. E. (2022). *Risky play in children's emotion regulation, social functioning, and physical health: an evolutionary approach. International Journal of Play,* 12(1), 127–139. https://doi.org/10.1080/21594937.2022.2152531

19. Harper, N. J. (2017). *Outdoor risky play and healthy child development in the shadow of the "risk society": A forest and nature school perspective.* Child & Youth Services, 38(4), 318–334. https://doi.org/10.1080/0145935X.2017.1412825

20. Sandseter, "Categorizing Risky Play," 237–252.

Threads To Ropes

1. United States Department of the Interior, Office of the Assistant Secretary – Indian Affairs. *Federal Indian Boarding School Initiative Investigative Report, Volume I: May 2022.* U.S. Department of the Interior, 2022.

2. https://nicoleapelian.com/blog/true-happiness-life-lessons-from-the-kalahari-san-bushmen/

3. Keeney, Bradford, and Hillary Keeney. *Way of the Bushman: Spiritual Teachings and Practices of the Kalahari Ju/'hoansi.* Bear & Company (an imprint of Inner Traditions), 2015.

4. Truth and Reconciliation Commission of Canada. *Honouring the Truth, Reconciling for the Future: Summary of the Final Report of the Truth and Reconciliation Commission of Canada.* Truth and Reconciliation Commission of Canada, 2015.

5. World Wide Fund for Nature and Zoological Society of London. *Living Planet Report 2022: Building a Nature-Positive Society.* Edited by R. E. A. Almond, M. Grooten, D. Juffe-Bignoli, and T. Petersen. WWF and ZSL, 2022.

6. WWF and ZSL, *Living Planet Report 2022.*

7. Guterres, "Opening Remarks at the COP15 Biodiversity Summit."

Fly The Baby

1. Lieberman, Matthew D. *Social: Why Our Brains Are Wired to Connect.* Crown Publishers, 2013.

2. Murthy, V. H. (2023, May 3). Our epidemic of loneliness and isolation: The U.S. Surgeon General's advisory on the healing effects of social connection and community. U.S. Department of Health and Human Services. Retrieved from https://www.hhs.gov/sites/defaul t/files/surgeon-general-social-connection-advisory.pdf

3. Rubin, Gretchen. *The Happiness Project: Or, Why I Spent a Year Trying to Sing in the Morning, Clean My Closets, Fight Right, Read Aristotle, and Generally Have More Fun.* HarperCollins, 2009.

4. Waldinger, Robert, and Marc Schulz. "The Harvard Study of Adult Development: Lessons from the Longest Study on Happiness." *Harvard Gazette,* 2017. https://news.harvard.edu/gazette/story/2017/04/over-nearly-80-ye ars-harvard-study-has-been-showing-how-to-live-a-healthy-and-hap py-life/

5. He, Ling, Yifan Zhai, Yan Wang, Yuwei Ma, Wei Yu, and Shuqin Li. "Effects of Morning Bright Light Exposure on Circadian Rhythm, Sleep, and Alertness: A Randomized Crossover Trial." *Scientific Reports* 13 (2023): Article 13129. https://doi.org/10.1038/s41598-02 3-40166-8

6. Burns, Annette C., Aysu Didikoglu, Clyde Francks, Luke C. Pilling, Colin Stroud, Mike J. Thrippleton, et al. "Genome-Wide Gene–Environment Study of Time Spent in Daylight and Sleep, Mental Health Outcomes." *Sleep* 46, no. 3 (2023): zsac287. https://doi.org/10.1093/sleep/zsac287

7. Razani, N., et al. "The Association of Knowledge, Attitudes and Access with Park Use Before and After a Park-Prescription Intervention for Low-Income Families in the U.S." *International Journal of Environmental Research and Public Health* 17, no. 3 (2020): 701. https://doi.org/10.3390/ijerph17030701

8. (A **targeted, small-group support** provided to students who are not successful with universal strategies alone.)

9. Kimmerer, Robin Wall. *Braiding Sweetgrass: Indigenous Wisdom, Scientific Knowledge, and the Teachings of Plants.* Milkweed Editions, 2013.

Jumping Monkeys

1. In occupational therapy, particularly in pediatric and sensory integration settings, a crash pad is a soft, cushioned mat or oversized foam-filled bag designed to provide safe, deep-pressure input through proprioceptive and vestibular play.

2. Gibson, James J. *The Ecological Approach to Visual Perception.* Hillsdale, NJ: Lawrence Erlbaum Associates, 1979.

3. John Medina, Brain Rules: 12 Principles for Surviving and Thriving at Work, Home, and School (Seattle: Pear Press, 2008).

4. *Bernie Krause has documented the sound decline in Sugarloaf Ridge State Park over 30 years, now finding total silence where once teemed biophany.*

5. Treasure, Julian. "5 Ways to Listen Better." TED Talk, July 2011.ht tps://www.ted.com/talks/julian_treasure_5_ways_to_listen_better

Relational Parenting

1. Narvaez, Darcia. "Undercare." *Kindred Media*, n.d. https://kindr edmedia.org/glossary/undercare/

The Attributes of a Good Human

1. Attributes of Connection (Jon Young and Gilbert Walking Bull) as written at the 2003 Mind of Mentoring Workshop: Quiet mind and health and well-being. Happiness of a child. Vitality and electricity in the body. Ability to listen deeply, and a commitment and drive to mentor others. Empathy for all living things. Intrinsic drive to be truly helpful & take initiative. Ability to live fully alive as if each day was our last and grieve fully. Ability to forgive and love deeply.

Speaking Belonging

1. A training I offer to staff of nature-connection programs and profes- sionals interested in incorporating nature into their work. Find more at, kathleenlockyer.com

The Trouble With Teens These Days

1. Cloutier, M. M. (2023). *Exploring trauma-informed wilderness therapy: A qualitative pilot study with adolescents. Psychological Trauma: Theory, Research, Practice, and Policy,* Advance online publication. Retrieved from https://repository.nusystem.org

2. Sachs, Ashby Lavelle, Eva Coringrato, Nadav Sprague, Angela Turbyfill, Sarah Tillema, and Jill Litt. 2022. "Rationale, Feasibility, and Acceptability of the Meeting in Nature Together (MINT) Program: A Novel Nature-Based Social Intervention for Loneliness Reduction with Teen Parents and Their Peers" International Journal of Environmental Research and Public Health 19, no. 17: 11059. https://doi.org/10.3390/ijerph191711059

3. The Journal of Positive Psychology

4. Liam Connolly, "Experiencing Awe May Help People with Long COVID Feel Better Mentally," *UC Davis Health*, June 23, 2025, https://health.ucdavis.edu/news/headlines/experiencing-awe-may-help-people-with-long-covid-feel-better-mentally/2025/06

The Village

1. This story is often attributed to African oral traditions (sometimes said to be from the Himba people of Namibia), though it circulates today more as a teaching parable than as a documented single-tribe practice.

When the World Paused

1. Robin Gurwitch, quoted in Tara Law, "Insurance Claim Data Show How Much Teen Mental Health Has Suffered During the U.S. COVID-19 Pandemic," Time, March 4, 2021, https://time.com/5943896/covid-19-teen-mental-health/.

2. Matthew D. Lieberman, Social: Why Our Brains Are Wired to Connect (New York: Crown, 2013), 279.

BIBLIOGRAPHY

Aamodt, Caitlin M., Madza Farias-Virgens, and Stephanie A. White. "Birdsong as a Window into Language Origins and Evolutionary Neuroscience." *Philosophical Transactions of the Royal Society B* 375 (2020): 20190060.

Adams, Maury, and Jennifer Morgan. "Mental Health Recovery and Nature: How Social and Personal Dynamics Are Important." *Ecopsychology* 10, no. 1 (2018): 44–52. https://doi.org/10.1089/eco.2017.0032.

American Occupational Therapy Association. *Occupational Therapy Practice Framework: Domain and Process*. 4th ed. Bethesda, MD: AOTA Press, 2020.

Ayres, A. Jean. *Sensory Integration and Praxis Tests*. Los Angeles: Western Psychological Services, 1989.

Ayres, A. Jean. *Sensory Integration and the Child: Understanding Hidden Sensory Challenges*. 25th anniversary ed. Los Angeles: Western Psychological Services, 2005.

Aviv, Rachel. "The Last of the Nightingales." *The New Yorker*, April 2025.

Barrett, Lisa Feldman. *How Emotions Are Made: The Secret Life of the Brain*. Boston: Houghton Mifflin Harcourt, 2017.

Barrett, Lisa Feldman. *Seven and a Half Lessons About the Brain*. Boston: Houghton Mifflin Harcourt, 2020.

Barrett, Lisa Feldman, and W. Kyle Simmons. "Interoceptive Predictions in the Brain." *Nature Reviews Neuroscience* 16 (2015): 419–29. https://doi.org/10.1038/nrn3950.

Belair, Sylvie. "Can Child Injury Prevention Include Health Risk Promotion?" *Injury Prevention*, Supplement 4, "Children Rise to Risk." n.d.

Berwick, Robert C., Gabriël J. L. Beckers, Kazuo Okanoya, and Johan J. Bolhuis. "A Bird's Eye View of Human Language Evolution." *Frontiers in Evolutionary Neuroscience* 4 (2012): 5. https://doi.org/10.3389/fnevo.2012.00005.

Bonfil Batalla, Guillermo. *Mexico Profundo: Toward a Decolonial Mexican National Identity*. Minneapolis: University of Minnesota Press, 1996.

Božanić Urbančič, Nataša, Špela Battelino, and Darja Vozel. "Appropriate Vestibular Stimulation in Children and Adolescents – A Prerequisite for Normal Cognitive, Motor Development and Bodily Homeostasis – A Review." *Children (Basel)* 11, no. 1 (2023): 2.

Brown, David W., Robert F. Anda, Valerie J. Edwards, Vincent J. Felitti, Shanta R. Dube, and Wayne H. Giles. "Adverse Childhood Experiences and Childhood Autobiographical Memory Disturbance." *Child Abuse & Neglect* 31, no. 9 (2007): 961–69.

Brown, David W., Robert F. Anda, Henning Tiemeier, Vincent J. Felitti, Valerie J. Edwards, Janet B. Croft, and Wayne H. Giles. "Adverse Childhood Experiences and the Risk of Premature Mortality." *American Journal of Preventive Medicine* 37, no. 5 (2009): 389–96.

Brown, Stuart. *Play: How It Shapes the Brain, Opens the Imagination, and Invigorates the Soul*. New York: Avery, 2009.

Bruns, Patrick. "Development and Experience-Dependence of Multisensory Processing." *Trends in Cognitive Sciences* 27, no. 9 (2023): 783–96.

Brussoni, Mariana, Lise L. Olsen, Ian Pike, and David A. Sleet. "Risky Play and Children's Safety: Balancing Priorities for Optimal Child Development." *International Journal of Environmental Research and Public Health* 9, no. 9 (2012): 3134–48.

Brussoni, Mariana, et al. "Position Statement on Active Outdoor Play." *International Journal of Environmental Research and Public Health* 12, no. 6 (2015): 6475–6505.

Burke Harris, Nadine. *The Deepest Well: Healing the Long-Term Effects of Childhood Adversity*. Boston: Houghton Mifflin Harcourt, 2018.

Burke Harris, Nadine. "How Childhood Trauma Affects Health Across a Lifetime." TED Conferences, 2014. https://www.ted.com/talks/nadine_burke_harris_how_childhood_trauma_affects_health_across_a_lifetime.

Carson, Rachel. *Silent Spring*. Boston: Houghton Mifflin, 1962.

Center on the Developing Child at Harvard University. "Serve and Return." Accessed November 17, 2025. https://developingchild.harvard.edu/key-concept/serve-and-return/.

Chen, Wei-Hsiang, and Yu-Hsuan Lin. "Effects of Deep Pressure Input on Autonomic Nervous System Activity during Wisdom Tooth Extraction in Adults." *Journal of Dental Sciences* 20, no. 1 (2025): 35–42.

Child, Brenda. "The History of Native American Boarding Schools Is Even More Complicated than a New Report Reveals." *Time*, 2022.

Ciucci, Enrica, Pamela Calussi, Ersilia Menesini, Alessandra Mattei, Martina Petralli, and Simone Orlandini. "Seasonal Variation, Weather and Behavior in Day-Care Children: A Multilevel Approach." *International Journal of Biometeorology* 57 (2013): 845–56. https://doi.org/10.1007/s00484-012-0612-0.

Connolly, Liam. "Experiencing Awe May Help People with Long COVID Feel Better Mentally." *UC Davis Health*, June 23, 2025. https://health.ucdavis.edu/news/headlines/experiencing-awe-may-help-people-with-long-covid-feel-better-mentally/2025/06.

Coventry, Peter A., Jennifer V. E. Brown, Jodi Pervin, Sally Brabyn, Rachel Pateman, Josefien Breedvelt, Simon Gilbody, Rachel Stancliffe, Rosemary McEachan, and Piran C. L. White. "Nature-Based Outdoor Activities for Mental and Physical Health: Systematic Review and Meta-Analysis." *SSM – Population Health* 16 (2021): 100934. https://doi.org/10.1016/j.ssmph.2021.100934.

Dizikes, Peter. "How Human Language Could Have Evolved from Birdsong." MIT News, February 21, 2013. https://news.mit.edu/2013/how-human-language-could-have-evolved-from-birdsong-0221.

Earp, Sarah E., and Donna L. Maney. "Birdsong: Is It Music to Their Ears?" *Frontiers in Evolutionary Neuroscience* 4 (2012): 14. https://doi.org/10.3389/fnevo.2012.00014.

Eberle, Scott G. Founding editor of the *American Journal of Play* and contributor to *Psychology Today*.

Erïk, Evren, Elif Esma Safran, and Ömer Şevgïn. "Effectiveness of Vestibular and Proprioceptive Exercises in Reducing Hyperactivity in Children with Autism Spectrum Disorder: A Randomized Controlled Trial." *Research in Autism* 123 (2025): 202543.

Escoffier, Nicolas, Christoph S. Herrmann, and Annett Schirmer. "Auditory Rhythms Entrain Visual Processes in the Human Brain: Evidence from Evoked Oscillations and Event-Related Potentials." *NeuroImage* 111 (2015): 267–76. https://doi.org/10.1016/j.neuroimage.2015.02.024.

Farias-Virgens, Madza. "Birdsong and Human Language." Interview. UC Berkeley Social Science Matrix, May 23, 2016. https://matrix.berkeley.edu/research-article/birdsong-and-human-language/.

Ferraro, Danielle M., Zachary D. Miller, Lindsay A. Ferguson, Brian D. Taff, Jesse R. Barber, Peter Newman, and Clinton D. Francis. "The

Phantom Chorus: Birdsong Boosts Human Well-Being in Protected Areas." *Proceedings of the Royal Society B* 287 (2020): 20201811.

Ferrè, Erminia Raffaella, and Patrick Haggard. "Vestibular-Somatosensory Interactions: A Mechanism in Search of a Function?" *Multisensory Research* 28, nos. 5–6 (2015): 559–79.

Ferrè, Erminia Raffaella, Giuseppe Bottani, and Patrick Haggard. "Vestibular Inputs Modulate Somatosensory Cortical Processing." *Brain Structure and Function* 217 (2012): 859–64.

Filion, L. B. Marie. *The Interrelationship between Sensorimotor Deficits and Maladaptive Behavior in the Classroom.* PhD diss., Walden University, 2023.

Gabor Maté. *The Myth of Normal: Trauma, Illness, and Healing in a Toxic Culture.* New York: Avery, 2022.

Garner, Andrew, Michael Yogman, Committee on Psychosocial Aspects of Child and Family Health, Section on Developmental and Behavioral Pediatrics, and Council on Early Childhood. "Preventing Childhood Toxic Stress: Partnering with Families and Communities to Promote Relational Health." *Pediatrics* 148, no. 2 (2021): e2021052582. https://doi.org/10.1542/peds.2021-052582.

Ghanizadeh, Ahmad, Farideh Firoozabadi, and Hossein Dehbozorgi. "Vestibular Therapy Improved Motor Planning, Attention, and Balance in Children with Attention Deficit Hyperactivity Disorders: A Randomized Controlled Trial." *Journal of Neuropsychiatry and Clinical Neurosciences* 30, no. 3 (2018): 214–21.

Grahn, Patrik. "Nature-based Therapy in Individuals with Mental Health Disorders, with a Focus on Mental Well-being and Connectedness to Nature – A Pilot Study." *International Journal of Environmental Research and Public Health* 20, no. 3 (2023): Article 2112.

Harrison, Laura A., Anastasiya Kats, Marian E. Williams, and Lisa Aziz-Zadeh. "The Importance of Sensory Processing in Mental Health: A Proposed Addition to the Research Domain Criteria (RDoC) and Suggestions for RDoC 2.0." *Frontiers in Psychology* 10 (2019): 103. https://doi.org/10.3389/fpsyg.2019.00103.

Harper, Nick J. "Outdoor Risky Play and Healthy Child Development in the Shadow of the 'Risk Society.'" *Child & Youth Services* 38, no. 4 (2017): 318–34.

Harper, Nick J., and Pam Obee. "Articulating Outdoor Risky Play in Early Childhood Education: Voices of Forest and Nature School Practitioners." *Journal of Adventure Education and Outdoor Learning* 21, no. 2 (2020): 184–94.

Harris, Nadine Burke. *The Deepest Well: Healing the Long-Term Effects of Childhood Adversity*. Boston: Houghton Mifflin Harcourt, 2018.

Jacobs, Laurence J., and Simon D. Giszter. "Integration of Proprioceptive and Vestibular Inputs in the Control of Locomotion." *Frontiers in Integrative Neuroscience* 15 (2021): 7867206.

Jamon, Marc. "The Development of Vestibular System and Related Functions in Mammals: Impact of Gravity." *Frontiers in Integrative Neuroscience* 8 (2014): 11. https://doi.org/10.3389/fnint.2014.00011.

Keeney, Bradford, and Hillary Keeney, eds. *Way of the Bushman: Spiritual Teachings and Practices of the Kalahari Ju/'hoansi*. Rochester, VT: Inner Traditions, 2015.

Keltner, Dacher, and M. Monroy. "Awe as a Pathway to Mental and Physical Health." *Perspectives on Psychological Science* 18, no. 2 (2023): 309–20. https://doi.org/10.1177/17456916221094856.

Kim, Dong-Min, Ji-Young Yoon, and Sung-Phil Kim. "Vestibular Nerve Stimulation Modulates the Intrinsic Functional Network Organization of the Anterior Insula and Anterior Cingulate Cortex." *Frontiers in Systems Neuroscience* 13 (2019): 14.

Kleppe, Rasmus, Ellen Beate Hansen Sandseter, Ole Johan Sando, and Mariana Brussoni. "Children's Dynamic Risk Management – A Comprehensive Approach to Children's Risk Willingness, Risk Assessment, and Risk Handling." *International Journal of Play* 13, no. 4 (2024): 395–409.

Krause, Bernie. *The Power of Tranquility in a Very Noisy World*. New York: Little, Brown Spark, 2024.

Krause, Bernie. "Bernie Krause Has Documented the Sound Decline in Sugarloaf Ridge State Park over 30 Years, Now Finding Total Silence Where Once Teemed Biophony." *The Guardian*, 2024.

Kross, Ethan, Marc G. Berman, Walter Mischel, Edward E. Smith, and Tor D. Wager. "Social Rejection Shares Somatosensory Representations with Physical Pain." *Proceedings of the National Academy of Sciences of the United States of America* 108, no. 15 (2011): 6270–75. https://doi .org/10.1073/pnas.1102693108.

Kielhofner, Gary. *Model of Human Occupation: Theory and Application*. 4th ed. Philadelphia: Lippincott Williams & Wilkins, 2008.

LaBelle Sr., James, and National Native American Boarding School Healing Coalition. *Stories of Trauma and Survival from Boarding School Survivors*. Washington, DC: Healing Coalition, 2022.

Li, Li M. W., Meng Liu, and Kenji Ito. "The Relationship between the Need to Belong and Nature Relatedness: The Moderating Role of Independent Self-Construal." *International Journal of Environmental Research and Public Health* 12, no. 6 (2015): 6475–6505. https://doi. org/10.3390/ijerph120606475.

Li, Liman Man Wai, Mengru Liu, and Kenichi Ito. "The Relationship between the Need to Belong and Nature Relatedness: The Moderating

Role of Independent Self-Construal." *Frontiers in Psychology* 12 (2021): 638320. https://doi.org/10.3389/fpsyg.2021.638320.

Lieberman, Matthew D. *Social: Why Our Brains Are Wired to Connect.* New York: Crown, 2013.

Lickliter, Robert. "The Integrated Development of Sensory Organization." *Clinics in Perinatology* 38, no. 4 (2011): 591–603. https://doi.org/10.1016/j.clp.2011.08.007.

Lin, Yung-Chi, Yi-Chen Lee, and Chun-Chih Lin. "Weighted Vest with Vibrotactile Stimulation for Anxiety Reduction in College Students." *Healthcare* 12, no. 17 (2024): 1745.

Louv, Richard. *Last Child in the Woods: Saving Our Children from Nature-Deficit Disorder.* Chapel Hill, NC: Algonquin Books, 2005.

Louv, Richard. *Our Wild Calling: How Connecting with Animals Can Transform Our Lives – and Save Theirs.* New York: Algonquin Books, 2019.

McClelland, Megan M., Shauna L. Tominey, Sara A. Schmitt, Brianne E. Hatfield, David J. Purpura, Christopher R. Gonzales, and Amanda N. Tracy. "Red Light, Purple Light! Results of an Intervention to Promote School Readiness for Children from Low-Income Backgrounds." Human Development and Family Sciences, Oregon State University, n.d.

McGruder, K. *Children Learn What They Live: Addressing Early Childhood Trauma Resulting in Toxic Stress in Schools.* Regional Office of Education #26, Illinois, n.d.

Medina, John. *Brain Rules: 12 Principles for Surviving and Thriving at Work, Home, and School.* Seattle: Pear Press, 2008.

Melillo, Robert, and Gerald Matthews. "A Retrospective Review of Parent-Reported Anxiety and Emotional Functioning in Children with Developmental Challenges after Participation in the Brain Balance Program." *Mental Health & Prevention* 18 (2020): 200180.

Merrick, Melissa T., Katie A. Ports, David C. Ford, Tracie O. Afifi, Elizabeth T. Gershoff, and Andrew Grogan-Kaylor. "Protective Factors and Resilience: Mitigating the Impact of Adverse Childhood Experiences." *Journal of Child Psychology and Psychiatry* 64, no. 2 (2023): 232–45.

Miyagawa, Shigeru, Robert C. Berwick, and Kazuo Okanoya. "The Emergence of Hierarchical Structure in Human Language." *Frontiers in Psychology* 4 (2013): 71. https://doi.org/10.3389/fpsyg.2013.00071.

Mitchell, Joni. "The Circle Game." Track on *Ladies of the Canyon*. Reprise Records, 1970.

Monroy, M., M. Amster, J. Eagle, et al. "Awe Reduces Depressive Symptoms and Improves Well-Being in a Randomized-controlled Clinical Trial." *Scientific Reports* 15 (2025): 16453. https://doi.org/10.1038/s41598-025-96555-w.

Monroy, M., and Dacher Keltner. "Awe as a Pathway to Mental and Physical Health." *Perspectives on Psychological Science* 18, no. 2 (2023): 309–20. https://doi.org/10.1177/17456916221094856.

Morris, Amanda S., and Jennifer Hays-Grudo. "Protective and Compensatory Childhood Experiences and Their Impact on Adult Mental Health." *World Psychiatry* 22, no. 1 (2023): 150–51.

Moyer, Melinda Wenner. "The Kids Are Not Alright." *The Cut*, March 15, 2021.

Narvaez, Darcia. *Neurobiology and the Development of Human Morality: Evolution, Culture, and Wisdom*. Foreword by Allan N. Schore. New York and London: W. W. Norton & Company, 2014.

Narvaez, Darcia. "Undercare." *Kindred Media*. Accessed November 17, 2025. https://kindredmedia.org/glossary/undercare/.

Park, Hang. "The Context of Experienced Sensory Discrepancies Shapes Multisensory Integration: Integration Bias Adapts to the Range of Experienced Spatial Discrepancies." *Cognition* 222 (2022): 105010.

Pew Research Center. "Most U.S. Teens See Anxiety and Depression as a Major Problem Among Their Peers." February 20, 2019. https://www.pewresearch.org/social-trends/2019/02/20/most-u-s-teens-see-anxiety-and-depression-as-a-major-problem-among-their-peers/.

Posner, Michael I., and Cristopher M. Niell. "Illuminating the Neural Circuits Underlying Orienting of Attention." *Vision* 3, no. 1 (2019): 6. https://doi.org/10.3390/vision3010006.

Pritchard, Adam, Miles Richardson, Danielle Sheffield, and Kathryn McEwan. "The Relationship between Nature Connectedness and Eudaimonic Well-Being: A Meta-Analysis." *Journal of Happiness Studies* (2019). https://doi.org/10.1007/s10902-019-00118-6.

Rajagopalan, Arunachalam, K. V. Jinu, K. S. Sailesh, S. Mishra, U. K. Reddy, and J. K. Mukkadan. "Understanding the Links between Vestibular and Limbic Systems Regulating Emotions." *Journal of Natural Science, Biology, and Medicine* 8, no. 1 (2017): 11–15.

Ramsay, Douglas S., and Stephen C. Woods. "Clarifying the Roles of Homeostasis and Allostasis in Physiological Regulation." *Psychological Review* 121, no. 2 (2014): 225–47. https://doi.org/10.1037/a0035942.

Riquelme, Inmaculada, Sami M. Hatem, Álvaro Sabater-Gárriz, Enrique Martín-Jiménez, and Pedro Montoya. "Proprioception, Emotion and Social Responsiveness in Children with Developmental Disorders: An Exploratory Study in Autism Spectrum Disorder, Cerebral Palsy and Different Neurodevelopmental Situations." *Children (Basel)* 11, no. 6 (2024): 719.

Robinson, Christopher, and Alicia Madeleine Brown. "Considering Sensory Processing Issues in Trauma Affected Children: The Physical Environment in Children's Residential Homes." *Scottish Journal of Residential Child Care* 15, no. 1 (2016).

Rosenfeld, Mark S. *Wellness and Lifestyle Renewal: A Manual for Personal Change*. Rockville, MD: The American Occupational Therapy Association, 1993.

Sandseter, Ellen Beate Hansen. "Categorizing Risky Play – How Can We Identify Risk-Taking in Children's Play?" *European Early Childhood Education Research Journal* 15, no. 2 (2007): 237–52.

Sandseter, Ellen Beate Hansen. *Scaryfunny: A Qualitative Study of Risky Play Among Preschool Children*. PhD diss., Norwegian University of Science and Technology, 2010.

Stanley, Elizabeth A. *Widen the Window: Training Your Brain and Body to Thrive during Stress and Recover from Trauma*. New York: Avery, 2019.

Sutton, D., and E. Nicholson. *Sensory Modulation in Acute Mental Health Wards: A Qualitative Study of Staff and Service User Perspectives*. Auckland, New Zealand: Te Pou o Te Whakaaro Nui, 2011.

Szepsenwol, Ohad, Jeffry A. Simpson, Vladas Griskevicius, Osnat Zamir, Ethan S. Young, Anat Shoshani, and Guy Doron. "The Effects of Childhood Unpredictability and Harshness on Emotional Control and Relationship Quality: A Life History Perspective." *Development and Psychopathology* (2021): 1–14. https://doi.org/10.1017/S0954579421001371.

Theirworld. "Games That School Children Play Around the World." Theirworld, June 9, 2017.

Thompson, Chris. "Into the Wild: The Soundscapes of Bernie Krause." *Wired*, July 2008.

Touloumakos, Athanasios K., and Alexandra Barrable. "Adverse Childhood Experiences: The Protective and Therapeutic Potential of Nature." *Frontiers in Psychology* 11 (2020): 597935. https://doi.org/10.3389/fpsyg.2020.597935.

Trajkovik, Vladimir, Toni Malinovski, Tatyana Vasilyeva-Stojanovska, and Marina Vasileva. "Traditional Games in Elementary School: Relationships of Student's Personality Traits, Motivation and Experience with Learning Outcomes." *PLOS ONE* 13, no. 8 (2018): e0202172.

Truth and Reconciliation Commission of Canada. *Honouring the Truth, Reconciling for the Future: Summary of the Final Report*. Winnipeg: Truth and Reconciliation Commission of Canada, 2015.

Treasure, Julian. "5 Ways to Listen Better." TED Talk, July 2011. https://www.ted.com/talks/julian_treasure_5_ways_to_listen_better.

Ureta, Sebastián, Thomas Lekan, and W. Graf von Hardenberg. "Baselining Nature: An Introduction." *EPE: Nature and Space* 3, no. 1 (2020): 3–19. https://doi.org/10.1177/2514848619898092.

U.S. Department of the Interior. *Federal Indian Boarding School Initiative Investigative Report*. Vol. 1, May 2022. Washington, DC: U.S. Department of the Interior, 2022.

U.S. Department of the Interior. *Federal Indian Boarding School Initiative Investigative Report*. Vol. 2, August 2024. Washington, DC: U.S. Department of the Interior, 2024.

Van Gordon, William, Edo Shonin, and Miles Richardson. "Mindfulness and Nature." *Mindfulness* 9 (2018): 1655–58.

Weaver, Simon. "Nature-based Therapeutic Service: The Power of Love in Helping and Healing." *Journal of Sustainability Education*, March 2015.

Wolf, Lynda, Jacquie Ripat, Ellen Davis, Pam Becker, and Jane MacSwiggan. "Applying an Occupational Justice Framework." *Canadian Journal of Occupational Therapy* 77, no. 5 (2010): 264–75. https://doi.org/10.2182/cjot.2010.77.5.3.

Young, Jon. *What the Robin Knows: How Birds Reveal the Secrets of the Natural World*. Boston: Houghton Mifflin Harcourt, 2012.

Young, Jon, Ellen Haas, and Evan McGown. *Coyote's Guide to Connecting with Nature*. 2nd ed. Shelton, WA: OWLink Media, 2010.

ABOUT KATHLEEN LOCKYER

 For nearly thirty years, Kathleen Lockyer is a licensed occupational therapist who for almost thirty years has been stepping outside to practice — following birdsong, children's laughter, and the wisdom of the wild to help people reclaim health, belonging, and resilience. She founded RxOutside™ and co-founded Outside Now! a California non-profit. Kathleen coined the words ecoception and NatureLed™, and created the NatureLed™ Approach—bridging neuroscience, sensory health, and ancestral wisdom.

Raised a little bit wild and a little bit cultured by a fisherman from Newfoundland, Canada, and a debutante from NYC, Kathleen sees the world through curiosity and forgiveness, always searching for the overlooked threads of connection. She has tracked animals with international experts, shared stages with bestselling authors, and played in wild places with children of every age. She laughs easily, loves fiercely, and when no trail is visible, she makes one.

Kathleen lives with her loving partner on a farm with their fabulous friends in the hills of the Central Coast of California, and with their emotional Pyrenees mix. She spends as much time with her grown daughters as they allow!

ABOUT HOLLY RINGLAND

Holly Ringland

Holly is an international best-selling author and TV presenter.

Her award-winning, internationally bestselling debut novel, The Lost Flowers of Alice Hart, has been published in 30 territories. In 2019, it won the Australian Book Industry Award General Fiction Book of the Year. In 2023, a 7-episode TV series adaptation of the same name streamed globally on Prime Video, starring Sigourney Weaver. The series broke records with the biggest opening weekend viewership globally for any Australian launch. It has reached the top five in 78 countries, and top 3 in 42 countries.

Holly's second novel, The Seven Skins of Esther Wilding, was published in 2022 and became an instant national bestseller. Booktopia named it their 2022 Book of the Year.

Holly's latest book, The House That Joy Built, is her first non-fiction title and has become a national bestseller. Published in 2023, it's part-memoir, part-research, and part-storytelling about the pleasure and power of giving ourselves permission to create. Readers have called it "life-changing". Apple Book Reviews called it a "non-fiction masterpiece".

In 2021, along with Aaron Pedersen, Holly co-hosted the factual ABC TV series, Back To Nature, which aired to critical acclaim. You can learn more about her and get her books at: https://hollyringland.com

Where To Learn More

Go to kathleenlockyer.com to find workbooks, courses, podcasts and other great resources about the NatureLed™ Approach.

www.ingramcontent.com/pod-product-compliance
Lightning Source LLC
Chambersburg PA
CBHW021214130626
46554CB00004B/1214